Business Management

Paul Hoang

PREPARE FOR SUCCESS ✓

FOR THE
IB DIPLOMA
PROGRAMME

Business Management

Paul Hoang

PREPARE FOR SUCCESS ✓

HODDER
Education

The Publishers would like to thank the following for permission to reproduce copyright material.

Photo credits

p. 21 © Tada Images/stock.adobe.com; **p. 36** © steheap/stock.adobe.com; **p. 41** © chartphoto/stock.adobe.com; **p. 69** © jon_chica/stock.adobe.com; **p. 72** © Cartoon-Designer/stock.adobe.com; **p. 89** © herraez/stock.adobe.com; **p. 90** © Visual Content/stock.adobe.com; **p. 102** © TSUNG-LIN WU/stock.adobe.com; **p. 104** © Bernd Kröger/stock.adobe.com; **p. 149** © cristianbalate/stock.adobe.com; **p. 159** © Rido/stock.adobe.com; **p. 163** © Jeff B/peopleimages.com/stock.adobe.com; **p. 166** *t* © rutchapong/stock.adobe.com, *b* © European Community; **p. 168** © Artem/stock.adobe.com; **p. 191** © vchalup/stock.adobe.com; **p. 201** © Gorodenkoff/stock.adobe.com; **p. 206** © kinwun/stock.adobe.com; **p. 210** © Ga_Na/stock.adobe.com; **p. 213** © lindacaldwell/stock.adobe.com

Acknowledgements

Every effort has been made to trace all copyright holders, but if any have been inadvertently overlooked, the Publishers will be pleased to make the necessary arrangements at the first opportunity.

Although every effort has been made to ensure that website addresses are correct at time of going to press, Hodder Education cannot be held responsible for the content of any website mentioned in this book. It is sometimes possible to find a relocated web page by typing in the address of the home page for a website in the URL window of your browser.

Hachette UK's policy is to use papers that are natural, renewable and recyclable products and made from wood grown in well-managed forests and other controlled sources. The logging and manufacturing processes are expected to conform to the environmental regulations of the country of origin.

Orders: please contact Hachette UK Distribution, Hely Hutchinson Centre, Milton Road, Didcot, Oxfordshire, OX11 7HH. Telephone: +44 (0)1235 827827. Email education@hachette.co.uk Lines are open from 9 a.m. to 5 p.m., Monday to Friday. You can also order through our website: www.hoddereducation.com

ISBN: 978 1 3983 5842 3

© Paul Hoang 2023

First published in 2023 by
Hodder Education,
An Hachette UK Company
Carmelite House
50 Victoria Embankment
London EC4Y 0DZ

www.hoddereducation.com

Impression number   10 9 8 7 6 5 4 3 2 1

Year   2027 2026 2025 2024 2023

Cover photo © Kalyakan/stock.adobe.com

Illustrations by Aptara Inc.

Typeset in India by Aptara Inc.

Printed in Spain

A catalogue record for this title is available from the British Library.

MIX
Paper | Supporting responsible forestry
FSC™ C104740
FSC
www.fsc.org

Contents

Introduction

How to use this book

This book will help you to plan your revision and work through it in a methodological way. It follows the IB Business Management syllabus topic by topic, with revision and exam practice questions to help you check your understanding.

■ Features to help you succeed

EXPERT TIPS

These tips give advice that will help you boost your final grade, in some cases including identifying typical mistakes that students make, and explaining how you can avoid them.

Key terms

Key terms appear in these boxes, and are highlighted and defined throughout the book. A glossary of essential terms is given at the end of the book.

KEY CONCEPTS

The four key concepts will be discussed in these boxes: change, creativity, ethics and sustainability.

WORKED EXAMPLES

Some parts of the course require you to carry out mathematical calculations, plot graphs, and so on. These worked examples show you how.

EXAM PRACTICE QUESTIONS

Exam practice is given for the types of questions you might get. For the longer essay questions, sample sentences and paragraphs are given to show what examiners are looking for in your essay answers. Use these questions to consolidate your revision and to practise your exam skills. Answers are available at **www.hoddereducation.com/ib-extras**

BUSINESS MANAGEMENT TOOLKIT

Guidance on the set of situational, planning and decision-making tools.

You can keep track of your revision by ticking off each topic heading in the book.

Use this book as the cornerstone of your revision. Do not hesitate to write in it and personalize your notes. Use a highlighter to identify areas that need further work. You may find it helpful to add your own notes as you work through each topic. Good luck!

Getting to know the exam

Exam paper	Duration	Format	Topics	Total marks
Paper 1	1 hr 30 mins	Structured questions based on a pre-released statement	All	30
Paper 2	1 hr 30 mins (SL) 1 hr 45 mins (HL)	Structured questions based on stimulus material	All	40 (SL) 50 (HL)
Paper 3 (HL only)	1 hr 15 mins	Unseen stimulus material about a social enterprise	All	25

At the end of your IB Business Management course, SL students will sit two papers – Paper 1 and Paper 2. Paper 1 is worth 35 per cent of the final marks and Paper 2 is worth 35 per cent of the final marks. The other assessed part of the course (the remaining 30 per cent) is made up of the Internal Assessment, which is marked by your teacher and externally moderated.

HL students will sit an additional paper – Paper 3, worth 25 per cent. For HL students, Paper 1 is worth 25 per cent of the final marks and Paper 2 is worth 30 per cent of the final marks. The other assessed part of the course (the remaining 20 per cent) is the Internal Assessment (or IA), which is marked by your teacher and externally moderated.

Countdown to the exams

4–8 weeks to go

- Start by looking at the syllabus and making sure you know exactly what you need to revise.
- Look carefully at the contents list in this book and use it to help organize your class notes and to make sure you have covered everything.
- Work out a realistic revision plan that breaks down the material you need to revise into manageable pieces. Each session should be around 25–40 minutes, with breaks in between. The plan should include time for some relaxation.
- Read through the relevant chapters of this book and refer to the Expert tips, Key terms definitions, and Worked examples.
- Tick off the topics that you feel confident about, and highlight the ones that need further work.
- Look at past exam papers. They are one of the best ways to check your knowledge and practise exam skills. They will also help you identify areas that need further work.
- Try different revision methods, for example summary notes, mind maps and flash cards.
- Test your understanding of each topic by working through the Exam practice questions.
- Make notes of any problem areas as you revise, and ask a teacher to go over them in class.

1 week to go

- Aim to fit in at least one more timed practice of entire past papers, comparing your work closely with the mark scheme.
- Examine the contents list of this book carefully to make sure you haven't missed any of the topics.
- Tackle any final problems by getting help from your teacher or talking them over with a friend.

The day before the examination

- Look through this book one final time. Look carefully through the information about each exam paper to remind yourself what to expect, including timings and the number of questions to be answered in each section of the papers.
- Check the time and place of the exams.

- Make sure you have all the equipment you need (for example extra pens, a pencil and a ruler for diagrams, a watch, tissues and water).
- Allow some time to relax and have an early night so you are rested and ready for the exams. There is a huge opportunity cost if you are not refreshed!

My exams

Paper 1

Date: ....

Time: ....

Location: ....

Paper 2

Date: ....

Time: ....

Location: ....

Paper 3 (HL only)

Date: ....

Time: ....

Location: ....

1 Introduction to business management

1.1 What is a business?

SL/HL content	Depth of teaching
The nature of business	AO1
Primary, secondary, tertiary, and quaternary sectors	AO2
Entrepreneurship	AO2
Challenges and opportunities for starting up a business	AO2

Diploma Programme *Business management guide* (May 2022)

The nature of business (AO1)

- A **business** is any organization set up to provide goods and/or supply services.
- Businesses aim to satisfy the needs and desires of their customers by selling them a good or providing a service.
- To produce goods and services, a business needs to combine human, physical, financial, and entrepreneurial resources. These resources are referred to as the **factors of production**, comprising land, labour, capital, and enterprise:
  - *Land*: natural resources used in the production process, for example wood, water, physical land, fish, metal ores, and minerals.
  - *Labour*: physical human effort and psychological intellect used in the production process.
  - *Capital*: non-natural (manufactured) resources used to further the production process, for example tools, equipment, machinery, vehicles, and buildings.
  - *Enterprise*: an individual with the necessary skills and ability to take risks in organizing the other factors of production to generate output in a profitable way.
- The production process adds value to the final goods and services sold to customers. **Value added** is the process of creating a product that is worth more than the cost of the inputs used to produce it, for example bottled orange juice is worth more than the original oranges grown in a farm.
- Value added is measured as the difference between the cost of the inputs in the production process and the price of the final output.
- Businesses strive to add value to a good or service so that the product better meets the needs and wants of their customers.
- The nature of business involves four distinct but interrelated functions: human resources, finance and accounts, marketing, and operations management.

EXPERT TIP

Be sure to know the difference between consumers and customers. **Consumers** are the people who use a good or service. **Customers** are the people who buy a good or service. Buyers and users are not necessarily the same entities.

■ Human resources

- Human resource management (HRM) refers to the management of an organization's staff (personnel).

- This function handles human resource issues, for example recruitment, dismissal, training and development, redundancies, appraisals, performance management, career planning, and the general welfare (wellbeing) of the organization's employees.
- The HRM department of a business must comply with employment legislation (labour laws), for example minimum wage legislation, rules about working hours, equal opportunities laws, and anti-discrimination regulations.

Finance and accounts

- The function of the finance department of an organization is to manage the firm's money.
- It processes payments for the organization's bills (for example invoices owed to suppliers and payments to the tax authorities) and arranges the financial compensation for the organization's employees.
- The finance department prepares the final accounts, such as income statements and balance sheets (see Chapter 3.4), as well as the various budgets of the organization (see Chapter 3.9) in order to improve its financial control.

Marketing

- The marketing department is responsible for identifying the needs and wants of its customers, and ensuring the organization's goods and services meet these demands in a profitable way.
- It conducts market research to identify the changing needs of the organization's customers.
- It arranges promotional activities to sell the firm's products at appropriate prices, distributed to customers at the right time and place.

Operations management

- Operations management, often referred to as production, is the process of making products from the available resources of the business.
- The operations department is responsible for manufacturing finished goods or providing services to the organization's customers.
- It is responsible for production targets and deadlines, stock control management, research and development (innovation), and meeting quality standards.

Primary, secondary, tertiary, and quaternary sectors (AO2)

The primary sector

- The **primary sector** is the first stage of production. It refers to businesses involved in the extraction of natural resources and raw materials, for example farming (agriculture), fishing, forestry, and mining.
- In less economically developed (low income) economies, the majority of people are employed in the primary sector.
- Value added in the primary sector is relatively low compared to the other sectors.

The secondary sector

- The **secondary sector** refers to businesses engaged in manufacturing and construction, which create finished and usable products.
- It involves businesses using and transforming primary products and components into finished goods for sale, for example car making, aerospace manufacturing, construction (road building and other forms of infrastructure), breweries and bottlers, engineering, and ship building.
- In many parts of the world, the use of mechanization and automation have caused a decline in employment in the secondary sector.

The tertiary sector

- The **tertiary sector** refers to businesses that focus on providing a service to consumers and other businesses, for example banking, insurance, security, catering, education, health care, retail, transportation, news media, law, leisure and tourism, and entertainment.
- The tertiary sector accounts for the largest sector (in terms of employment and the value of output) in economically developed (high income) countries.

> **EXPERT TIP**
>
> It is wrong to assume that those working in the tertiary sector are paid more than those in the primary or secondary sectors. While value added is higher in the tertiary sector, plenty of people working in the tertiary sector, such as in the retail and fast food industries, earn minimum wages. Engineers in the secondary sector and fishermen or miners in the primary sector are often very well paid.

The quaternary sector

- The **quaternary sector** refers to businesses engaged in the creation or sharing of knowledge or information.
- Value added is high in both the tertiary and quaternary sectors.
- Sectoral change happens over time, because as a country develops, it shifts the majority of its output from the primary sector to manufacturing (the secondary sector), and then eventually to the tertiary and quaternary sectors.

Entrepreneurship (AO2)

- **Entrepreneurship** is the term for individuals who take calculated risks and initiative in the start-up of a new business or commercial project.
- An **entrepreneur** is someone who is willing to take financial risks by investing in a business idea. Entrepreneurs are usually self-employed, and they develop new products or services mainly for their own benefit.
- The entrepreneur brings together the factors of production necessary to produce goods and services to meet the needs and desires of customers.
- The economic success of countries worldwide is largely the result of encouraging and rewarding an entrepreneurial culture. It is entrepreneurs who take the risk of business management in search of profit. They provide employment opportunities, satisfy the needs of customers, and contribute to the overall prosperity of the economy.

- Entrepreneurs are unique in that they are capable of bringing together the necessary finance, skilled labour and manufacturing, land and buildings facilities required in order to produce a good or service. They are also capable of planning, executing and managing the marketing of that particular good or service.

- Entrepreneurs devise appropriate strategies to create new businesses and commercial ideas, as well as to rejuvenate existing ones. This can include identifying untapped markets, developing new goods or services, and/or creating new business processes.

- Entrepreneurship is a rare trait that requires a profound skills set: time management, creativity, communications, leadership, teamwork, business planning, and risk management.

- Effective management and leadership skills (see Chapter 2.3) are essential for the success of any entrepreneurial pursuit. Successful entrepreneurs must be able to effectively communicate their vision, motivate and manage teams, and make strategic decisions in order to survive and thrive.

- An entrepreneurial mindset is important for generating a successful and sustainable business. This involves a combination of the skills of creativity and critical thinking, as well as the ability to adapt to changing business environments.

> **KEY CONCEPTS**
>
> Discuss the role of **creativity** for the **sustainability** of a business organization.

Opportunities for starting up a business (AO2)

The opportunities for starting up a business refer to the benefits of or reasons for business start-ups. These reasons or opportunities include, but are not limited to, the following:

- *To be your own boss.* Wanting to work for themselves is a key reason many people start up their own business. Some people do not like working for others and natural-born entrepreneurs may feel that they are not able to work for someone else. They prefer the opportunity to be their own boss, along with enjoying the freedom to make independent decisions. This can help individuals to meet their self-actualization needs on Maslow's hierarchy of needs (see Chapter 2.4).

- *Challenges.* Setting up a business involves obstacles and opportunities that employees would not otherwise face if they worked for someone else. Some people are motivated by, and thrive on, personal challenges. They enjoy gaining knowledge and developing new skills.

- *Personal interests, engagement, and enjoyment.* Some people have a desire to pursue their personal interest as a business opportunity. Doing something you are passionate about every day is a key motivation for entrepreneurs. The goal is not always primarily to make a profit. Many new businesses start from the innovative and creative ideas of entrepreneurs, as seen in the examples of Red Bull and The Walt Disney Company.

- *Niche-market opportunities.* Some people identify business opportunities or gaps in the market, so start their own business to fill these gaps. Examples of entrepreneurs who identified such gaps include Stelios Haji-Ioannou (of easyJet) and Tony Ryan (of Ryanair). They both saw huge business opportunities in the low-budget European airline industry. Recognizing a niche in the market can help the business to gain a first-mover advantage.

- *Family tradition.* Being entrepreneurial is often a family trait, as seen in the cases of the Walton family (Walmart), the Mars family (Mars Inc.), and the Hilton family (Hilton Hotels).
- *Flexibility.* Setting up and running your own business often means you can set your own deadlines and get things done in your own way. This may be a major motivator for entrepreneurs.
- *Money.* The key driving force for starting up a business or an enterprise can be the opportunity to earn a lot of money through hard work and determination.

Challenges for starting up a business (AO2)

- *Planning.* Poor market research can result in a flawed business idea, and the product may fail to meet the needs and wants of customers. The set-up procedures can be time consuming, especially if there are complicated legal aspects to deal with.
- *Finance.* Inability to raise sufficient start-up finance or to maintain liquidity in the business (see Chapter 3.7) can cause financial problems. Start-up businesses often struggle to secure external sources of finance from banks and other lenders to fund their operations. In some cases, set-up costs can prove to be unaffordable.
- *Marketing.* Start-ups have a limited budget available for promotion and advertising. The product might lack differentiation or a distinctive selling point, thus failing to gain recognition and market share. A small customer base is likely to cause liquidity issues.
- *Human resources.* New, unestablished businesses may struggle to recruit suitable and experienced employees.
- *Operations management.* New businesses may lack the benefit of an established relationship with suppliers, which can cause delivery and distribution problems. Some new businesses lack the necessary finance to fund research and development, so are at a disadvantage against established businesses.
- *Strategic thinking.* Entrepreneurs may lack experience in strategic decision making, which can cause major problems for a start-up business. Their business plans are often not convincing or detailed enough to secure the necessary finance to get the business started.

BUSINESS MANAGEMENT TOOLKIT

Discuss the importance of business plans for business start-ups.

1.2 Types of business entities

SL/HL content	Depth of teaching
Distinction between the private and the public sectors	AO2
The main features of the following types of organizations: sole traders, partnerships, privately held companies, and publicly held companies	AO3
The main features of the following types of for-profit social enterprises: private sector companies, public sector companies, and co-operatives	AO3
The main features of the following types of non-profit social enterprise: non-governmental organizations (NGOs)	AO3

Diploma Programme *Business management guide* (May 2022)

Distinction between the private and the public sectors (AO2)

- The private sector is the commercial sector of the economy, and is mainly owned and run by private individuals and organizations that typically strive for a profit.

- Examples of private sector businesses include sole traders, partnerships, limited liability companies, co-operatives, franchises (see Chapter 1.5), and multinational companies (see Chapter 1.6).

- Organizations in the public sector are owned and controlled by regional and/or national governments.

- The public sector provides goods and services deemed to be essential and of benefit to its citizens, including, for example, transportation and communications networks, health care services, education, social housing, and national defence.

The main features of the following types of for-profit organizations (AO3)

▨ Sole traders

> **Key term**
>
> **Unlimited liability** means that the owner(s) of a business are personally liable for any and all of the business's debts. This means the owner(s) may need to pay for the debts by selling off their personal belongings and assets.

- A **sole trader** (or **sole proprietorship**) is a commercial business owned by a single person (known as the sole trader). The sole trader can employ as many people as required, but remains the only owner of the business.

- It is run as an unincorporated business, which means there is no legal distinction between the owner and the business organization itself. Hence, a sole trader has **unlimited liability** and is responsible (liable) for any debts of the business, which may need to be paid from the sole trader's personal assets if necessary.

- All or most of the finance needed to run the business is provided by the owner.

- The individual owner of the business accepts all the risks of running the organization, including possible losses or business failure. However, the owner receives all of the profits if the business does succeed.

■ **Table 1.1** Advantages and disadvantages of sole traders

Advantages of sole traders	Disadvantages of sole traders
• A sole trader is quick to create, without long and expensive set-up procedures; it is the easiest form of business organization to set up.	• The sole trader bears all risks and has unlimited liability as the firm's finances are not separate from the owner's.
• The owner has complete control and is free to make decisions without any consultation with others.	• Finance is limited as the main source is provided by the owner; access to external finance is difficult as the firm represents high risk, so expansion is difficult.
• Decision making is quick.	
• The owner enjoys tax advantages as a small business.	• There is no one else to share ideas, burdens or responsibilities with, limiting the extent to which sole traders can benefit from specialization and division of labour.
• The owner enjoys privacy as the business does not need to publish its financial accounts to the general public (only the tax authorities need to see these).	

• There is flexibility, as the sole trader can introduce new trading activities or change what the business does with relative ease. • There are motivational impacts as the owner has a sense of achievement from running their own business.	• Running a business as a sole owner often means having to work long hours due to high workload, and this can result in extra stress. • If the owner is sick or wants to take a break, there can be a lack of continuity and the business may struggle as a result. • A sole trader cannot exploit economies of scale, making it hard to gain cost advantages. This often means that sole traders have to charge higher prices for their products.

Partnerships

- A **partnership** is a commercial business owned by two or more people. In an **ordinary partnership**, there are usually between 2 and 20 owners (depending on the country's laws on partnerships). These owners are called **partners**.
- As an unincorporated business, at least one partner will have unlimited liability, although it is usual for all the partners to share responsibility for any losses incurred by the partnership.
- It is possible for some businesses, such as law firms and health care clinics, to operate with more than 20 partners.
- To prevent potential misunderstandings and conflict, most partnerships draw up a legal contract between the partners, known as a **deed of partnership**, stating their responsibilities, voting rights, and how profits are to be shared between the owners.
- Partnerships are usually found in professional services (such as doctors, solicitors, dentists and accountants) and in family-run businesses.

■ **Table 1.2** Advantages and disadvantages of partnerships

Advantages of partnerships	Disadvantages of partnerships
• With up to 20 owners (depending on the country), partners are able to raise more finance than sole traders. • The partners can benefit from having more ideas and expertise between them, along with shared workloads and responsibilities. • They can also benefit from specialization and the division of labour. • Business affairs are kept confidential, so only the tax authorities need to know about the financial position of the partnership. • There is improved continuity as the partnership can remain in business if a partner is ill or goes on holiday. • Silent partners can provide additional sources of finance without having an active role in the running of the business.	• As there is more than one owner, there might be disagreements and conflict between the partners, which can undoubtedly harm the running of the firm. • Any profits made must be shared between all the partners. • The death or departure of a partner can cause the organization to cease operating until a new partnership agreement is legally created. • In most cases, partners have unlimited liability (silent partners are exempt). • There is limited ability to raise capital compared with limited liability companies; access to finance is limited by the number of partners in the business.

▣ Privately held companies and publicly held companies

- Companies (or corporations) are commercial businesses with limited liability and are owned by their **shareholders**. Hence, any profits must be shared among the shareholders.

- Being incorporated businesses, there is a divorce of ownership and control in privately and publicly held companies. This means there is a legal separation between the owners of a company and the business as an entity itself. Hence, shareholders enjoy the benefit of having limited liability.

- Limited liability protects shareholders as, in the event of the company going bankrupt, they cannot lose more than the amount they invested in the company.

- Typically, to set up a limited liability company, the owners must submit two important documents:

  - The **Memorandum of Association** – a relatively short document that records the name of the company, its registered business address, the amount of share capital and an outline of the company's operations (what it does).

  - The **Articles of Association** – a longer document that contains information about:
    - the details and duties of the directors of the company
    - shareholders' voting rights
    - the transferability of shares
    - details and procedures for the Annual General Meeting
    - how profits are to be distributed (dividend policy)
    - procedures for winding up (closing) the company.

- Once the authorities are satisfied with the paperwork, a Certificate of Incorporation is issued to the limited liability company so that it can begin trading as a legal entity.

- The shareholders elect a board of directors (BOD) to take charge of the strategic direction of the company on behalf of its owners.

- There are two types of limited companies: privately held companies and publicly held companies (see Table 1.3).

▣ **Table 1.3** Features of privately held companies and publicly held companies

Features of privately held companies
• Usually smaller businesses than publicly held companies.
• Shares can only be transferred (bought or sold) privately, and all shareholders must agree on the sale/transfer.
• Typically, shares are owned by family, relatives, and close friends.
• The shares cannot be advertised for sale nor be sold via a stock exchange.
• Examples include Mars and IKEA.

Features of publicly held companies
• Shares in a publicly held company can be bought by and sold to any member of the public or institution.
• The first time that shares in a publicly held company are sold via a **stock exchange** is called the initial public offering (IPO).
• There is no legal maximum number of shareholders; the company can have as many shareholders as its share capital can accommodate.
• Publicly held companies tend to be the largest type of business organizations.
• They are strictly regulated and are required by law to publish their complete financial accounts (see Chapter 3.4) on a yearly basis.
• Examples include Apple, Toyota, and Samsung.

Key term

A **stock exchange** (or **stock market**) is a place for buying and selling shares in publicly held companies. It oversees the IPO of new companies and subsequent share issues of existing companies. It is also the marketplace for buying and selling secondhand shares.

■ **Table 1.4** Advantages and disadvantages of privately held companies

Advantages of privately held companies	Disadvantages of privately held companies
• Control of the company cannot be lost as shares cannot be bought without the agreement of existing shareholders. • More finance can be raised compared to a sole trader or a partnership business. • Privately held companies tend to have more privacy than publicly held companies. • There is continuity in the event of the departure or death of one of the key shareholders. • Owners have limited liability so can only lose up to the sum of their investment.	• Shares cannot be sold to the general public, limiting finance compared with a publicly held company. • Legal fees and auditing fees mean it is more expensive to set up compared to a sole trader or partnership business. • The company can become vulnerable to a takeover offer by a larger company. • There is a lack of privacy as the company's financial accounts must be made available upon request.

■ **Table 1.5** Advantages and disadvantages of publicly held companies

Advantages of publicly held companies	Disadvantages of publicly held companies
• It is relatively easy to obtain finance for growth and evolution (see Chapter 1.5) by selling additional share capital. • It is also easier for large publicly held companies to secure external sources of finance from banks and other investors or lenders. • They can enjoy the benefits of being large, e.g. economies of scale, market power, and market dominance. • Owners enjoy limited liability. • As with privately held companies, there is continuity even if one of the principal shareholders leaves or passes away.	• The financial information becomes public, as people have access to the financial information of a publicly held company. • They are the most administratively difficult, time consuming, and expensive type of commercial business to set up. • There are high costs to complying with the rules of the stock exchange. • There is the potential threat of a hostile takeover by a rival company. • There is the possibility of the firm becoming too large to manage efficiently, and so suffering from diseconomies of scale, i.e. higher average costs of production.

Types of for-profit social enterprises (AO3)

- A social enterprise is an organization that uses commercial business practices to improve communities, the environment, and human wellbeing, rather than focusing on profits for owners or shareholders.

- Some social enterprises are run for profit (for example, co-operatives and microfinance providers), while others are run as non-profit organizations (for example, non-governmental organizations).

- Non-profit organizations can earn a surplus from selling goods and services, but they reinvest this back into the business and/or local community (to meet their social objectives), rather than distributing the extra money to shareholders.

▣ Private sector companies

● Social enterprises can be operated in the private sector as sole traders, partnerships, or limited liability companies. Some social enterprises are run as private sector companies to give shareholders the protection of limited liability.

● Social enterprises operated as private sector companies seek to earn a profit and succeed commercially, although they use any financial surplus to meet their social objectives.

● They operate in all sectors of the economy, producing and selling a broad range of consumer goods and services such as cafés, cleaning services, discount food stores, health care providers, recycling projects, restaurants, and waste-management companies.

● Creative agencies and arts organizations often operate as private sector companies. For example, film companies set up as social enterprises often focus on providing opportunities and training for young people to develop youth talent.

● One example of a for-profit social enterprise organized as a private sector company is Change Please. The company sells coffee in multiple countries and strives for a world without homelessness. Change Please recruits and trains people experiencing homelessness as baristas at its coffee outlets, offering them full-time employment, accommodation, and support with mental health.

▣ Public sector companies

● As the term suggests, public sector companies are limited liability companies that are owned by, or have the majority of their shares owned by, the government. Being in the public sector, these organizations are more likely to have social objectives as well as financial ones.

● Examples include the Indian Oil Corporation Limited, owned by the Indian government, and the Industrial and Commercial Bank of China (ICBC), owned by the Chinese government. Both are large and profitable companies owned by their respective governments.

● Some companies may be jointly owned by the private and public sector, such as with public–private sector partnerships.

● A public–private partnership (PPP) is an organization jointly established by the government and at least one private sector organization, for example the Hong Kong government owns 51 per cent of the stake in Hong Kong Disneyland, while The Walt Disney Company owns the other 49 per cent stake. A PPP is run as a public sector company.

● A public–private sector company benefits from private sector expertise and investment, which is often needed to provide the necessary resources to get the joint project completed, such as constructing an airport or motorway (highway). The private sector company benefits from the revenues generated from the project, such as tolls on bridges and motorways, fees from the government, and/or charges for maintenance.

● Public–private sector companies have been used for a wide range of projects that benefit local communities and societies, such as schools, hospitals and health care services, public transportation networks, prisons, parks, and convention centres.

- Once a particular project is built or completed, it is usually maintained by the private sector contractor on a medium- to long-term basis (typically up to 30 years), after which time there is the option to renew the partnership, or the asset returns to public ownership.
- According to the World Bank, more than half the countries around the world now operate public–private sector companies.

> **EXPERT TIP**
>
> Do not confuse a publicly held company with a public sector company. The former is owned by shareholders and operates in the private sector, whereas the latter is wholly or predominantly owned by a government operating in the public sector.

Co-operatives

- Co-operatives are for-profit social enterprises owned and run by their members, such as employees, managers, and customers. They strive to provide a service and to create value for their members, rather than a financial return for their member-owners.
- Like a limited liability company, a co-operative is run as a separate legal entity from the members. Shareholders, directors, managers, and employees have limited liability so are not personally liable for any debts incurred by the co-operative.
- All members have equal voting rights, irrespective of their position in the organization or the amount they have invested in the co-operative.
- All shareholders or members are expected to help run the business.
- Co-operatives promote a democratic style of managing the organization, with a culture of promoting the concepts of sharing resources and delegation in order to increase the organization's competitiveness.

■ **Table 1.6** Advantages and disadvantages of co-operatives

Advantages of co-operatives	Disadvantages of co-operatives
• It is usually straightforward and inexpensive to set up a co-operative.	• It can be difficult to attract potential members/shareholders, as co-operatives are not formed to generate a financial return on investment.
• All members and shareholders must be active stakeholders of the co-operative, making it more likely to succeed.	• There are limited resources, as the financial strength of co-operatives depends on the capital contributed by their members (membership fees are limited, so they are unable to raise a large amount of finance).
• Shareholders have equal voting rights (all members are equally important for the society), making the organization more democratic and harmonious.	
• Members have limited liability.	• Employees and managers may not be highly motivated, due to the lack of financial rewards and benefits.
• Members own and control the business rather than the business being governed by external investors.	• As co-operatives are managed by their members only, employees may not have any managerial skills, so inefficiencies can hinder the success of the business.
• Any surplus is spent for the welfare of the members and a portion is kept for reserves as an internal source of finance.	
• Governments often provide special financial assistance to help co-operatives.	• Although some members have more responsibilities, they still only get one vote, which may be deemed unfair.

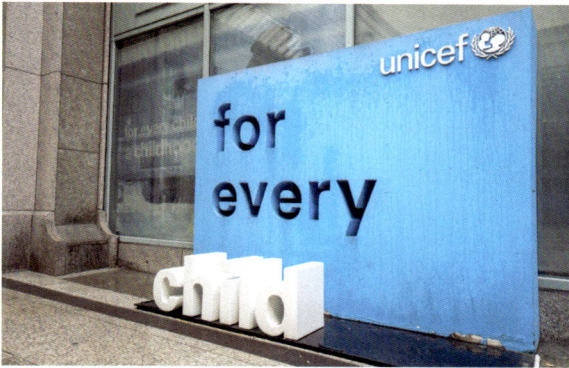

■ **Figure 1.1** The UNICEF sign outside the social enterprise's headquarters in New York

Types of non-profit social enterprises (AO3)

- Social enterprises are organizations that generate revenue, but act with community objectives (for the wellbeing of others) at the core of their operations.
- A non-profit social enterprise behaves in a commercial business-like way but does not distribute any profits (financial surplus) to its owners or shareholders. Instead, the organization uses the surplus to pursue its mission or vision.
- Examples of non-profit social enterprises include non-government organizations such as UNICEF, World Vision, BRAC (formerly Bangladesh Rehabilitation Assistance Committee), Save the Children, and the UN's World Food Programme (WFP).

■ **Table 1.7** Advantages and disadvantages of non-profit social enterprises

Advantages of non-profit social enterprises	Disadvantages of non-profit social enterprises
• They are exempt from paying income taxes and corporate taxes. • They qualify for government grants and subsidies. • They exist for the benefit of local communities and societies, such as through fundraising, donations, and humanitarian aid. • As part of government incentives to encourage donors, non-profit social enterprises qualify for tax concessions on their donations.	• In order to protect the general public, there are restrictions and strict guidelines that must be followed, including on the types of trading activities allowed. • Earnings of workers are often lower, as it would be regarded as unethical if they were paid similar to those in for-profit companies. • They are often reliant on donations and external support in order to survive. • Cost and financial control may not be stringent, as there is no expectation to earn a profit.

EXPERT TIP

HL candidates must pay attention to this section of the syllabus, as Paper 3 focuses explicitly and exclusively on social enterprises.

■ Non-governmental organizations (NGOs)

- A non-governmental organization (NGO) is a type of non-profit social enterprise that is neither part of a government nor a traditional for-profit business, but is instead run by a voluntary group.
- They may be funded by governments, international organizations, charities, commercial businesses, or private individuals.

- NGOs can operate at a local, regional, national or international level, but are not usually affiliated with any government.
- The majority of NGOs are run to promote a social cause, such as human rights, animal rights, environmental protection, disaster relief, or development assistance.
- They exert pressure and influence on governments to support their cause and/or a wide range of global issues.

1.3 Business objectives

SL/HL content	Depth of teaching
Vision statement and mission statement	AO2
Common business objectives including growth, profit, protecting shareholder value, and ethical objectives	AO2
Strategic and tactical objectives	AO3
Corporate social responsibility (CSR)	AO3

Diploma Programme *Business management guide* (May 2022)

Vision statement and mission statement (AO2)

■ Table 1.8 Vision statements and mission statements

Vision statement	Mission statement
<ul><li>An abstract statement that outlines what the organization ultimately wants to be/do.</li><li>Concentrates on the future direction of the organization.</li><li>A source of inspiration (driving force) for internal stakeholders.</li><li>A statement of the purpose of the organization, in terms of its core values or ideals.</li><li>Provides guiding beliefs about how things should be done within the organization.</li><li>Informs strategic planning, i.e. where the organization wants to be.</li><li>Vision statements don't change, even as business models adapt over time.</li><li>Broad statements.</li></ul>	<ul><li>A concrete and practical statement intended to state the purpose and guide the actions of an organization.</li><li>A declaration of an organization's reason for being, i.e. why it exists.</li><li>Symbolises an organization's philosophies, goals and ambitions.</li><li>Enables the organization's stakeholders to understand the desired level of performance.</li><li>Incorporates meaningful and measurable criteria, e.g. expectations of growth and profitability.</li><li>Describes how an organization will execute its vision, i.e. the tactics that make the vision a reality.</li><li>Narrow and specific statements.</li></ul>

EXPERT TIP

Not all businesses have separate vision and mission statements. For example, Facebook combines its vision and mission as: 'Facebook's mission is to give people the power to share and make the world more open and connected'. Amazon's vision and mission statements are also combined as: 'To be Earth's most customer centric company; to build a place where people can come to find and discover anything they might want to buy online'.

KEY CONCEPT

For an organization of your choice, investigate how the vision or mission statement has influenced change in the organization.

Common business objectives including growth, profit, protecting shareholder value, and ethical objectives (AO2)

Objectives

- Objectives are the targets an organization is trying to achieve, for example to protect or maximize shareholder value.
- Objectives can be *strategic* (long term), *tactical* (medium term) or *operational* (short term).
- They are often set as SMART goals (**s**pecific, **m**easurable, **a**chievable, **r**ealistic and **t**ime constrained), for example to achieve sales growth of $250m by 2027, or to increase market share by 3 per cent within five years.
- They can give a sense of direction to employees, managers, departments, and the organization as a whole.
- Objectives can define both the purpose and the aspirations of an organization.
- They can be communicated through the organization's mission statement.

EXPERT TIP

Objectives are vital for any business organization, so that stakeholders know where it is going, and are able to measure the business's progress towards its goal. Objectives give departments and the organization a sense of common purpose, making it easier to create a team spirit and co-ordinate the business.

The common (or generic) business objectives in the IB syllabus are (i) growth, (ii) profit, (iii) protecting shareholder value, and (iv) ethical objectives.

Growth

- Growth refers to an increase in the size of a business, in terms of measures such as sales revenue, number of employees, capital employed, and market share.
- If a firm grows, it should be able to enjoy improved brand awareness, more economies of scale (see Chapter 1.5), increased market power, and it should also earn higher profits.
- A larger business is also better positioned to spread risks, such as being safer from a takeover bid by a competitor (because a larger organization tends to be more expensive to acquire).
- Growth can benefit owners and shareholders in the long term by providing greater profits and dividends.
- Employees and managers can benefit from being offered higher salaries and better job security.

Profit

- **Profit** is the quantitative difference between a firm's total sales revenue and its total costs for any given time period, that is to say, profit is the financial surplus that is generated from business activities.
- It is a common business objective for for-profit business organizations.
- Profit is the conventional measure of business success.
- It is used as a source of internal finance for investment purposes and/or paid to the owners (shareholders) of the business.
- Employees and managers may have their remuneration (bonus or reward) linked to the value of profits that the business generates during the year. This can help to motivate workers and managers to meet or exceed performance targets.
- For relatively new businesses, it can take several years before any profit is earned, as it takes time and money to establish a business, its products, and brand. Nevertheless, a business cannot survive in the long term without earning any profit.

Protecting shareholder value

- **Shareholders** are the owners of companies (privately held and publicly held companies). Directors and senior managers are responsible for protecting the interests of the company's owners – the shareholders.
- Shareholder value is comprised of two elements: (i) capital gain and (ii) dividends.
- **Capital gain** on the value of shares means there is a financial gain in the value of the shares that shareholders bought in the business, meaning there is a sustained increase in share price over time.
  - The price of a company's shares will increase if there is higher demand for its shares. This is based on the level of profits that the company is expected to earn in the future.
  - Share prices are also dependent on the perceived quality of the senior management team and the strategic plans that directors have in place.
  - Confidence in the stock market is also dependent on external influences, such as the outlook for the market, as well as the state of the economy in general.
- **Dividends** paid on the shares. Dividends are a share of a company's profits that is distributed to its owners. Shareholders will be interested in the amount of dividends paid each year.
  - The company directors need to consider what proportion of any profits earned by the company during the year should be distributed to shareholders.
  - Whatever is passed on to shareholders in the form of dividends cannot be used as retained earnings as an internal source of finance to fund investment expenditure.
- In some companies, the dividend payment to shareholders is relatively low, because the focus is on investment and long-term growth. In other businesses, there is more focus on short-term dividend payments to shareholders, who may be highly influential owners of the company.

Ethical objectives

- Ethical objectives are business targets that are based on moral principles of what is deemed to be right. This is shaped by internal factors (such as a firm's vision or mission statement) and external factors (such as societal norms and expectations).

- Examples of ethical objectives include the fair treatment of workers, protecting the environment through the use of sustainable production techniques, and ensuring that suppliers receive fair and prompt payment.
- There is increasing interest in the ethical behaviour of businesses from many stakeholders. This is largely due to education and the influence of mass media, including social media.
- Pursuing ethical objectives may be well received by the various stakeholders of a business, including customers, employees, suppliers, the local community, and the government.
- Ethical business objectives can help a business to build a more reputable and respected brand. This can, in the long term, lead to increased sales, improved customer loyalty, and higher staff retention, as well as attract more investments.
- However, there are high costs of compliance and implementation. For example, some businesses may choose to pay workers more than the legal minimum wage (an ethical act to safeguard the wellbeing of their employees), but this increases production costs.

Strategic and tactical objectives (AO3)

◼ Strategic objectives

- Strategies are the ways in which an organization intends to achieve its strategic business objectives.
- Strategic objectives are long term, with overall corporate decisions made by the senior management team or executive board.
- Examples of strategic objectives include goals to expand overseas, to change the business's location, to acquire a competitor firm, or to diversify the product portfolio in order to develop competitive advantages.

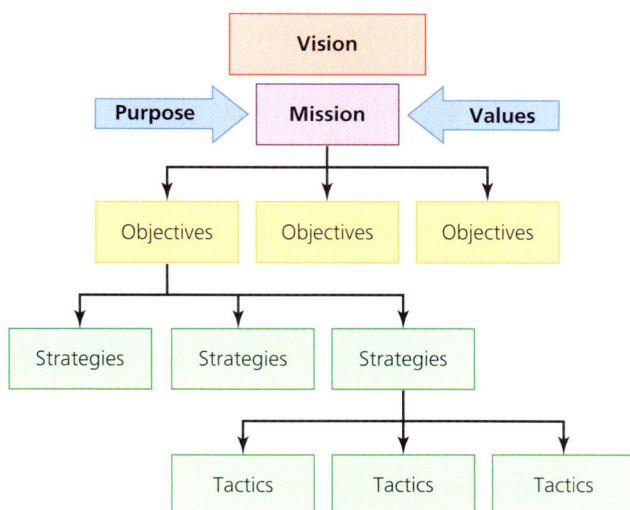

◼ Tactical objectives

- Tactics are short-term, smaller-scale or routine decisions about how an organization intends to achieve its business objectives on a day-to-day or routine basis. The responsibility for making these decisions is usually delegated to employees lower down in the hierarchy, to motivate and inspire workers.
- Tactics are concerned with achieving narrowly defined and measurable goals.
- Tactical objectives have specific targets and timelines, enabling managers to assess if or when these targets have been achieved.
- They are used to support firms in achieving the strategic objectives of the organization.

◼ **Figure 1.2** The relationship between objectives, strategies, and tactics

Corporate social responsibility (CSR) (AO3)

- **Corporate social responsibility (CSR)** refers to the obligation and engagement of a business in committing to behaving ethically and responsibly towards its different stakeholders (see Chapter 1.4).

- Examples of CSR include improving the quality of work life for employees, adopting green technologies to protect the natural environment, and using socially responsible marketing strategies (see Chapter 4.1).

- CSR includes the voluntary actions a business takes that are over and above compliance with minimum legal requirements. This can help to improve its competitiveness and the interests of the wider community.

- CSR is based on what is deemed to be morally correct (or ethical) according to societal norms and values.

- As a business becomes more established and grows, the scale of its operations enlarges. For example, more workers are needed. As a result, organizational objectives and priorities may need to change or evolve.

- The opportunity cost for a large multinational company that does not act ethically is potentially huge, especially when compared to an unknown and small sole trader that operates in a remote town.

- Modern business practice in many countries has shown that CSR plays an important role in determining the market position (see Chapter 4.2) of an organization.

- Attitudes towards CSR can change over time. What was previously considered socially acceptable, such as getting a new plastic bag each time you buy something at the supermarket, may no longer be the case today. Environmental protection was not a major corporate priority until the 1980s.

- Hence, changes in societal norms, expectations, and values mean that organizations may need to review their CSR policies and practices from time to time.

Some of the reasons why businesses engage with corporate social responsibility (CSR) are listed below:

- Media exposure, pressure group action, and educational awareness have all ensured that an increasing number of businesses are actively implementing CSR and pursuing ethical business objectives.

- Setting and pursuing CSR can increase employee motivation and productivity. Businesses might also find it easier to recruit and retain employees because they are regarded as ethical employers.

- CSR can help to reduce negative publicity from the mass news media and pressure groups.

- The growing use of social media makes it easier for the general public to demand transparency and ethical business behaviour.

- Having a good corporate image with customers and a good corporate reputation with the government enables a business to gain competitive advantages. Hence, CSR can be profitable in the long term (the ultimate aim of for-profit organizations).

- Pursuing CSR is a form of self-regulation and ethical business behaviour. This helps to avoid government intervention and unwanted media attention.

However, there can be limitations or drawbacks to pursuing CSR. Some of these impacts are listed below:

- Compliance costs of acting in socially responsible ways and the extra management time required to implement such practices can put the organization at a competitive disadvantage, at least in the short term.

- This can mean lower profits being available to distribute to shareholders (in the form of dividends). This might therefore create some resentment and conflict with investors.
- Furthermore, as competitors are in pursuit of similar socially responsible practices, any unique selling point (USP) might be short lived, which means using CSR to gain competitive advantages is not necessarily sustainable.

EXPERT TIP

It is incorrect to assume that only non-profit organizations (NPOs) and social enterprises set ethical business objectives such as corporate social responsibility. NPOs may have different objectives because they are not profit seeking. However, for-profit organizations may choose to implement CSR and pursue ethical business objectives for humanitarian and altruistic reasons.

KEY CONCEPT

Discuss how CSR facilitates businesses to compete in **sustainable** ways.

EXPERT TIP

The nature of CSR is further complicated when organizations operate in overseas markets. What is considered socially acceptable in one country might not be in others. For example, Australia and the UK have very strict laws on tobacco advertising, whereas Japan and Greece are far more relaxed about this.

EXAM PRACTICE QUESTION

Explain the purpose of a vision statement for the employees of an organization.   [2]

1.4 Stakeholders

SL/HL content	Depth of teaching
Internal and external stakeholders	AO2
Conflict between stakeholders	AO2

Diploma Programme *Business management guide* (May 2022)

Internal stakeholders (AO2)

> **Key word**
>
> **Stakeholders** are individuals, organizations, or groups with a direct interest in the operations and performance of a particular business. They have varying degrees of influence on the organization.

- **Employees** are the people who work within an organization. They can have a significant influence on the organization, such as through their level of motivation and productivity. Employees seek to improve their remuneration and the terms and conditions of their employment, for example competitive levels of pay, job security, good working conditions, and opportunities for professional advancement.
- **Managers** and **directors** are people hired to be in charge of certain departments or operations within an organization. They may aim to maximize profits, improve operational efficiency, and enhance customer relations. They also strive to improve their own conditions of employment and financial rewards, such as bonuses, share options schemes, performance-related pay, and fringe benefits (see Chapter 2.4).
- **Shareholders** are individuals or organizations who hold shares in a company, thereby owning a part of the business. As part-owners of the company, shareholders have

rights to a portion of any profits the business earns (these payments are known as dividends), as well as having voting rights at the company's Annual General Meeting (AGM) to decide who serves on the company's board of directors. Shareholders also expect the company to earn an acceptable return on their investment, thereby providing them with shareholder value.

EXPERT TIP

Shareholders can be classified as internal or **external stakeholders**. For example, employees and directors may hold shares in the company so are **internal stakeholders**. However, the general public and other organizations may also own shares in the company, but these stakeholders are external to the business.

EXPERT TIP

Do not confuse the terms 'shareholders' and 'stakeholders'. The latter is a much broader term and includes more than shareholders. All shareholders of a business are stakeholders, but not all stakeholders are shareholders.

External stakeholders (AO2)

- **Customers** are the clients of a business. They want value for money – competitive prices that reflect the quality of the goods and services purchased, products that are safe and fit for their purpose, good customer care, and the provision of after-sales support.

- **Suppliers** provide the goods and support services for other businesses. For example, Coca-Cola supplies supermarkets with carbonated soft drinks. Suppliers are important stakeholders, as they can decide what credit terms or discounts (if any) are offered to the business. They are interested in securing reasonable prices for their goods and services, regular orders, and prompt payment from their business clients.

- **Competitors** are the rival organizations of a particular business. As external stakeholders, they are interested in the business competing in a fair and honest way. Competitors set their own targets and strategies based on the actions of other businesses in the same industry.

- The **local community** is interested in businesses acting in a socially responsible way, such as creating job opportunities, protecting the natural environment, and supporting local residents and firms, such as with sponsorship of public events.

- **Pressure groups** are organizations or groups of people who have a common interest and push for change. They try to influence governments and public opinion in favour of their cause, such as environmental protection, fair trade, animal welfare, or human rights. Therefore, these special interest groups put pressure on businesses to work in socially responsible, ethical, and sustainable ways.

- **Financiers** are commercial banks and other creditors that provide sources of finance for businesses (see Chapter 3.2). They are external stakeholders interested in the financial wellbeing of a business in terms of its ability to repay debts such as bank loans and mortgages. They can do this by using quantitative techniques such as liquidity (see Chapter 3.7) and investment appraisal (see Chapter 3.8).

- The **government** is a key external stakeholder of all businesses. It is keen to see that firms operate legally and in a socially responsible way. The government affects businesses directly by its policies, such as the tax system, employment legislation, consumer protection rights, and environmental protection laws.

Conflict between stakeholders (AO2)

As outlined earlier, stakeholder groups have different interests in the activities of a business. In practice, it is difficult to satisfy all stakeholder groups at the same time, all of the time. There may be areas of mutual benefit, but there may also be disagreements or differences in opinions with others. For example, business growth may create jobs, thus generating positive impacts on the local community, such as more choice for consumers. However, business expansion in the local community might also create traffic congestion and cause more pollution, which conflicts with the interests of environmental pressure groups. Other examples of possible conflict between stakeholders' interests are listed below:

- Owners of the business may be reluctant to pay higher wages to employees as they seek to use the financial surplus to distribute profits instead.

- Directors may want large bonuses, but this may conflict with the desire of shareholders to have higher dividend payouts.

- In general, customers may want lower prices, but shareholders may prefer higher prices as this would generate greater profit margins.

- In the pursuit of efficiency and productivity gains, employers may invest in new machinery, but this may result in redundancies (job losses) for employees.

- Shareholders may demand a greater proportion of profits to be distributed as dividends, yet this leaves less funds for managers to use for marketing, product development, or to improve working conditions for their employees.

- Pressure groups might deem the corporate profits of some large multinational companies to be too high, although the management team would argue the profits are necessary to remain competitive in the future.

- Acting in a socially responsible way, such as reducing and recycling waste, can help a business to please the local community, but this could upset directors and shareholders due to the high costs of compliance and implementation.

- To some extent, stakeholder conflict is likely to always exist, so the varying interests of stakeholders must always be carefully managed.

In order to deal with potential stakeholder conflict, businesses often use **stakeholder mapping** (see Figure 1.3) as a management tool to determine the key stakeholders. Stakeholder mapping (or **stakeholder analysis**) involves organizing the various stakeholders of the business into a matrix, based on their degree of power (influence) and their level of interest in the business.

The stakeholder group(s) with a high degree of power and interest are known as the **key stakeholders**. Successful businesses strive to fulfil as many of the needs and interests of various stakeholder groups as possible, but give priority to satisfying the needs and interests of their key stakeholder group(s). Due to the complexities of running and managing large businesses, handling potentially conflicting stakeholder interests tends to be simpler in smaller businesses.

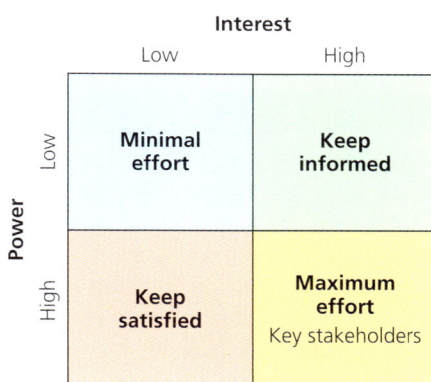

■ **Figure 1.3** Stakeholder mapping

Possible methods to handle stakeholder conflicts include the following:

- Using a **conciliation** service (see Chapter 2.7) to align the conflicting interests of different stakeholder groups.

- Using an **arbitrator** to assess the conflicting interests, with the stakeholders agreeing to accept the judgement of the independent arbitrator (see Chapter 2.7).

- Hiring **public relations** (PR) consultants (or using an internal PR team) to communicate with the local community and to keep other stakeholders informed of the positive aspects of the organization's operations or planned changes.
- Improving **communications** with the different stakeholder groups, for example keeping stakeholders informed of new developments and communicating the rationale for change.
- Using **financial rewards** linked to employee productivity gains. This helps to motivate workers to perform more effectively, thereby enabling the business to earn more profits. Shareholder value is also improved, as higher profits should lead to higher dividend payments and increased share prices.
- Ensuring wider representation of stakeholders in the decision-making process, for example the involvement of a trade union representative in strategic decision making, or including an employee representative at the board of directors' meetings.

In resolving conflict, the outcome of negotiations is largely influenced by the relative bargaining power of the various stakeholder groups. For example, employees who are backed by powerful labour unions may be in a better position to secure improved terms and conditions of employment. International pressure groups, such as Greenpeace and Friends of the Earth, can exert huge pressure on businesses, because they have greater backing from the general public and media.

However, it is possible to meet the potentially conflicting interests of different stakeholder groups. For example, offering competitive financial rewards and improved terms and conditions of employment for all workers can result in a highly motivated, loyal, and productive workforce. This leads to lower staff turnover (see Chapter 2.4) and greater output. It can also result in an improved corporate image, thereby helping with the organization's marketing and recruitment. By contrast, not managing conflict effectively, such as conflicts between management and the workforce, can lead to industrial action (see Chapter 2.7). Ultimately, resolving potential conflicts between stakeholders leads to improved efficiency and higher profits.

EXPERT TIP

While different stakeholder groups have different objectives, some stakeholders belong to multiple groups. For example, managers are employees of the organization and might also be shareholders of the company. Hence, stakeholder analysis is a difficult balancing act of trying to meet the potentially conflicting interests of different stakeholder groups.

EXAM PRACTICE QUESTION

In November 2022, Twitter announced that half of its global workforce of 7,500 employees would be losing their jobs. The move came shortly after Twitter was taken over by Elon Musk, CEO of Tesla and SpaceX. Musk admitted that Twitter was losing over $4 million per day, so mass redundancies were necessary due to the loss in advertising revenues on the social media platform. Advertising accounts for 90 per cent of Twitter's revenues. Analysts suggested the move would reduce the return on investment for Twitter's shareholders, at least in the short run. Musk had purchased Twitter for $44 billion, a price which was far higher than Twitter's valuation at the time.

a   Identify **two** stakeholders of Twitter.   [2]
b   Explain **two** conflicts following Twitter's decision to reduce its global workforce.   [4]

KEY CONCEPT

Discuss the importance of **ethics** for various stakeholder groups in an organization of your choice.

1.5 Growth and evolution

SL/HL content	Depth of teaching
Internal and external economies and diseconomies of scale	AO2
The difference between internal and external growth	AO2
Reasons for businesses to grow	AO3
Reasons for businesses to stay small	AO3
External growth methods: mergers and acquisitions (M&As), takeovers, joint ventures, strategic alliances, and franchising	AO3

Diploma Programme *Business management guide* (May 2022)

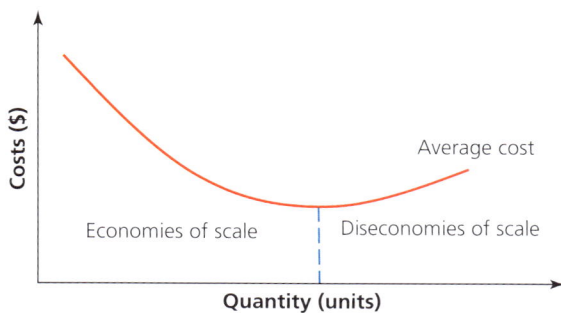

■ **Figure 1.4** Economies and diseconomies of scale

Internal and external economies and diseconomies of scale (AO2)

- **Economies of scale** are the cost-saving benefits of operating on a large scale, i.e. the reduction in unit costs of production as an organization grows.

- By contrast, **diseconomies of scale** arise when the cost per unit of output increases due to the organization being too large and inefficient, for example problems with communication and co-ordination.

- **Internal economies of scale** are created and enjoyed within an organization when it operates on a larger scale. Examples include:
  - *Financial economies.* Larger firms can obtain finance more easily and at lower interest costs due to their relatively lower risk.
  - *Managerial economies.* Larger organizations can afford greater numbers of specialized managers, thereby boosting productivity and output.
  - *Production economies.* Fixed costs of production are spread out over a larger volume of output, thereby reducing the average fixed costs of production.
  - *Marketing economies.* Marketing costs per unit fall when sales volume grows, as the larger firm can market its entire product range.
  - *Purchasing economies.* Buying larger quantities of raw materials, components and stock, thereby reducing the organization's average costs.

- **External economies of scale** arise from having specialized back-up services available in a particular region where firms are located. For example, Silicon Valley in California, USA, is home to many of the best-known high-tech companies.

- **Diseconomies of scale** occur when an organization becomes too large to manage effectively, so its unit costs begin to increase. For example, if a firm increases its factor inputs by 50 per cent, but the subsequent output only increases by 20 per cent, then it experiences higher average costs of production.

- **Internal diseconomies of scale** are caused by problems of co-ordination, control, and communication within a firm. For example:
  - As firms get larger, managers find it more difficult to co-ordinate, control, and communicate with a larger workforce, resulting in higher costs per unit of output.
  - When fixed costs increase, for example through the purchase of additional premises as a firm grows. This substantially increases its average costs of production if output is unable to increase by at least the same proportion.

Key terms

Internal economies of scale refer to the fall in unit costs of production for a single organization as it grows and evolves, for example managerial and financial economies of scale.

External economies of scale refer to the fall in unit costs of production for all organizations in an industry as it experiences growth and evolution.

- **External diseconomies of scale** affect all firms in an industry, resulting in higher per unit costs. Examples include:
  - ○ Traffic congestion causing delays and therefore causing costs to increase.
  - ○ Higher costs of rent due to the high demand for firms locating in a particularly popular area.
  - ○ Labour shortages in a certain location, thereby leading to higher labour costs.

EXPERT TIP

Students often state that costs of production will fall as a firm increases the scale of its operations. This is not quite accurate – clearly it is cheaper to produce 1,000 cans of Coca-Cola than it is to produce 500,000 cans! However, it is cheaper to produce each can of Coca-Cola on a larger scale; in other words, economies of scale reduce the average costs of production.

EXAM PRACTICE QUESTION

Candy's Candies has monthly fixed costs of $4,800 and variable costs of $1.50 per unit. Demand for its candies is 4,000 units each month. The average unit price is $4.

a Distinguish between internal and external economies of scale. [4]

b Calculate the average cost for Candy's Candies each month. [2]

c Calculate the profit made by Candy's Candies each month. [2]

EXPERT TIP

Candidates need to demonstrate that they clearly understand the distinction between internal economies of scale (which relate to a specific firm) and external economies of scale (which relate to the whole industry).

The difference between internal and external growth (AO2)

- **Internal growth** (also known as **organic growth**) occurs when an organization expands using its own resources, without involving other organizations. For example, a business can grow internally by using Ansoff's growth matrix strategies (see the Business management toolkit section), such as market penetration and product development.

- **External growth** (also known as **inorganic growth**) occurs when a business relies on third-party organizations for growth. Examples of such methods include mergers, acquisitions, takeovers, and franchising.

- Key indicators of growth include an increase in an organization's sales revenue, its market share (see Chapter 4.1), and the number of employees hired.

■ **Table 1.9** Differences between internal and external growth

External growth
• External growth is usually the quickest method of growth.
• Ordinarily, it requires external sources of finance (see Chapter 3.2).
• It often results in the dilution of ownership and control.
• It is far more bureaucratic, especially with mergers and acquisitions (M&As) and takeovers.
• It involves more financial risk.
• In the case of M&As, external growth reduces or eliminates competition.

Internal growth

- The brand identity and corporate culture can be maintained.
- It is less risky, especially if financed by retained profits (see Chapter 3.2).
- Higher levels of production mean the business can benefit from internal economies of scale (lower average costs), whereas external growth can create diseconomies of scale, especially if there is a culture clash.

Reasons for businesses to grow (AO3)

The following list includes some of the reasons why businesses may want to grow (the merits of being a larger organization):

- Larger firms benefit from economies of scale, so may be able to offer lower prices, yet offer greater choice to customers.
- Greater access to financial resources; having more capital than their rivals means that larger businesses have scope for further growth.
- They can attract better-skilled staff as they can offer better career development and remuneration packages.
- Customers tend to be attracted to larger, well-known brand names as they recognize and trust these businesses more than smaller, unknown brands.
- Large firms are less likely to fail so represent lower risk for owners, investors, and financiers. Small firms are more vulnerable during an economic recession.
- The above advantages combine to give larger businesses a competitive edge over their smaller rivals.

Reasons for businesses to stay small (AO3)

The following list includes some of the reasons why businesses may choose to stay small (the merits of being a smaller organization):

- Small businesses are easier to set up and this can be done at a much lower cost.
- Owners of small businesses enjoy independence in decision making – there is freedom to operate independently from the demands of directors and shareholders.
- The owner(s) can maintain control and ownership of the business.
- In general, smaller businesses are more flexible in responding to changes in the marketplace, as there is less bureaucracy.
- They can serve specialized niche markets that are potentially highly profitable, without attracting the attention of larger businesses.
- Small businesses tend to have a closer relationship with their customers.
- The financial accounts of the business can be kept private; only the tax authorities need access to these.

> **EXPERT TIP**
>
> Students are not expected to give a definitive verdict about small versus large organizations. Both large and small businesses can thrive; the important thing is to consider size in a critical way and in the context of the organization. There are other factors to also consider, for example size might not matter as much as the firm's vision and the organizational culture.

External growth methods (AO3)

Methods of external growth include (i) mergers and acquisitions (M&As), (ii) takeovers, (iii) joint ventures, (iv) strategic alliances, and (v) franchising.

▥ Mergers and acquisitions (M&As)

- A **merger** is a form of external growth that occurs when two or more independent businesses voluntarily agree to combine to form a new, single legal entity. Typically, these businesses operate in the same industry, so the merger gives the new firm greater market power.

- An **acquisition** is a form of external growth that occurs when one company buys a controlling interest in another company; that is, it purchases enough shares in the company to acquire a majority stake. This is typically done with the agreement of the board of directors of the target company.

- For example, in July 2015, British publishing giant Pearson sold the *Financial Times* to Japanese media firm Nikkei for £844 million ($1.27bn) in cash. Interestingly, the *FT* had been founded through a merger in 1888.

■ **Table 1.10** Advantages and disadvantages of M&As

Advantages of M&As	Disadvantages of M&As
• A range of economies of scale can be gained through M&As.	• Resistance from employees, trade unions, managers, and shareholders (who are unwilling to sell their shares).
• It enables the new, larger firm to share costs, expertise, and risks.	• M&As are not always successful, especially when the firms pursue a high-risk diversification strategy.
• It is a quick way for a firm to enter new industries and geographic markets.	• M&As are generally very expensive, especially if there are delays in the process; in some cases, the purchase price ends up being unaffordable.
• M&As offer instantaneous growth, as they are quicker than methods of organic growth.	• Corporate culture clashes, such as contrasting management styles and organizational structures, can cause huge problems for M&As.
• The cutting of costs and synergies from M&As allow the business to earn higher profits and/or gain market share.	• Diseconomies of scale may occur due to the loss of cost control and the loss of focus of the company's core activities.
• The newly formed business gains market power to influence prices and output in the industry.	
• A merger or acquisition could be the only way that a business can survive due to its poor cash flow or financial difficulties.	

▥ Takeovers

- As with an acquisition, a **takeover** is a form of external growth that occurs when one company buys a controlling interest in another company, although this is usually done in a hostile way (hence, takeovers are often referred to as **hostile takeovers**).

- An example is Elon Musk's takeover of Twitter for $44 billion in 2022.

- Takeovers often result in mass redundancies (job losses) in the target firm, due to cost savings desired by the purchaser. For example, Elon Musk made more than half of Twitter's workforce redundant after his takeover, including all members of the board of directors at the time.

- The advantages and disadvantages of M&As (see Table 1.10) also apply to takeovers.

Joint ventures

- A **joint venture** (JV) is an arrangement between two or more separate parties, to pool their resources together to form a new legal entity.

- An example is Hong Kong Disneyland, a joint venture between the Hong Kong government (which owns 51 per cent of the JV) and The Walt Disney Company (with a 49 per cent stake).

- The companies engaged in a JV share resources (financial, capital, and human), such as personnel, assets, and costs in pursuit of profits.

■ **Table 1.11** Advantages and disadvantages of joint ventures

Advantages of joint ventures	Disadvantages of joint ventures
• The firms combine their resources, such as technology and capital, creating synergies and strengthening their position in the market.	• Conflict and disagreements are common due to the different corporate cultures and management styles of the firms involved in a JV.
• Financial risks of the project are shared between the partner companies.	• Compromises are often made with JVs, and this can lead to suboptimal outcomes for both parent companies. By contrast, execution of business strategy is more decisive with acquisitions and takeovers.
• Local firms can enable the JV to overcome cultural difficulties that a foreign company may encounter.	
• JVs enable companies to become larger and thus to benefit from economies of scale.	• Diseconomies of scale may occur due to operations on a larger scale, e.g. additional meetings and administrative processes, and communications problems.
• The firms in the JV enjoy the advantages of growth without losing their separate identities.	• JVs are generally more difficult to terminate due to the lawfully binding obligations of the newly created legal entity.
• Firms in the JV can avoid the high administrative and legal costs associated with M&As.	

Strategic alliances

- Strategic alliances (SAs) are formed when two or more businesses join forces to benefit from growth without any fundamental changes to their own long-term strategies.

- Unlike joint ventures, the formation of a strategic alliance does not create a new business organization.

- Examples include the SA between Starbucks and Barnes & Noble (a coffee shop chain and a bookstore) which started in 1993. Apple has partnered with Sony, Motorola, Phillips, and AT&T. The Star Alliance consists of 27 airlines, forming the world's largest global SA in the airline industry.

■ **Table 1.12** Advantages and disadvantages of strategic alliances

Advantages of strategic alliances	Disadvantages of strategic alliances
• Like JVs, firms in a strategic alliance can benefit by sharing expertise and resources with other businesses in the SA.	• Unlike joint ventures, strategic alliances are easier to enter and exit, so can be less stable or committed.
• Businesses in the SA remain separate legal entities, without the relatively high costs of forming a new company.	• Strategic alliances are sometimes only short-term, temporary agreements.
• Synergies and economies of scale can be gained by the partner firms in the SA.	• It can make a business vulnerable to mistakes or malpractice by partner businesses in the SA.

▨ Franchising

- **Franchising** refers to an agreement between a business (the franchisor) that gives the legal rights to other organizations (the franchisees) to sell products under the franchisor's brand name.
- Examples of multinational companies that use franchising include McDonald's, Subway, Starbucks, Pizza Hut, KFC, and Hotel Inn.

■ **Figure 1.5** McDonald's is a famous global franchise. The branch shown here is located in Xian, China

■ **Table 1.13** Advantages and disadvantages of franchising

Advantages of franchising	Disadvantages of franchising
• The franchisor can expand the business without the need to raise finance and invest their own funds to make the business grow (as the franchisee pays for the expansion); hence, it is a cheaper method of expansion than organic growth.	• Not all businesses have the expertise to properly manage the franchising model in terms of quality control and marketing activities.
• The franchisor receives royalties based on a predetermined percentage of the franchisee's sales revenues.	• It can be very expensive for the franchisee in terms of start-up costs and running costs, as they must pay a percentage of sales revenues to the franchisor.
• It is a relatively fast method of external growth that can strengthen the brand name quickly.	• The franchisee is also usually charged an annual fee by the franchisor, so this can substantially cut the franchisee's profit margin.
• The franchisor does not need to closely monitor or control the day-to-day operations of the franchisee (whereas monitoring and control must take place with directly owned stores).	• The franchisee lacks flexibility in decision making, as they need to follow the corporate rules and policies of the franchisor, including what they can and cannot sell, and the marketing used to promote the firm's goods and services.
• The franchising model is usually a tried and tested one, so the success rate is high; hence, there can be large profits made for the franchisee and franchisor.	• Diseconomies of scale can arise, even with franchises, especially if the franchise over-expands in too short a timescale.
• Economies of scale, such as purchasing economies of scale, can be gained and passed on to franchisees when buying products to be sold.	• Incompetent, substandard or dishonest franchisees can easily damage the corporate image and reputation of the franchisor's brand.
• The franchisee receives ongoing support from the franchisor, e.g. marketing, market research, staff training, and distribution networks.	

EXPERT TIP

Buying a franchise is not an easy thing to accomplish. Franchisors use a thorough vetting process to assess the limited number of franchisees granted a license each year. For the franchisor, their brand name and reputation is at risk, and legally removing an incompetent franchisee is both challenging and costly.

1.6 Multinational companies (MNCs)

SL/HL content	Depth of teaching
The impact of MNCs on the host countries	AO3

Diploma Programme *Business management guide* (May 2022)

The impact of MNCs on the host countries (AO3)

Key term

A **multinational company (MNC)** is an organization that operates, owns, or controls production and/or service facilities in two or more countries. Typically, the headquarters (or head office) of the MNC is in its home country.

The following list gives some of the reasons for the growth of **multinational companies (MNCs)**:

- MNCs benefit from access to larger markets in overseas countries.
- Many MNCs operate on a large, global scale with well-established brand names.
- The size of MNCs means they can benefit from economies of scale (see Chapter 1.5), especially as they grow.
- Other cost-saving benefits of operating in overseas countries include access to cheaper labour, lower rates of tax, access to cheaper raw materials and components, and/or being closer to global customers.
- MNCs spread risk by operating in other markets, not just within their own domestic country.
- MNCs expand overseas as a market development strategy (see Ansoff's matrix in the Business management toolkit section) when other markets are saturated.
- MNCs can exploit the potential growth opportunities in certain overseas markets that are still untapped.

EXPERT TIP

MNCs are not without their complications and limitations. They are, for example, exposed to additional risks when operating in overseas markets. Risks include cultural differences in business practices, legal differences, political risks and volatility with fluctuating foreign exchange rates.

◼ Positive impacts of MNCs on the host countries

The impacts of MNCs on the host countries can be positive or negative. Positive impacts of MNCs on the host countries include the following:

- MNCs provide a significant number of employment opportunities, helping to raise the quality of life in the host country.
- The host nation benefits from having a more skilled labour force. Domestic workers also gain invaluable employment skills.

- MNCs are likely to buy local raw materials and components, thereby providing extra revenue for local suppliers and supporting local industries (such as packaging and distribution services).

- Consumers in the host country do not have to rely only on local suppliers, as they have more choice from MNCs. They also have access to higher quality products, thus helping to raise standards of living.

- Similarly, increased competition from MNCs can force domestic businesses to improve their operational efficiency, quality, customer care, and prices.

- The transfer of technical knowledge and benchmarking practices (see Chapter 5.3) from MNCs can also benefit domestic firms.

- Profitable MNCs will be taxed by the host government, thus providing added tax revenues to benefit the host economy.

■ Negative impacts of MNCs on the host countries

Negative impacts of MNCs on the host countries include the following:

- Domestic businesses may lose customers, market share, and profits due to the competition from foreign MNCs.

- Foreign companies may not be socially responsible, especially if rules and regulations are more relaxed in overseas markets, which might result in employees being exploited, scarce resources being depleted, or damage being done to the natural environment.

- The existence of large and powerful MNCs can destroy domestic businesses as they do not have the financial and human resources to compete successfully.

- Not all domestic people and businesses will welcome the presence of foreign companies, especially if it results in a cultural shift in the way of life, and this may lead to social and political tensions.

- Quite often, the profits of the MNC are repatriated to the headquarters in the home country, so the money leaves the host country. Without the profits being reinvested within the host country, employment and gross domestic product (GDP) will be lower.

- Many MNCs are extremely large organizations so can have significant influence over the governments of some host countries. Governments have also struggled to reach agreements on how to tax MNCs in equitable and transparent ways.

> ### KEY CONCEPT
>
> Investigate how **sustainability** or **creativity** has impacted the growth and evolution of a multinational company of your choice.

2 Human resource management

2.1 Introduction to human resource management

SL/HL content	Depth of teaching
Role of human resource management	AO2
Internal and external factors that influence human resource planning (for example, demographic change, change in labour mobility, immigration, flexitime, and gig economy)	AO2
Reasons for resistance to change in the workplace	AO2
Human resource strategies for reducing the impact of change and resistance to change	AO3

Diploma Programme *Business management guide* (May 2022)

Role of human resource management (AO2)

- **Human resource management** (HRM) is the management function of using and developing an organization's personnel (employees) in efficient ways, so as to meet its business objectives.

- It also involves human resource planning, recruitment and selection, training and development, employee relations, monitoring and maintaining professional relations between employees and employers, as well as legal compliance with employment legislation.

- Human resource planning is the management process of forecasting an organization's future workforce needs, and determining how to meet those needs. It is important to ensure that the organization has the right number of employees in the right roles at the right time.

- Recruitment and selection are important human resource roles, in order to ensure the business employs the right candidates for the right positions in the organization. This includes creating job descriptions, advertising vacant positions, conducting job interviews, and making job offers to the right people.

- Training and development are required to improve the skills and productivity (performance) of an organization's employees. This includes identifying the different training needs of different employees, creating appropriate training programmes, and evaluating the effectiveness of training and development programmes.

- Employee relations are important for maintaining positive and professional relationships between employees and the employer. This includes dealing with employee grievances and complaints, conflict in the workplace, as well as implementing policies and procedures to promote a positive working environment.

- Legal compliance means human resource managers must ensure that the organization obeys all relevant employment laws and regulations. This includes equal opportunities employment laws and anti-discrimination regulations.

Key term

Human resource planning is the management process of anticipating and meeting an organization's current and future staffing needs.

Internal and external factors that influence human resource planning (AO2)

- **Human resource planning** involves analyzing and forecasting the numbers of workers and the skills of those workers that will be needed by the organization. For example, new recruits are needed as a business expands, or because existing employees leave.

- Human resource planning aims for the effective management of an organization's workforce in order to achieve its objectives.

- Aspects of human resource planning include recruitment, induction (of new staff), retention, dismissal, redundancies, training, and performance appraisals.

- Human resource planning involves an analysis of historical data relating to the size of the workforce, the workload and mobility (flexibility) of employees, labour turnover rates, and demographic trends in society.

- Human resource planning is also needed to deal with instances of absenteeism. This refers to the number of staff away from work as a percentage of the firm's total workforce, per time period.

- Successful human resource planning helps a firm to develop a competitive advantage by matching human resource needs with the organization's strategic direction. It enables workers to be properly trained so that they perform at their best, which also helps to improve staff motivation.

- Internal and external factors that influence human resource planning include demographic change, changes in labour mobility, immigration, flexitime, and the gig economy. These factors can create opportunities and threats to different businesses.

▨ Demographic change

- Demographic change refers to developments and trends in the population that influence human resource planning, for example the average age of the population, gender distribution, educational attainment levels, and average household income.

- In some countries, such as France and Britain, the official retirement age has been increased due to the longer life expectancy of workers.

- The combination of lower birth rates, falling death rates and increased life expectancy in many economically developed countries has led to an aging population (an increase in the average age of the population). This has several implications for human resource planning, including:
  - ○ reduced labour mobility
  - ○ lower labour productivity levels
  - ○ changing consumption patterns.

- In many countries, there has been an increased number of women in the workforce. Women are opting to participate in the workforce and pursue their professional aspirations as well as having a family.

▨ Change in labour mobility

- **Occupational mobility** refers to the ease and flexibility of workers in moving from one job to another due to their ability and willingness to switch.

- By contrast, occupational immobility is the inability of workers to move from one job to another, due to a lack of skills, expertise, or qualifications.

- **Geographical mobility** refers to the extent to which workers are able and willing to relocate to another area for employment purposes.
- Geographical immobility is the reluctance of workers to move to another location. This might be due to personal reasons (such as family ties) or financial factors (such as relocation costs, property prices, or the higher costs of living in new locations).
- International labour mobility is even more difficult to achieve. Expatriate workers are often highly remunerated as an incentive for them to relocate overseas.
- Labour mobility can be improved by the business offering training and development programmes to its employees.

Immigration

- Migrants usually move to other countries in search of employment opportunities.
- Recruiting more migrant and temporary workers can help employers to fill short-term gaps in labour markets, such as during seasonal or peak trading periods.
- Highly skilled workers are more likely to be able and willing to migrate for employment purposes, as they have a greater chance of securing well-paid jobs overseas.
- The migration of skilled workers has increased due to globalization (such as the widespread growth of multinational companies) and internet technologies that enable better flows of information to workers looking for job opportunities overseas.

Flexitime

- Flexitime is a variable work schedule, requiring employees to work a set number of hours, but giving employees the right to choose when they work. There is normally a core (peak) period during the day when employees must be at work. This is common in the high-tech industry.
- Flexitime and part-time workers have led to a fall in the numbers of full-time workers in several industries, for example in supermarkets, retail, and fast food.
- Flexible work practices can help to increase employee morale and productivity by improving the way they operate, such as having the option to work from home (WFH).
- Flexitime has cost implications for the business, as managers need to supervise and monitor the hours actually worked by all flexitime employees.

■ **Figure 2.1** Many people rely on the gig economy as a source of income

Gig economy

- The gig economy refers to individuals who work in temporary positions, often through multiple online platforms such as Uber, Deliveroo, or TaskRabbit.
- Businesses that operate in the gig economy rely on independent contractors and outsourced workers, rather than traditional, permanent employees hired by the organization.
- Opportunities in the gig economy include increased flexibility and autonomy for workers, as they can choose when, where, and how often they work.
- However, it can lead to a decrease in job security traditionally associated with full-time employment. Furthermore, workers in the gig economy do not qualify for the same employment benefits and perks as their full-time counterparts.

- A growing number of people rely on the gig economy as their primary or secondary source of income. Hence, the gig economy is expected to continue growing in all regions of the world, with an increasing number of people participating in opportunities provided by the gig economy.

Reasons for resistance to change in the workplace (AO2)

- *Self-interest.* The pursuit of self-interest often takes priority over organizational objectives. Workers are often more interested in or concerned with the implications of change for themselves, rather than how it might benefit the organization. Hence, they may feel that change is unnecessary and requires too much effort unless it directly benefits them.

- *Low tolerance.* A lack of open-mindedness about change often happens because people fear or dislike disruptions and uncertainties. They might also fear failure in adapting to change so naturally resist it.

- *Misinformation.* A lack of understanding can cause resistance to change when the purpose of change has not been communicated effectively. Employees often feel that change is not necessary, especially when things are going well for the organization.

- *Interpretation of circumstances.* Management and employees may disagree on the purpose and benefits of change. Different interpretations of a particular situation can cause conflict and, in turn, resistance to change.

Human resource strategies for reducing the impact of change and resistance to change (AO3)

- *Communicating the change.* Effective communication of the purpose of and rationale behind change is vital to get support from staff. This means communicating in a clear and timely manner, so as to inform employees about the need and urgency for change, as well as the benefits of change (how change aligns with the firm's mission or vision and how it will help the organization to meet its business objectives).

- *Getting agreement/ownership.* Allowing workers to be involved in the decision-making process and giving them ownership of their work can help to prevent misunderstandings and misinterpretations of the purpose of change.

- *Recognition and rewards.* Similarly, recognizing and rewarding employees for their positive contributions to the change process can help to increase the overall level of staff motivation and engagement.

- *Planning and timing the change.* Rapid change is often poorly communicated and executed. Effective change management needs careful planning, including considerations regarding the timing of change. Training needs should be considered to facilitate the impact of change in the organization.

- *Managing resistance to change.* Despite the plans put in place, there is still likely to be some degree of resistance to change in the workplace. Hence, it is important to anticipate and manage resistance to change. This can be done by addressing the restraining forces against change and strengthening the driving forces in favour of change (see force field analysis in the Business management toolkit section).

KEY CONCEPT

Investigate how **ethics** have impacted the human resource planning for an organization of your choice.

2.2 Organizational structure

SL/HL content	Depth of teaching
The following terminology in relation to different types of organizational structures: delegation, span of control, levels of hierarchy, chain of command, bureaucracy, centralization, decentralization, delayering, and matrix structure	AO2
The following types of organization charts: (i) flat or horizontal, (ii) tall or vertical, hierarchical, and (iii) by product, by function, or by region	AO2, AO4
Appropriateness of different organizational structures given a change in external factors (for example, project-based organization and Charles Handy's 'shamrock organization') (HL only)	AO3

Diploma Programme *Business management guide* (May 2022)

Terminology in relation to different types of organizational structures (AO2)

- Small businesses are often characterized by informal organizational structures, while larger businesses need to adopt more formal structures due to the larger numbers of staff involved.

- As a business grows, it needs to organize staff into formal organizational structures to ensure effective communications, increased efficiency, and clear expectations of accountability and responsibility.

- The following terms help to facilitate understanding of different types of organizational structures: delegation, span of control, levels of hierarchy, chain of command, bureaucracy, centralization, decentralization, and delayering.

■ Delegation

> **Key term**
>
> **Delegation** is the process of entrusting and empowering a subordinate to successfully complete a task, project, or job role.

- As a business grows, it becomes inevitable that managers need to relinquish some of their roles and responsibilities. This is known as **delegation**.

- Delegation involves a line manager passing on control and authority while still holding the subordinate accountable for their actions. The overall responsibility still remains with the line manager.

- Delegation makes people accountable for their actions. Accountability is the extent to which a particular individual is held responsible for the success or failure of a job role or activity.

- Decision making can be delegated, but responsibility remains with the executive directors as they are ultimately responsible for the organization's strategy.

- Delegation can be a motivational tool for employees, as it recognises their talent, ability, and potential. Staff who are empowered may feel inspired to perform well. They feel a sense of achievement and pride in their work. Morale is high as they feel trusted and valued by management.

- Delegation can, but does not always, come with extra financial rewards, for example pay rises.

- Successful delegation frees up managers to attend to other important tasks such as strategic decision making.

> **EXPERT TIP**
>
> While delegation empowers a worker with decision-making rights and authority, responsibility cannot be delegated – the line manager remains responsible for the work or tasks delegated to others.

Span of control

- The **span of control** is inversely proportional to the number of hierarchical layers in an organization.
- A wide span of control means a manager is responsible for many subordinates. By contrast, a narrow span of control indicates that fewer workers directly report to the line manager.
- Having a narrow span of control can improve communication and control of different teams in the business.
- The wider the span of control, the greater the need for strong leadership and clear lines of communication.
- A wider span of control makes the organization flatter, whereas a narrower span of control makes the organization taller.
- Organizations with wider spans of control (and hence flatter structures) require fewer managers, which can lower costs of production. However, a narrower span of control means that managers have greater control and supervision over their employees, which can lead to improved performance and higher productivity.

Levels of hierarchy

- Hierarchical structures show where each person within an organization fits, and hence their roles and responsibilities.
- Hierarchical structures can be tall, with a narrow span of control, but may have many **levels of hierarchy**.
- Alternatively, organizations can be flat, with wider spans of control, but with fewer levels in the hierarchical structure.

Chain of command

- The **chain of command** in an organizational structure is usually shown as a vertical line of authority indicating how decisions and responsibility are passed down the hierarchical layers.
- Instructions and commands flow downward along the chain of command, while accountability flows upward in the organizational structure.
- The clearer the chain of command, the more effective the decision making tends to be.
- A clear and established chain of command improves the efficiency of communications in the workplace.
- Businesses with fewer levels in the hierarchy (flat structures) have a shorter chain of command.

Bureaucracy

- Bureaucratic organizational structures have a number of layers of management, with decisions passed down from senior executives to regional managers, departmental managers, supervisors and operative workers.

- In bureaucratic organizations, authority and decision making is generally centralized. This way, strategic decisions can be made more quickly, as fewer people are involved in decision making.
- **Bureaucracy** often leads to excessive administration, paperwork, and other formalities.
- It encourages a culture focused on rules and standards, where daily operations are rigidly controlled with close supervision and accountability.
- This rigidity means that bureaucratic organizations are often slow to react to changes in the external environment. It also discourages creativity and innovation.
- This reduces flexibility and discourages creativity in the organization, thus leading to inefficiencies and slower decision making.

Centralization

- In centralized organizations, the importance of subordinates is reduced, while the importance of senior executives is increased.
- Centralized structures are favoured by management theorists such as FW Taylor (see Chapter 2.4), who prefer faster decision making and better control.
- **Centralization** is associated with an autocratic or paternalistic style of leadership (see Chapter 2.3).
- Rapid decision making can result in fewer conflicts due to consistent policies coming from the top few highly experienced managers.
- Costs are also reduced, as there is less need to hire more specialists or departmental managers.
- However, centralized structures are highly inflexible, put added pressure on senior managers, and can be demotivational for employees.

> **EXPERT TIP**
>
> Evaluation skills require candidates to demonstrate 'thinking' skills (part of the ATL skills in the IB). Make sure you apply your understanding to the context of the business in question. For example, bureaucracy is not suitable for highly creative industries that require autonomy and independent decision making. By contrast, the emergency services (fire, police, and ambulance services) would require centralized structures and strict chains of command to ensure that the services are carried out properly without endangering the safety of the general public.

Decentralization

- **Decentralization** involves passing responsibility and authority away from the board of directors and senior executives, to individual departments.
- In decentralized structures there is shared decision-making authority and responsibilities.
- Decentralization is associated with fewer tiers (flatter structures) in an organizational structure and wider spans of control.
- Unlike centralized structures, which have a 'top-down' approach to management and decision making, decentralized structures are seen as 'bottom-up' and democratic.
- The larger the business, the more decentralized its organizational structure tends to be.
- Decentralized structures are often found in organizations with an informal corporate culture.

- Delegation and empowerment – vital aspects of decentralization – can result in better motivation for employees.
- Decentralization also results in quicker and more flexible decision making.
- However, decentralized structures can result in poor decision making due to the lack of experience and expertise of less senior staff.

The decision to have a more centralized or decentralized organizational structure is influenced by several factors, such as the corporate culture, the size of the organization, and the nature of the decisions to be made (whether they are strategic or routine decisions).

Delayering

> ### Key terms
>
> **Delayering** is the process of removing one or more layers in the organizational hierarchy to make the structure flatter.
>
> A **matrix structure** is a flexible organizational structure that uses teams of employees from across traditional departments for a specific business project.

- **Delayering** results in flatter structures and managers having wider spans of control.
- Reasons for delayering include improving communication in the organization, having shorter chains of command, and cutting costs, as there are few levels of management.
- The biggest disadvantage of delayering is the potential stress and anxiety of subordinates due to the added workload.
- Firms may choose to downsize or delayer because it improves or speeds up communication and is cheaper due to fewer layers of management.
- The move towards flexible working practices (see Chapter 2.1) means less of a need for traditional hierarchical structures.

Matrix structure

- **Matrix structures** combine individuals across different functional teams to work on different projects. This means employees work in functional and product-based teams, which creates greater flexibility for the organization.
- Such flexible structures also enable managers to oversee multiple projects simultaneously.
- Matrix structures are suitable for organizations that operate in dynamic and rapidly changing environments, such as in the high-tech or research and development (R&D) industries.
- This type of organizational structure encourages and relies on collaboration between different departments.
- Matrix structures are a popular way of organizing highly skilled and experienced staff. They help to utilize the synergies created from interactions among staff in the matrix.
- However, matrix structures can lead to confusion and/or conflict over roles and responsibilities, because employees have two or more different line managers at the same time. Hence, matrix structures may cause challenges for decision making.

Types of organization charts (AO2, AO4)

Flat or horizontal

- A flat (or horizontal) organization has few layers of management (see Figure 2.2).
- Line managers have a wide span of control in flat hierarchical structures. This gives the manager a lot of authority over decision making, but also places added pressure on their level of responsibility.

- Organizations with flat structures are suitable when employees are highly experienced, multi-skilled, and can organize their own work effectively.
- Flatter structures have shorter chains of command, which improves communication in the organization.

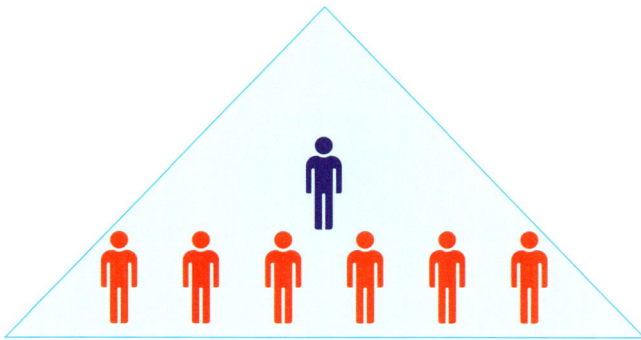

■ **Figure 2.2** A flat organizational chart

- The culture of relationships in flat structures is often open and informal. This is partly because there is minimal control over individual employees, which allows employees to take responsibility for their own work.
- With a large and wide span of control in horizontal structures, it can prove difficult to have tight control and close supervision of workers. This is because managers in a flat organizational structure with a wide span of control directly supervise a relatively large number of people.

■ Tall or vertical

- There are many layers in an organization in a tall (or vertical) hierarchical organizational structure (see Figure 2.3). Such structures organize people within an organization in terms of their rank.
- The person directly above an employee on the next hierarchical level is known as the **line manager**. The line manager supervises and manages the subordinates on a day-to-day basis.
- It is suitable when job roles are straightforward and routine, as output can be easily measured and checked because there are clear lines of accountability.
- Roles, responsibilities, and departments tend to be highly specialized.
- Generally, taller hierarchical structures are characterized by a narrow span of control, with each manager being responsible for fewer subordinates.

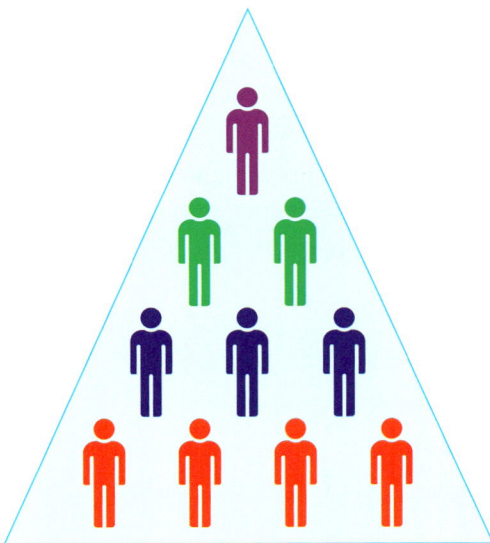

■ **Figure 2.3** A tall organizational structure

- Vertical structures are hierarchical, with clear chains of command. Rules, policies, and procedures are written and formalized. This reduces the chances of making mistakes.
- Such structures can be motivational for junior staff, as there are prospects for promotion and moving up the hierarchical structure.
- Tall, hierarchical structures are rigid and bureaucratic, so responding to changes in the internal or external business environment (see STEEPLE analysis in the Business management toolkit section) can be slow.
- A key drawback of vertical structures is the potential for miscommunication problems due to the large number of layers in the organization. Hence, decision making can be slow, due to formal, inflexible, and bureaucratic structures.
- They tend to be overly administrative and bureaucratic, so employees can feel rather distanced due to the impersonal nature of the hierarchical structure.

Organization by product

Key term

Organization by product occurs when an organization groups its human resources based on the distinct goods or services it sells.

- **Organization by product** is suitable for large businesses that have a broad product line of goods or services, as this requires specialized expertise in marketing and operations.
- Each product group has its own internal structure related specifically to that particular product line (see Figure 2.4).
- For example, the Volkswagen Group would have different executives responsible for different divisions of its business and product range, for example Volkswagen, Audi, Porsche, and Bugatti. Each executive would be responsible for all products under that division.
- The main advantage of this type of organizational structure is that products created using completely different and separate processes are better managed and controlled.

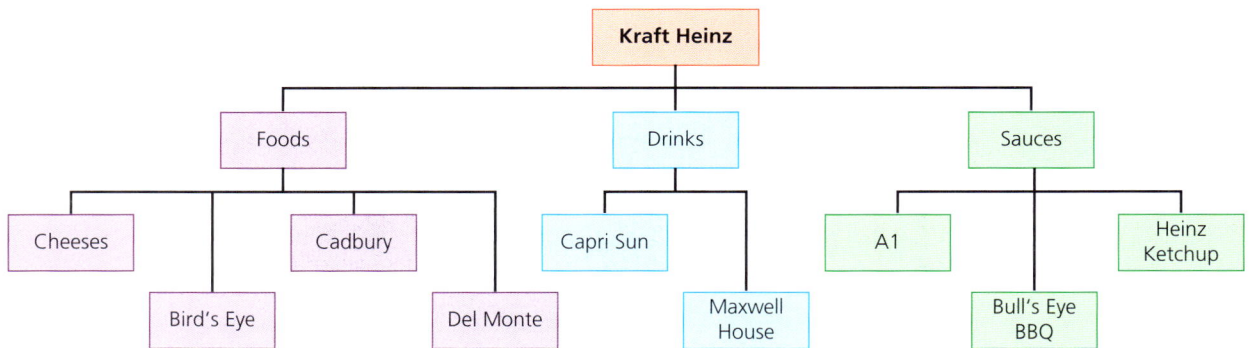

■ **Figure 2.4** Example of a product organizational chart for the Kraft Heinz Company

Organization by function

Key term

Organization by function involves establishing the organizational structure according to business functions such as marketing, production, and finance.

- Functional organizational structures arrange individuals by specific functions performed, for example human resources, finance, operations management, and marketing (see Figure 2.5).
- **Organization by function** is the most common form of organizational structure.
- Managers of different functional areas report to the respective director or vice president who holds overall responsibility for the department or division. For example, marketing managers report to the marketing director.
- The advantage of this type of structure is that functions are separated by expertise, but the challenges come in when different functional areas turn into silos that focus only on their area of responsibility and don't support the function of other departments.

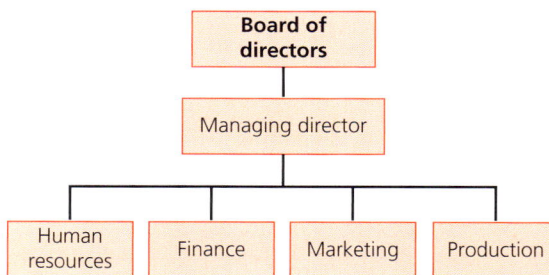

■ **Figure 2.5** Organization by function

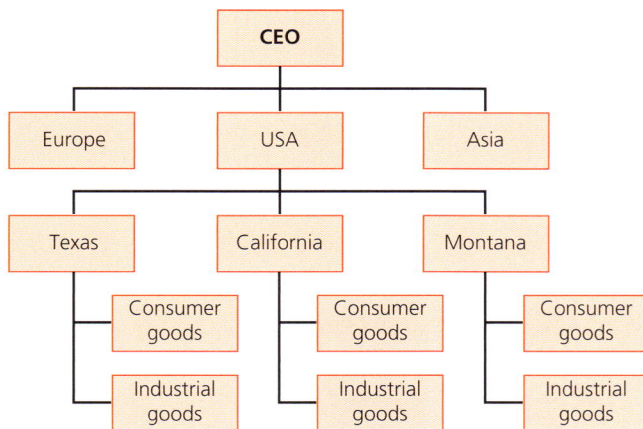

■ **Figure 2.6** Organization by region

Organization by region

- **Organization by region** is suitable for businesses that are located in several different geographic regions within a country or around the world (see Figure 2.6).

- Typically, under this system, operations are managed and overseen by a regional director.

- There are efficiency gains and operational benefits to organizing people by different regions, for example to better support and meet the needs of customers in different locations.

- Organization by region can support logistical demands and differences in different geographical locations.

> **Key term**
>
> **Organization by region** refers to establishing the organizational structure according to different geographical areas.

Appropriateness of different organizational structures given a change in external factors (AO3)

In reality, organizational structures are not static. Changes in the internal and external business environments mean that organizational structures need to be more flexible and adaptable. Examples include project-based organization and shamrock organization.

Project-based organization

> **Key term**
>
> **Project-based organization** refers to the organization of human resources around specific projects that need to be completed, rather than traditional functional departments.

- Unlike matrix structures that can be permanent, **project-based organization** is established only for the completion of a specific project.

- Project-based organization is suitable for organizations that engage in large, complex, and one-off projects, such as product development or the construction of bridges, buildings, and motorways (highways or freeways).

- Using project-based organization involves the temporary use of teams of the most suitable employees from different departments (functional areas) for a particular project.

- As a flexible organizational structure, project-based organization is conducive to a democratic leadership style (see Chapter 2.3) as it encourages the generation of new and creative ideas from team members.

- Project-based organizational structures create opportunities for job enlargement and job enrichment (see Chapter 2.4), thus boosting staff morale and motivation.

- However, project-based organization can create problems for the business, because staff may have some uncertainties about prioritizing tasks when they have more than one line manager at the same time.

- Similarly, there can be difficulties in controlling team members from various departments in the project who have conflicting interests and priorities.
- Project-based organizational structures can cause some staff to be demoralized due to the added workload and pressures of working on different projects.
- Additional resources and finance will be needed to facilitate the running of the projects.

▨ Handy's shamrock organization

- Irish scholar Charles Handy's shamrock organization (1991) is a model that suggests organizations face continual change so need to adapt accordingly.
- The changing organization is comprised of three 'leaves' (or types) of workers, as shown in Figure 2.7. These are the core workers (professional core), peripheral workers (contingent workforce), and outsourced workers (or outsourced vendors).

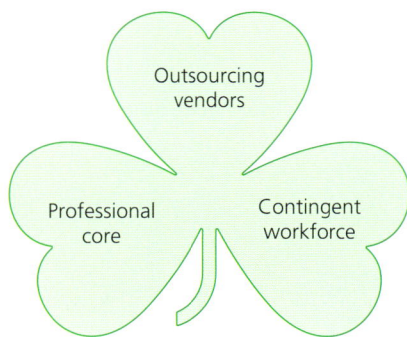

  - The **professional core** consists of full-time, experienced, and essential staff needed for the organization's operations and survival. With improvements in technology and the trend for downsizing and delayering, there is less of a need for so many core staff in an organization.

  - The **contingent workforce** refers to peripheral workers, for example the temporary and portfolio workers employed by organizations on a short-term basis. However, this often causes job insecurity and low staff morale.

  - **Outsourced vendors** are individuals or businesses hired on a contract basis to do specific tasks such as an advertising campaign. They are specialists in their field so can be expensive to employ. This also includes workers in the gig economy (see Chapter 2.1).

■ **Figure 2.7** The shamrock organization

- The model emphasises the growing practice of outsourcing non-essential activities, as well as the recognition of flexible working practices (see Chapter 2.1).
- The model presents cost savings and greater flexibility for organizations. For example, labour costs are cheaper because only the core staff receive full employment perks (benefits), whereas peripheral and outsourced workers do not.
- Handy's academic work on organizational structures has shaped the thinking behind present-day organizational structures in many business organizations around the world.

EXPERT TIP

While this section of the syllabus looks at formal organizational structures, it is important for managers to be aware of and understand the informal structures that are likely to exist. Informal structures can help to promote a sense of belonging in the workplace. Knowledge and skills are unevenly spread in an organization, so informal networks can help to identify and exploit different sources of knowledge and skills.

KEY CONCEPTS

Investigate how **change** has impacted the organizational structure for a business of your choice.

2.3 Leadership and management

SL/HL content	Depth of teaching
Scientific and intuitive thinking/management (HL only)	AO2
Management and leadership	AO2
The following leadership styles: autocratic, paternalistic, democratic, laissez-faire, and situational	AO3

Diploma Programme *Business management guide* (May 2022)

Scientific and intuitive thinking/management (HL only) (AO2)

Business management is essentially about problem solving and decision making. There are two broad approaches to problem solving and decision making – scientific and intuitive thinking/management.

▣ Scientific thinking/management

- Scientific thinking/management is based on quantitative data, facts and figures, in order to make objective decisions.

- This involves managers having to do thorough research in order to gather relevant and sufficient data. Only after careful data analysis can a decision be made.

- Scientific thinking/management is rational and logical, rather than subjective and based on personal preferences.

- Many of the quantitative tools studied in the course form part of scientific thinking/management, such as investment appraisal (Chapter 3.8), break-even analysis (Chapter 5.5) and decision trees (Business management toolkit section).

- Data and information to support scientific decision making can also be gathered through both primary and secondary research methods (see Chapter 4.4).

- This approach is likely to be used for non-routine decisions, such as whether to acquire a competitor firm.

- It helps to reduce the risks of decision making, especially for major decisions that are influenced by factors beyond the control of the organization.

- Advances in technology, such as management information systems (see Chapter 5.9), have made it easier and cheaper to collect and analyze data. For example, the widespread use of customer loyalty programmes enables businesses to know far more about their customers, including their spending habits and purchasing habits.

- However, scientific thinking/management is not free of errors. Using past data and trends to make predictions about the future does not always work; indeed, the past is not necessarily representative of the future, especially in fast-changing and dynamic markets.

- Furthermore, data collection and analysis can be expensive and time consuming. The reliability of the data and information also needs to be considered.

- Hence, managers and decision makers have to judge the costs and benefits of scientific thinking/management for each situation.

▨ Intuitive thinking/management

- Intuitive thinking/management relies on the past experience, insights, and gut feeling (intuition) of managers in the decision-making process.
- Intuitive thinking/management is based on personal opinion, perspectives, and preferences, rather than on rational and logical thinking based on research.
- This approach is likely to be used for routine and straightforward decisions.
- It is also appropriate when a quick decision is needed, rather than relying on a lengthy process of gathering and analyzing data.
- It is used by managers when making decisions based on factors within the control of the organization.
- Intuitive thinking and management are more appropriate when decision makers have a wealth of experience in the area.
- Such an approach is also appropriate when data or information is not readily available, or is prohibitively expensive to access.
- However, as this approach is based on feelings and instincts (hunches), it can lead managers to make illogical and irrational decisions, which increases the risk of such decisions. However, do note that intuitive thinking/management is predominantly based on logic and rationality, especially when the decision maker has much experience and knowledge or insight into a particular issue.

Management and leadership (AO2)

- **Management** refers to the process of planning, organizing, and controlling different business operations.
- **Leadership** refers to the art of guiding and inspiring other people within an organization, in order to achieve agreed organizational objectives.
- Management and leadership are vital to the success of a business. They have implications across all areas of the organization and shape its organizational culture.
- Table 2.1 outlines some of the differences between management and leadership.

■ **Table 2.1** Management versus leadership

Management	Leadership
• Follow the culture of the organization	• Set the culture of the organization
• Manage others	• Inspire others
• Plan, organize, control, command, co-ordinate, and set objectives	• Cope with and promote change, with a more emotional dimension to inspire and align people
• Focus on the present	• Focus on the future
• Work within the parameters of organizational policies and procedures	• Instigators of change, setting the strategic direction of the organization
• Focus on operational objectives	• Focus on vision and mission statements
• Mainly concerned with processes	• Mainly concerned with people
• Tactical decision making	• Strategic decision making
• Deal with individual needs of staff	• Focus on common needs
• Policy makers and decision makers	• Risk takers and decision makers
• More involved with administrative aspects of the organization	• Optimistic, innovative, inspirational, entrepreneurial and creative
• Confirmative capacity (learning to do)	• Adaptive capacity (learning to learn)

Leadership styles (AO3)

Leadership style refers to the way in which managers and leaders provide direction, implement organizational plans, and motivate people. There are five leadership styles specified in the syllabus: (i) autocratic, (ii) paternalistic, (iii) democratic, (iv) laissez-faire, and (v) situational.

Autocratic

- Autocratic leaders are authoritative. This means there are formal systems of command and control.
- They avoid discussions and negotiations as they do not believe that employees should be involved in decision making.
- Delegation and consultation are non-existent.
- Communication is top-down and one way – managers order and instruct their subordinates.
- It is most likely to be used when employees are unskilled, inexperienced, lack initiative, and/or cannot be trusted.
- An autocratic approach may also be suitable or necessary when critical decisions must be made, such as with the emergency services (police, fire, and ambulance services) or in the military and navy.
- The success of the organization very much relies on the ability and direction of the leader.

■ **Table 2.2** Advantages and disadvantages of autocratic leadership

Advantages of autocratic leadership
• Ensures there is control and close oversight within the organization.
• Quick decision making takes place.
• Employees have a clear sense of direction.
• Effective when deadlines are imminent or major decisions need to be made.

Disadvantages of autocratic leadership
• Stifles initiative and creativity as employees are not involved in decision making.
• Demotivates workers as their ideas are not valued.
• Does not nurture future leaders among employees, so can damage competitiveness in the long term.
• Subordinates are usually ineffective if the leader is absent from work.

Paternalistic

- Paternalistic leaders see the workforce as an extension of the family, so make decisions that they perceive to be in the interest of their employees.
- It is often effective in family-run businesses.

- It is used in organizations where the leader is highly experienced and genuinely values the workers.
- There is close supervision of employees and their work (comparable to a parent's traditional control over their children).

■ **Table 2.3** Advantages and disadvantages of paternalistic leadership

Advantages of paternalistic leadership
• It is a softer form of autocratic leadership which often results in improved staff motivation and lower staff turnover.
• Feedback is invited, so this can improve relationships at work, as employees' social needs are emphasized.
• There is often commitment and loyalty to leaders when workers perceive they will take care of their staff's wellbeing.

Disadvantages of paternalistic leadership
• Employees can become dissatisfied as their viewpoints are often ignored (decisions are made by top management), so it does not help to develop their careers.
• Communication is mostly downward.
• Paternalistic leaders can become too dictatorial and make poor decisions (does a parent or leader always know what is best?).

■ Democratic

- Democratic leaders involve workers in the decision-making process – consultation and collaboration are considered to be important to the organization.
- Leaders encourage discussion and employee participation, although they have the final say overall.
- Leaders delegate authority and empower their staff.
- Democratic leadership is likely to be effective when used with skilled, experienced, and creative employees.

■ **Table 2.4** Advantages and disadvantages of democratic leadership

Advantages of democratic leadership
• Can be motivational as workers feel their opinions and input are valued, thus creating a greater sense of belonging and staff loyalty.
• The collaborative environment often results in better-informed solutions to challenges and problems.
• There is two-way communication, so this encourages the sharing of ideas in the workplace.

Disadvantages of democratic leadership
• Decision making is slower, as employees have greater involvement in the process.
• Reaching a consensus over decisions can be time consuming and costly.
• The possibility of disagreement among internal stakeholders during the discussion process can negatively affect day-to-day operations.
• It is inappropriate during times when urgent decisions need to be made.

EXPERT TIP

It is common in exams for students to claim that democratic leaders are better than autocratic ones, stating that the former are 'nicer' than the latter. This suggests a lack of critical thinking, as the most effective leadership style depends on the context of the organization, its workers, and the task at hand. Managers and leaders are not there to be popular or liked, but to get things done.

Laissez-faire

- Laissez-faire leaders delegate responsibility and authority to their staff, enabling them to complete tasks in their own way (although the leader sets broad goals and clear parameters within which the employees must operate).

- Staff are given the freedom to work without supervision from the management, as there is a deliberate attempt to delegate power and authority.

- At a polar opposite to autocratic leaders, the success of laissez-faire leadership primarily depends on the aptitude and attitude of the employees.

- Laissez-faire leadership is suitable for mundane and routine tasks which do not require managerial supervision.

- It is also suitable when staff can be trusted, are highly talented, self-motivated, and creative, as with, for example, the staff at Google and Disney.

■ **Table 2.5** Advantages and disadvantages of laissez-faire leadership

Advantages of laissez-faire leadership
• The freedom given to employees can allow them to excel in what they do best, without any constraints imposed by the management team.
• Provides opportunities for employees with vision, talent, and willpower.
• Autonomy in decision making can have positive impacts on staff motivation, productivity, and staff retention levels.

Disadvantages of laissez-faire leadership
• Individual goal setting can conflict with organizational objectives, especially as there is a lack of management control.
• Laissez-faire leadership is often criticized for the poor definition of the role/purpose of management.
• As the management team takes a 'hands-off' approach, monitoring and controlling the organization's operations becomes extremely challenging.

Situational

- Situational leaders adapt their style of leadership according to differences in circumstances.

- In situational leadership, it is regarded that there is no single-best leadership style, but rather different styles are suitable depending on the context or situation.

- Relationships at work play a key role in the success of situational leadership.

- It relies on the skills and level of experience of the leader.

■ **Table 2.6** Advantages and disadvantages of situational leadership

Advantages of situational leadership
• It recognizes the need for leaders to be flexible in their style, given the dynamic nature of business management.
• It is practical and applies across a range of industries and business problems.
• Workers can benefit from the mix of support from leaders when appropriate, and directive activities at other times.

Disadvantages of situational leadership
• Most managers and leaders have a preferred or natural style, so expecting them to change their style according to different situations can be difficult.
• Employees may have grown accustomed to a particular leadership style in the workplace, so staff may become disoriented and unsettled if the leader changes his/her style.
• The inconsistent approach can mean the leader loses credibility with the employees.

2.4 Motivation and demotivation

SL/HL content	Depth of teaching
The following motivation theories: Taylor, Maslow, and Herzberg (motivation–hygiene theory)	AO3
The following motivation theories: McClelland's acquired needs theory (HL only), Deci and Ryan's self-determination theory (HL only), equity theory and expectancy theory (HL only)	AO3
Labour turnover (HL only)	AO2, AO4
The following types of appraisal (HL only): formative, summative, 360-degree feedback, and self-appraisal	AO2
Methods of recruitment (HL only)	AO2
Internal and external recruitment (HL only)	AO3
The following types of financial rewards: salary, wages (time and piece rates), commission, performance-related pay (PRP), profit-related pay, employee share ownership schemes, and fringe payments	AO2
The following types of non-financial rewards: job enrichment, job rotation, job enlargement, empowerment, purpose/the opportunity to make a difference, and teamwork	AO2
The following types of training: induction, on the job, and off the job	AO2

Diploma Programme *Business management guide* (May 2022)

Motivation theories (AO3)

An important role of management is to motivate the workforce to ensure that they are efficient and productive. **Motivation** exists when people do something because they want to do it, not because they have to do it. Motivation is therefore the desire to achieve something. It influences people to behave in a certain way and has a direct impact on the outcomes of that behaviour. By contrast, **demotivation** exists when an employee has no interest in, or desire for, their work.

> **EXPERT TIP**
>
> One of the difficulties with this topic in the syllabus is the large number of key terms. Use revision strategies that will help you to remember the definitions of the key terms in this unit, such as the use of flash cards, crosswords, glossaries, and online tools such as Quizlet.

■ Taylor

- Frederick Winslow Taylor (1856–1917) was an American engineer and management consultant who sought to improve efficiency and productivity.

- In his book *The Principles of Scientific Management* (1911), Taylor argued that 'we do not want any initiative. All we want of them [workers] is to obey the orders we give them, do what we say, and do it quick.' His approach to management was based on three factors:
  - *measurement* of what can be done better and how
  - *monitoring* to ensure targets are met, and
  - *control* by using rigorous analysis of the firm's inputs, outputs, and costs.

- Taylor argued that people work for only one reason: money. By motivating workers to become more efficient and productive, the business would generate more profit, thus enabling employees to be paid higher wages.

- Taylor advocated payment systems that reward those who meet or exceed output targets, and penalize those who do not. Such a payment scheme became known as **piece rate**. Taylor claimed that 'what the workmen want from employers beyond anything else is higher wages.'

- Taylor argued that employers must reward the behaviour they seek and punish the behaviour they discourage in order to raise productivity.

- He introduced rest breaks to the working day so that workers could recover from tiredness and hence a loss of productivity.

- Henry Ford (founder of Ford Motor Company) used Taylor's theory by introducing scientific management in his factories, for example the use of the division of labour and purpose-built machinery, such as conveyor belts, for mass production, in order to increase efficiency and productivity. Today, many firms offer 'zero hours' contracts – no work equals no pay.

- Despite being criticized for being authoritarian and treating people as though they were machines, Taylor believed his scientific management of human resources was in the best interests of his staff.

- There are limitations to Taylor's theory:
  - Not all workers are motivated in the same way, and the most efficient way of working for one person can be inefficient for another.
  - Taylor's approach does not acknowledge the complications of human behaviour, such as personal preferences and interpersonal difficulties.
  - Working harder due to scientific management practices can still mean people are dissatisfied with the work environment.

> **Key term**
>
> **Piece rate** is a payment system, advocated by Taylor, which rewards workers based on their level of output (productivity), for example earning $1 per batch produced or 5 per cent per product sold. Piece rate is used to motivate and reward workers who are more productive.

Maslow

- Abraham Maslow (1908–70) was an American social psychologist who wrote about a **hierarchy of needs**, as he believed that people are motivated by a series of needs (see Figure 2.8 and Table 2.7).
- *Physiological needs* (also known as *basic needs* for human survival) are those thought to be the most important, so must be met first.
- *Safety needs* are the factors that make people feel secure, such as personal and financial security. They are vital to a person's wellbeing.
- *Social needs* are about being accepted by others. They are the love and belonging needs that people desire.
- *Esteem needs* are about people feeling respected and having self-respect. Self-esteem exists when a person feels good about themselves and feels valued by others.
- The highest level in Maslow's hierarchy of needs refers to the realization of a person's full potential. In his book, *Motivation and Personality* (1954), Maslow defined self-actualization needs as, 'To become everything that one is capable of becoming', and, 'What a man can be, he must be.'

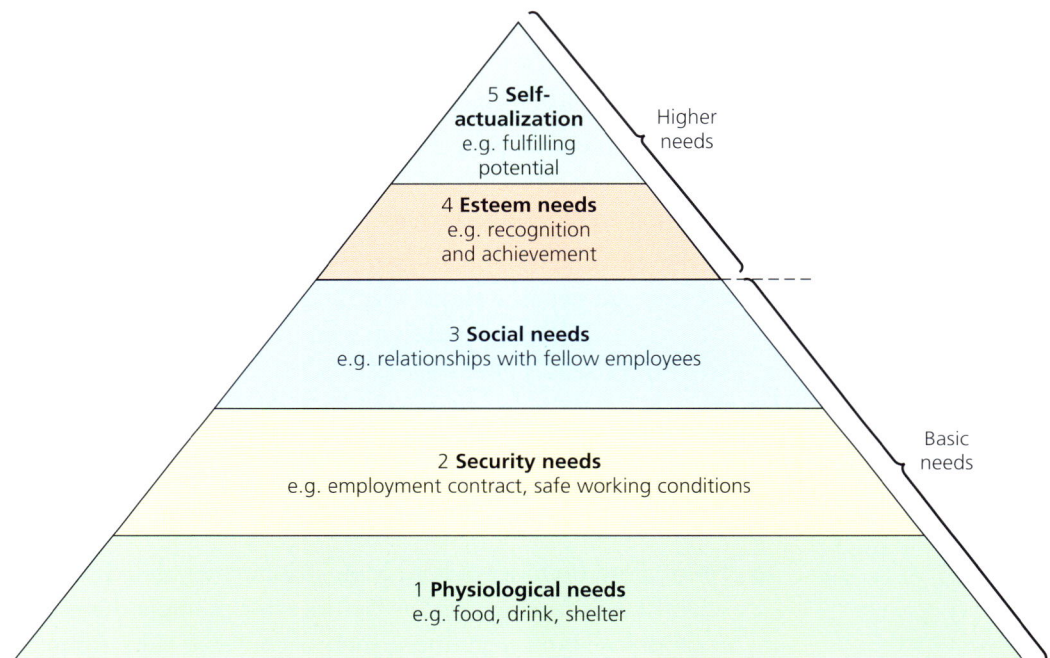

■ **Figure 2.8** Maslow's hierarchy of needs

■ **Table 2.7** Examples and business implications of Maslow's hierarchy of needs

Levels of human needs	Examples	Business implications
Physiological needs (basic needs)	Food, clothing, water, warmth, and shelter	Pay award systems and decent working conditions
Safety needs	Physical security, financial security, economic stability, health, and wellbeing	Job security, grievance procedures, insurance policies, and clear job descriptions
Love and belonging needs	Friendship, intimacy, social contact, and social acceptance	Teamworking, co-workers, mentors, and social facilities
Esteem needs	Status, recognition, competence, self-respect, and independence	Status (job titles), power, trust, and recognition of achievements
Self-actualization	Self-fulfilment, mastery, and life accomplishment	Job opportunities to develop new skills and meet new challenges

- Maslow argued that it is important for employers to understand that when one level of needs is satisfied then it no longer motivates. Hence, businesses need to devise strategies to satisfy the higher-level needs of their employees.
- Lower-order needs consist of physiological, security, and love and belonging needs. Higher-order needs consist of self-esteem and self-actualization. Nevertheless, Maslow argued that the different levels in the hierarchy are interrelated rather than separate.
- There are some criticisms of Maslow's theory:
  - There is debate about whether all humans have the same needs.
  - People place different levels of importance on different needs. For example, not everyone is motivated by job promotional opportunities, so may prefer other ways to achieve esteem needs.
  - It is not realistic for most workers to achieve real self-actualization – can everyone's motivational needs be truly and fully satisfied?

■ Herzberg (motivation–hygiene theory)

- Frederick Herzberg (1923–2000) was an American psychologist and a highly influential person in the field of business management.
- Professor Herzberg defined motivation as 'the will to work due to enjoyment of the work itself.'
- In his book *Work and the Nature of Man* (1966), Herzberg argued that removing factors that cause dissatisfaction in the workplace was a prerequisite to positively increasing motivation.
- Contrary to the findings of Taylor, Herzberg found that employee satisfaction did not stem from extrinsic factors (such as salary) as these are easily forgotten and become an expectation.
- Influenced by the work of Maslow, Herzberg suggested that humans have two levels of needs, which employers should seek to satisfy at work:
  - Lower-level needs to meet people's physical needs in order to avoid pain and deprivation. Herzberg called these needs **hygiene factors**.
  - Higher-level needs to meet people's psychological needs and to enable them to grow psychologically. Herzberg called these needs **motivators**.

Key terms

Hygiene factors are aspects of a job that can lead to workers being dissatisfied. These factors need to be addressed in order to prevent dissatisfaction, but they do not motivate.

Motivators are factors that help workers to gain job satisfaction, for example recognition and opportunities for personal advancement. These factors satisfy the psychological needs of employees. Herzberg's motivators correspond with Maslow's higher level of needs and the nature of the job or work itself.

■ **Table 2.8** Herzberg's motivation–hygiene theory

Hygiene factors	Motivators
Company policy	Advancement
Conditions of employment	Nature of the job
Inability to develop	Opportunities to improve
Pay (wages and salaries)	Personal growth
Relationship with colleagues	Promotional opportunities
Relationship with management	Recognition (of achievement)
Treatment at work	Responsibility

EXPERT TIP

Remember that according to Professor Herzberg, motivation is enhanced by improving **motivators**, for example recognition, responsibility, and opportunities for advancement. By contrast, improving hygiene factors simply prevents dissatisfaction, but does not boost morale or motivation in the workplace.

- Herzberg suggested that as people work better due to the work being intrinsically interesting, the work provides employees with opportunities for psychological growth.
- Herzberg introduced the ideas of job enrichment, job enlargement, and job rotation to improve employee performance (see the text later in this chapter on types of non-financial rewards).
- Critics of Herzberg's theory are doubtful about the role of wages and salaries being a hygiene factor, which could perhaps appear to be in both sets of needs. Indeed, many people seek promotional opportunities due to the higher financial rewards. Herzberg argued that pay is only a short-term, not long-term, motivator.

Motivation theories (HL only) (AO3)

There are four additional theories that HL students need to understand. These are outlined below.

■ McClelland's acquired needs theory

- Dr David McClelland (1917–98) was an American psychologist, best known for his acquired needs theory. He argued that an individual's motivation depends on their varying needs.
- McClelland argued that there are three types of motivational needs: the need for achievement (n-Ach), the need for authority/power (n-Pow), and the need for affiliation (n-Aff).
- Those with n-Ach have a need for a sense of accomplishment and strive for excellence.
  - They are likely to avoid low-risk situations due to the lack of reward or satisfaction from meeting unchallenging goals.
  - Equally, they tend to avoid overly high-risk situations due to the fear of not being able to achieve the targets. Hence, people with n-Ach aim to attain realistic, but challenging, goals.
- Those with n-Pow have a need for authority and power.
  - They are motivated by having the power and ability to direct or manage other employees to accomplish the organization's objectives.

- ○ They may also want to have more responsibility and higher status within the organization.
- Those with n-Aff have a desire for acceptance, integration, and harmonious relationships within the organization.
  - ○ They are motivated by working with other people who accept them and recognize their value or input, as well as their social interactions.
  - ○ These employees often work successfully in teams, including marketing departments and customer service departments.

Deci and Ryan's self-determination theory

- American psychologists Professors Edward L Deci (b. 1942) and Richard M Ryan (b. 1953) developed the self-determination theory of motivation (1985).
- **Self-determination** refers to an individual's ability to think independently, to manage themselves, and to make expert decisions. Deci and Ryan argued that a person must have self-determination in order to be motivated to carry out their work and to complete set tasks and projects.
- Self-determination theory is based on the assumption that people seek personal growth, such as mastering challenges and embracing new experiences.
- Self-determination theory focuses mainly on intrinsic motivation (internal sources of motivation), such as learning to gain independence and knowledge.
- The outcome of intrinsic motivation is that the work is done for reasons of self-satisfaction, interest, and enjoyment rather than reward (such as pay and status) or the threat of punishment.
- Deci and Ryan's research suggests that people have three universal and fundamental psychological prerequisites:
  - ○ *Autonomy.* This is the desire to have a sense of independence and self-control. This may be achieved by empowering workers to make independent decisions and well-informed choices in the workplace.
  - ○ *Relatedness.* This is the desire to be connected with others and to experience a sense of belonging. Hence, businesses can improve motivation by encouraging and supporting teamworking within the workplace.
  - ○ *Competence.* This is the desire to feel proficient in tackling challenges and work itself. Providing employees with appropriate and adequate training can help to meet this need. Firms can also avoid setting employees tasks that are too complex or ambitious.
- Fulfilling these three internal desires is critical for developing an individual's self-determination and hence their sense of wellbeing and motivation.

Equity theory

- John Stacey Adams (b. 1925), a behavioural psychologist, devised the equity theory of motivation (1963). He suggested that people seek a fair balance between their inputs (effort put into a job) and outputs (what they get out of it).
- **Equity** suggests people place emphasis on what is perceived to be fair and reasonable. For example, highly demotivated students may not think it is worth putting in the effort to study if they believe the output (exam grades) will be low.
- Examples of inputs include employee effort, experience, loyalty, adaptability, and commitment.

- Examples of outputs include financial remuneration, recognition, praise, credibility (reputation), job security, responsibilities, and promotional opportunities.
- Equity theory helps to explain why wages and salaries alone do not determine motivation, as workers compare their input-to-output ratio with that of others in order to establish their own interpretation of equity (fairness) in the workplace.
- If workers feel that their inputs are fairly and adequately rewarded by outputs, then motivation will be high. By contrast, if workers feel their inputs outweigh the outputs, then demotivation occurs. Adams argues that the extent of demotivation is generally proportional to the perceived inequity in an organization.
- Critics of the equity theory argue that perceptions of fairness are highly subjective – equity is a matter of opinion and partiality. Measuring equity in the workplace is therefore a meaningless task.

▨ Expectancy theory

- The expectancy theory of motivation (1964) was developed by Professor Victor Vroom (b. 1932). He argued that motivation depends on employees' expectations or assumptions of the results of their efforts.
- Vroom suggested that if employees know what they want from an outcome (be it a financial reward, recognition, or self-satisfaction, for example), and they believe they can realistically achieve that particular outcome, they will be motivated.
- Vroom's model of motivation consists of three elements, as illustrated in Figure 2.9:

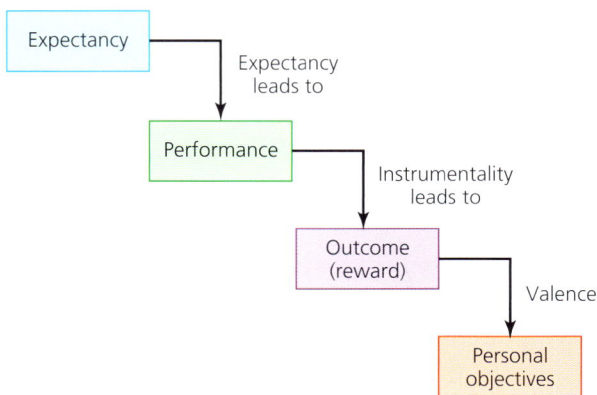

■ **Figure 2.9** Victor Vroom's expectancy theory

○ *Expectancy.* This refers to the belief that employees have in their ability to complete a particular activity or task to the required standard. Demotivation would result if workers felt they were not capable of completing the task to the expected standard, including doing so in a timely manner.

○ *Instrumentality.* This refers to the means or methods by which employees feel they can complete a particular task. In a situation of high instrumentality, the employee has confidence that specific tasks will result in the achievement of a valued reward. High instrumentality means that employees recognize a clear link between their actions and rewards, and have confidence that they will receive the rewards for achieving their targets.

○ *Valence.* This represents the strength of a person's desire to achieve a specific outcome. Valence is positive if a person prefers the outcome to not achieving it. If the person is indifferent to the outcome, then valence will be zero. High values of valence mean that an outcome is highly attractive to employees and has great potential to motivate. In such circumstances, managers can use the possibility of attaining this outcome as a means of motivation. For example, a salesperson may find the prospect of a monetary bonus for achieving an agreed sales target very desirable. The salesperson must have confidence in their ability to achieve the number of sales necessary to receive the bonus.

It is important that you remember the names of the different motivational theorists and their theories included in the IB syllabus:

- Taylor – Scientific management
- Maslow – Hierarchy of needs
- Herzberg – Motivation–hygiene theory
- McClelland – Acquired needs theory (HL only)
- Deci and Ryan – Self-determination theory (HL only)
- Adams – Equity theory (HL only)
- Vroom – Expectancy theory (HL only)

EXAM PRACTICE QUESTION

Virgin Group allows its staff parental leave on full pay for up to one year after the birth or adoption of a child. However, the offer only applies to employees at Virgin Management, the company's investment and brand licensing division. Staff must also have worked at Virgin Management for at least four years to qualify for full pay during their parental leave.

Vodafone has a global policy on maternity benefits of at least 16 weeks of leave on full pay for expectant mothers, even in countries where employment laws do not require it to do so.

Maternity leave rules vary significantly around the world. In Hong Kong, for example, maternity leave is 14 weeks with partial payment, the USA offers 12 weeks of unpaid leave, and the UK offers up to 39 weeks of partially paid leave.

a Explain **one** advantage and **one** disadvantage of providing fringe benefits beyond what is stipulated in employment laws. [4]

b Using appropriate motivation theory, explain the likely effects on employee motivation of the employment benefits at Virgin Management and Vodafone. [6]

Labour turnover (HL only) (AO2, AO4)

Key term

Labour turnover measures the rate of change of human resources within an organization, per period of time.

- **Labour turnover** is calculated using the formula:

$$\frac{\text{Number of staff leaving per year}}{\text{Average number of staff}} \times 100$$

- Labour turnover is inevitable in an organization, as some employees leave for personal or professional reasons, for example to have a baby or spend more time with their young children, to retire, or to pursue better opportunities elsewhere.

- Retaining staff in the organization is important, as there are significant costs to recruiting new staff, training them, and getting them acclimatized to the organizational culture.

- Causes of high labour turnover include:
  - an unhappy and discontented workforce
  - better pay and working conditions offered by rival firms
  - employees being overwhelmed by the amount of work
  - poor relationships with colleagues and/or managers
  - staff being inadequately trained, leaving them feeling incompetent and demotivated
  - toxic organizational culture.

- Businesses try to avoid having a high labour turnover rate, because this leads to higher costs of recruitment (and retention). It also uses up a large amount of management time.

- Having a large number of new workers also means there is greater downtime, when employees are less productive, simply because they have yet to acclimatize to their new working environment, policies, procedures, and processes.

- High labour turnover also raises concerns about the stability and continuity of the business.

EXAM PRACTICE QUESTION

Duffy & Wong Ltd employs 86 people. Thirteen of the employees resigned during the year. Calculate the firm's labour turnover rate. [2]

Types of appraisal (HL only) (AO2)

> **Key term**
>
> **Appraisal** refers to the formal assessment of an employee's performance, with reference to the roles and responsibilities set out in their job description.

- **Appraisals** are conducted for several reasons, including:
  - assessing an employee's performance against pre-agreed targets
  - identifying training needs of the individual employee
  - helping the management team to reward high-achieving employees.

- Target setting (or goal setting) is an integral part of staff appraisals. Targets should be SMART: **s**pecific, **m**easurable, **a**chievable, **r**ealistic, and **t**ime bound.

- If an employee's performance is deemed to be less than satisfactory, it should be followed by providing relevant training or counselling. Such appraisals do not necessarily result in severe or demotivating measures such as warning letters or dismissal.

- Different organizations use different appraisal systems, namely formative, summative, 360-degree feedback, and self-appraisal.

Formative appraisals

- Formative appraisals take place on an ongoing basis to enable employees to improve their job performance.

- The goal is to monitor worker performance in order to provide ongoing feedback to help them improve.

- It helps to identify an employee's strengths and weaknesses in a specific role, or the progress made in a particular task or project.

- It helps the organization to identify the specific training needs of an individual employee.

Summative appraisals

- Summative appraisals take place periodically, for example quarterly or annually, and are conducted by the line manager, who summarizes the personal performance and achievements of the appraisee.

- The purpose is to evaluate worker performance at the end of a given time period by comparing this against a chosen standard or benchmark.

- The appraisee is held accountable for the outcome of their work, including identifying any areas for improvement.

360-degree feedback

- 360-degree feedback is an appraisal system that involves getting comments, opinions, and information about the person being appraised from the various groups of people who work with, or are in direct contact with, that person, including, for example, their peers, line managers, subordinates, and customers.

- 360-degree feedback is usually obtained using questionnaires, surveys, observations, or interviews.

- In some cultures, such an approach to appraisal (where a senior member of staff is appraised by a junior colleague) would be deemed inappropriate and might not produce open and truthful discussions.

Self-appraisal

- Self-appraisal involves employees evaluating themselves against a predetermined set of criteria or performance targets.

- The appraisee reflects on their strengths and weaknesses (areas for development) in order to set new targets for themselves.

- To avoid potential bias and any inconsistencies, self-appraisals are often used in conjunction with an appraisal conducted by the line manager.

Methods of recruitment (HL only) (AO2)

Key terms

A **job description** is a document that provides details of a particular job, including, for example, the job title, roles, duties, and responsibilities.

The **person specification** is a document that gives the profile of the ideal candidate for a job, and includes a description of the desired qualifications, skills, experience, knowledge, and other attributes.

- Recruitment refers to the human resource management process of selecting and hiring employees.

- Two important documents used in the recruitment process are the **job description** and **person specification**.

- **Job analysis** is the process of identifying what a particular job entails, in terms of the tasks, roles, responsibilities, and skills required. From this analysis, the job description and person specification can be created.

- Job advertisements are typically released after a job analysis has been completed, and after the job description and person specification have been produced.

- Candidates often have to complete an application form for a job. The form can be in physical format, although most businesses now use online application forms.

- Job applicants may also need to include a **curriculum vitae** (or résumé) – a document that outlines the applicant's educational achievements, professional qualifications, employment history, skills, accomplishments, hobbies, and interests.

- **Shortlisting** is the systematic process of identifying and selecting the few most suitable candidates from all the applicants for an interview, because they best fit the profiles in the job description and person specification. Shortlisting eliminates unsuitable candidates from the recruitment process.

- Shortlisted candidates are then invited for interviews and (in some cases) testing, in order to select the most suitable candidate for the vacant position.

- Testing is used for some jobs to ensure the best candidate is recruited. Examples include the following:
  - *Aptitude tests.* A method of assessing the skills and abilities of a candidate to do a particular job, for example typing speed for a receptionist, or driving ability for a driving instructor.

    ○ *Psychometric tests.* Used to assess the attitudes and personality traits of candidates, for example their level of drive (or motivation) and their ability to deal with stressful situations. These tests are used to ensure the chosen candidate is a good match with the organizational culture.

    ○ *Trade tests.* Industry-specific assessments used to examine the candidate's skills and expertise in a specific profession.

    ○ *Intelligence tests.* Used to assess a candidate's skills of numeracy, literacy, general knowledge, and problem solving.

● Background checks are made with **referees** (one of which is likely to be the current or last employer), to ensure that information declared by the applicant is truthful and to get a character reference so the business can assess the suitability of the candidate.

● A **job offer** is then made to the most suitable candidate prior to issuing a contract of employment.

Internal and external recruitment (HL only) (AO3)

Internal recruitment

● Internal recruitment is the hiring of people from within the organization to fill a job vacancy.

● It is commonly used for targeting suitable employees for supervisory or management positions.

■ **Table 2.9** Advantages and disadvantages of internal recruitment

Advantages of internal recruitment	Disadvantages of internal recruitment
• Lower risk, as the employer already knows the strengths and suitability of the existing worker. • Relatively lower costs of recruitment compared to external recruitment. • It is generally quicker to complete than external recruitment. • It strengthens the loyalty of employees, as there are career development opportunities within the organization. • It reduces or eliminates the need for induction as existing workers are already familiar with the organization's policies, practices, and culture.	• 'Dead wood' (outdated practices) might exist in the organization, so an external candidate could bring in new ideas. • Similarly, external candidates may be more skilled, have more experience, or be better qualified. • A lower number of applicants can mean the employer has fewer candidates to choose from. • It can create unnecessary internal competition and conflict between existing workers who apply for a particular job. • Hiring someone internally means there is a vacancy created, so another person still has to be recruited.

External recruitment

● External recruitment is the hiring of people from outside the organization.

● It requires placing job advertisements using a range of media to attract potential applicants. Advertisements could be included in newspapers, on websites, and in specialist trade magazines.

● Interviews are the main method of selection for both internal and external recruitment.

- In some cases, specialist recruitment agencies in a particular industry take responsibility for advertising, interviewing, selecting, and hiring suitable people. In return, they charge a fee for their services.

- The advantages and disadvantages of external recruitment are the opposite to those of internal recruitment (see Table 2.9). For example, it can be difficult to determine the suitability of an external candidate to fit into the culture of the organization.

Types of financial rewards (AO2)

- Financial rewards are the combination of an organization's pay structures for its employees. These have to be carefully designed in order to:
  - ○ help to recruit staff in a competitive labour market
  - ○ motivate employees to improve their performance
  - ○ retain workers/prevent staff from leaving for rival firms.

- The following types of financial rewards are stated in the Diploma Programme *Business management guide* (May 2022): salary, wages (time and piece rates), commission, performance-related pay (PRP), profit-related pay, employee share ownership schemes, and fringe payments.

▩ Salary

- A salary is an annual sum of compensation, paid in monthly instalments, for doing a job.

- It is a fixed amount, irrespective of how long it might take to do a job, or the number of hours a person works. Salaried staff do not receive payments for any overtime.

- Salaries are therefore a fixed cost for businesses. For example, full-time teachers are paid a fixed monthly salary, irrespective of the number of lessons they teach in a particular month or the amount of homework they mark.

- Salaries are often part of the appraisal process (see Chapter 2.4) and can reflect any changes to a worker's job description.

▩ Wages (time and piece rates)

- **Wages** are a type of financial payment that rewards workers based on time or output. Wages can be paid as time rate or piece rate, such as workers in the gig economy.

- **Time rate** is a method of paying wages based on the number of hours worked. For example, someone may earn $12 per hour working at a restaurant.

- **Piece rate** is a method of paying wages based on the number of products made or items sold. For example, someone might earn $1.50 per kilo of fruits packed at a farm. Wages therefore represent a variable cost for businesses.

■ **Table 2.10** Advantages and disadvantages of piece rate payment systems

Advantages of piece rate	Disadvantages of piece rate
• Workers are paid purely on results so this should reduce slack (waste) in the workplace.	• Quality control can become an issue if employees rush their work.
• Can increase staff motivation (encourages staff to work harder).	• Can create unnecessary internal competition between workers.
• Reduces perceived inequalities – more productive staff are better rewarded.	• There is less stability for workers, often due to external factors beyond their control.
• Can improve cash flow as fewer wages are paid if there is a decline in sales.	• It becomes more difficult for the firm to monitor and control its (variable) costs.

Commission

- **Commission** is a form of financial reward paid to workers each time they sell a good or service.
- It is typically paid as a percentage of the value of the good or service sold, thereby encouraging staff to sell more products.
- It is a common payment system used for sales staff, such as real estate agents.
- Businesses usually pay employees a base salary plus commission.

■ Table 2.11 Advantages and disadvantages of commission

Advantages of commission	Disadvantages of commission
• Acts as an incentive for workers to produce or sell more.	• Commission can be detrimental to teamworking if it encourages internal rivalry.
• Customer service (customer satisfaction) is likely to improve in order to boost sales.	• Customer service may decline if workers focus on the number of clients served.
• Can help to identify staff who might need more training/skills development.	• Can encourage a hostile culture and a lack of security, thus causing high labour turnover.
• During times of low demand, commission can help firms to adjust their labour costs.	• Commission may motivate workers in the short term, but may not do so in the long term.

EXAM PRACTICE QUESTION

A real estate (property) agent earns a monthly salary of $2,500 plus 0.25% commission per completed transaction. Calculate her total pay if she manages to sell $3.4m worth of real estate in a month. [2]

Performance-related pay (PRP)

- **Performance-related pay** (PRP) is a financial reward system used to pay people whose work reaches or exceeds a required standard or performance target.
- Performance appraisals occur regularly, usually at least once per year, against agreed objectives and performance targets.
- PRP often comes in the form of cash bonuses and/or an increase in the wage rate or salary.

Profit-related pay

- **Profit-related pay** is a financial reward system for employees based on the extent to which staff meet profit targets within a predetermined time period.
- It is paid in addition to the regular pay of employees. It can be applied to individuals, a team, or the whole organization.
- Profit-related pay is common in the private sector, such as in the banking and finance industry.

■ **Table 2.12** Advantages and disadvantages of PRP and profit-related pay

Advantages of PRP and profit-related pay	Disadvantages of PRP and profit-related pay
• Can motivate people to be more productive in order to reach profit or performance targets.	• Profit and performance targets might be set too high, so this becomes a form of demotivation.
• Can promote teamwork and team spirit to meet organizational objectives.	• These reward systems can create competitive rivalry between colleagues if not managed well.
• Can be costly for the business, as it needs to distribute a proportion of profits to the staff.	• The payout from the organization's profits may be minimal (insignificant).
• PRP can be useful for rewarding individuals, which reflects their personal circumstances.	• There may be disagreements about how performance is measured objectively.

EXPERT TIP

While profit-related pay and PRP sound very similar, the firm's profit is highly unlikely to be attributable to any individual employee. Hence, the former tends to be used for rewarding teams. By contrast, PRP is often used as part of the appraisal process to reward individuals.

Employee share ownership schemes

- An **employee share ownership scheme** is a financial incentive that rewards employees with shares in the company they work for.
- This is usually in recognition of their value to the company, such as their performance, loyalty, or trust.
- Share ownership can encourage employees to improve their performance even more, because more profit means more dividend payments for them as shareholders. There is also the potential for capital gain if improved profitability causes the share price to increase.
- However, having more shareholders dilutes ownership in the company and can prolong the strategic decision-making process due to the likelihood of more disagreements emerging.

> **Key term**
>
> **Remuneration** refers to the entire package of financial rewards received by an employee, including, for example, their basic salary, commission, bonuses, share options, housing allowance, and other fringe benefits.

Fringe payments (perks)

- **Fringe benefits** (or **perks**) are any type of **remuneration** awarded to employees in addition to their basic pay.
- Examples of common fringe benefits include staff discounts on purchases, health insurance, education assistance, fitness (gym) membership, cafeteria services (free or subsidized food and drink for restaurant staff, for example), and pension contributions.
- Examples of fringe benefits offered by some well-known companies include:
  - Patagonia provides employees with company bikes and has on-site volleyball courts and yoga lessons.
  - Starbucks in the USA pays full tuition fees for its staff following an online degree course from Arizona State University.
  - Yahoo! offers 16 weeks of paid maternity leave and $500 cash for new parents.

■ **Figure 2.10** Bikes are just one of the fringe benefits that Google employees enjoy

○ In many countries, McDonald's offers its store managers a company car.

○ Google offers its employees free food, drinks, gym, bowling alleys, climbing walls, bikes, and electric scooters to get around the office.

■ **Table 2.13** Advantages and disadvantages of providing fringe benefits

Advantages of providing fringe benefits	Disadvantages of providing fringe benefits
• Tax benefits, e.g. some fringe benefits are exempt from income tax. • Health care coverage ensures that employees stay healthy. • Firms that offer a variety of fringe benefits can build a better corporate image as employers.	• Fringe benefits are essentially financial rewards, so represent expenses for the business. • Administrative fees are also incurred, e.g. administering health care or staff membership. • Fringe benefits may not apply to all workers, e.g. maternity leave or company cars.

KEY CONCEPTS

For an organization of your choice, discuss how **change** has affected staff motivation.

Types of non-financial rewards (AO2)

- Non-financial rewards are the various forms of compensation given to employees that do not involve direct cash or monetary payments.
- Businesses with attractive non-financial rewards can entice, motivate, and retain skilled employees.
- Examples of non-financial rewards include job enrichment, job rotation, job enlargement, empowerment, purpose (the opportunity to make a difference), and teamwork.

EXPERT TIP

In today's world, non-financial rewards can have an even more significant impact on employee motivation than traditional financial rewards. Recent research from Hay Group, a global management consulting firm, found that people value the work climate, career development, and recognition as key reasons for employee satisfaction.

■ Job enrichment

- Job enrichment involves improving and developing the experiences of employees through a wider variety of tasks, some of which carry greater responsibilities and/or complexities.
- It enables workers to have the potential to manage their own workload and to build their competence. Thus, it can help to create a sense of achievement in the workplace and boost the morale of employees.
- Employers benefit from having a more appreciative, motivated, and loyal workforce.
- However, job enrichment usually costs the business more money to implement, including the costs of training and professional development of its employees.
- It is not suitable for smaller businesses such as sole traders, because of the associated costs.

■ Job rotation

- **Job rotation** is a management technique that assigns staff to various tasks and departments over a period of time.
- It widens the range of activities of workers who switch between different roles and assignments. This helps to increase their level of knowledge, interest, and motivation in the workplace.

■ **Table 2.14** Advantages and disadvantages of job rotation

Advantages of job rotation	Disadvantages of job rotation
• Reduces the monotony (repetitiveness or boredom) of a routine job.	• There is a greater need for training, which costs money and takes time.
• Helps with succession planning so that knowledge and skills are not lost if workers leave the organization.	• It can reduce labour productivity if workers are expected to do too many tasks, especially if they are unfamiliar with the tasks.
• Develops a wider range of expertise within the organization.	• It encourages job generalization, rather than specialization.
• Enables workers to be more flexible (adaptable and multi-skilled).	• Productivity can fall when employees step out of their comfort zones and are more prone to making mistakes.
• Makes it easier to cover for absent colleagues, who may be sick or attending off-the-job training.	• It is not suitable in industries where labour needs to be highly specialized, such as doctors, accountants, teachers, and lawyers.

Job enlargement

- Job enlargement involves broadening the work of employees by increasing the number of similar tasks, in other words, it occurs at the same hierarchical level of responsibility and complexity.

- By widening the range of tasks that need to be performed, employees experience less repetition (a drawback of division of labour).

- It enables workers to have a greater scope in their jobs, thereby reducing the monotony (boredom) of repetitive job tasks.

- However, a key drawback is that job enlargement is sometimes viewed by workers as an obligation to do more work for the same amount of pay.

Empowerment

- Empowerment is a form of non-financial reward that involves giving employees more responsibility and autonomy in their job.

- It allows workers to make independent decisions without having to consult their line manager. This enables employees to develop a sense of ownership in their job roles, and to take responsibility for the outcome of their work.

- Empowerment shows that managers respect and trust their employees, thereby improving their level of motivation and job satisfaction.

- It is suitable for laissez-faire management (see Chapter 2.3), as it gives managers more time to concentrate on other operations of the organization and to focus on strategic decision making.

Purpose (the opportunity to make a difference)

- Purpose as a non-financial reward refers to meaningful work.

- Working for a good cause can be motivating, as can be the case for health care workers, teachers, and those in the emergency services, all of whom do not necessarily do their jobs because of the pay.

- Purpose reminds employees about why they are doing a particular job, for example to look after others in society, to protect people's physical and emotional wellbeing, or to educate the next generation.

- People driven by purpose are intrinsically motivated by the social good that comes about as a result of their efforts.

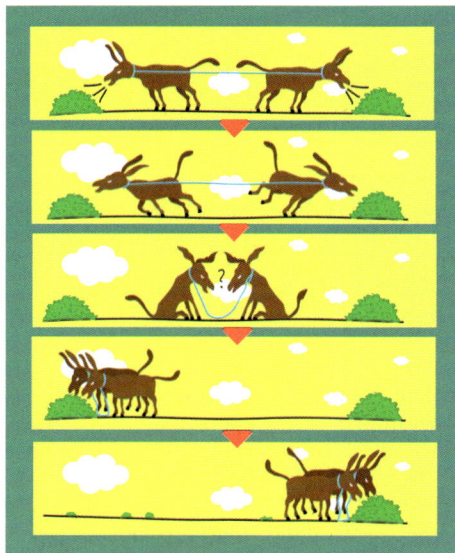

Figure 2.11 The benefits of teamwork

Teamwork

- Teamwork is about the organization of human resources into groups or clusters, working in specific departments or working on a particular project.

- Productivity should increase due to group dynamics, such as the various skills and expertise of different team members. It provides greater worker flexibility and co-operation.

- Teamworking involves social interaction and support from team members. This helps to promote a sense of belonging in the workplace.

- Teams are often empowered to set targets to achieve and make their own decisions. This can have positive impacts on staff motivation and self-esteem.

- Teamwork also helps to remove the drawbacks of internal rivalry between individuals because the performance of the team is more important than any individual's own accomplishments.

- Nevertheless, teamworking can still create non-productive rivalry between team members and it does not necessarily suit everyone.

> **KEY CONCEPT**
>
> For an organization of your choice, discuss the extent to which the organization's non-financial rewards system can be regarded as **ethical**.

> **BUSINESS MANAGEMENT TOOLKIT**
>
> With reference to Hofstede's cultural dimensions (HL only), discuss how financial and non-financial rewards may affect job satisfaction, motivation, and productivity in different cultures.

> **EXPERT TIP**
>
> Note that all the motivational theorists in the Business Management syllabus (Taylor, Maslow, Herzberg, McClelland, Deci and Ryan, Vroom, and Adams) are from North America. Do consider possible alternative perspectives – what motivates people in one part of the world may not necessarily motivate those in other regions.

Types of training (AO2)

- Training is the process of teaching employees new knowledge or a particular new skill in order to develop their competence in the workplace. The purpose is to match the skills of employees with the needs of the organization.

- It is important, as it improves the productivity of workers, boosts motivation, and reduces labour turnover. Training can also help to improve customer service and customer relations.

- A business that invests in its people can benefit from an improved reputation, which helps to attract good quality candidates in the recruitment process.

- The main types of training are induction, on the job, and off the job.

Induction

- **Induction** as a type of training is intended for employees who are new to the organization.

- It aims to support new staff in getting acquainted with the people, plans, policies, and processes of the firm.

- It can help new workers to avoid costly mistakes by familiarizing them with standard procedures, formalities, and codes of conduct.

- Induction training can be costly, as it takes valuable management time to set up and run the training for new staff.

On the job

- **On-the-job training** is conducted within the workplace, while the employee is working. For example, this could be a line manager showing, demonstrating, or instructing trainees how to do a certain task or job.

- It is used to increase productivity and efficiency in the workplace and to get workers accustomed to the corporate culture of the organization.

- Typically, on-the-job training involves workers shadowing more experienced employees and then moving on to completing these tasks with some degree of supervision.

■ **Table 2.15** Advantages and disadvantages of on-the-job training

Advantages of on-the-job training	Disadvantages of on-the-job training
• Cheapest form of training if the firm uses in-house specialists to provide the training.	• Trainees may pick up bad working habits from the trainer.
• Training is relevant as it is targeted at specific issues related to the firm's needs.	• Internal staff may lack the necessary skills, confidence, and experience to deliver the training.
• Fewer disruptions to daily operations as the trainees are still at work.	• Internal trainers cannot get their own work done while planning or delivering the training.
• Can help to build better relationships at work due to teamworking.	

Off the job

- **Off-the-job training** is conducted by specialists away from the workplace.

- Examples of off-the-job training include the following:

  - *Day release*. Employees take time off work to attend training at a local college, training centre or conference centre. For example, IB teachers attend three-day workshops as part of their professional reflection and development.

  - *Distance learning*. Employees undertake self-study courses to improve their skills and qualifications, perhaps by attending evening classes or doing an online training course.

  - *Seminars*. Staff attend a lecture or meeting as part of their professional learning and training.

■ **Table 2.16** Advantages and disadvantages of off-the-job training

Advantages of off-the-job training	Disadvantages of off-the-job training
• A wider range of skills and qualifications can be obtained. • Staff can learn from specialists or experts, none of whom may work within the organization. • Employees are not distracted from the daily operations in the workplace.	• It is more expensive than on-the-job training, e.g. training course fees. • Lost productivity during time when staff attend the training. • Employees gaining new skills and qualifications may decide to leave the firm for better jobs elsewhere.

2.5 Organizational (corporate) culture (HL only)

HL content	Depth of teaching
Organizational culture	AO1
Types of organizational culture, for example Charles Handy's 'gods of management'	AO2
Cultural clashes when organizations change, including but not limited to, when organizations grow and merge and when leadership styles change	AO3

Diploma Programme *Business management guide* (May 2022)

Organizational culture (AO1)

- The term **corporate culture** was coined by T Deal and A Kennedy (1982), referring to the set of values, attitudes, norms, and beliefs in an organization.

- Organizational culture is influenced by numerous factors, including the size of the organization, the personalities and behaviour of senior managers, traditions in the organization, management attitudes towards risk taking, and societal cultural norms.

- An organization's culture is formed over many years. However, external shocks such as a hostile takeover can change the organizational culture in a relatively short period of time.

- Organizational culture underpins all operations and systems in the workplace, such as communication channels, organizational structures, reward systems, and workforce planning.

- A strong and cohesive corporate culture creates a sense of belonging for both management and employees. It also minimizes potential misunderstandings and miscommunications in the workplace.

- Similarly, corporate culture is directly associated with the corporate or brand image. Hence, a positive corporate culture (as with Google, for example) can create competitive advantages, thereby attracting customers and prospective employees.

Types of organizational culture (AO2)

- Charles Handy's model of organizational culture (1999) shows four types of corporate cultures: power, role, task, and person. These are represented in the model as the 'gods of management'.

- A **power culture** (represented by the Greek god Zeus) exists in centralized decision-making organizations (see Chapter 2.2), where authority is concentrated in the hands of a few senior managers.
  - ○ It features centralized decision making from the senior leaders, with decisions made swiftly without slow bureaucratic processes.
  - ○ A potential negative is the impact on staff esteem, as they have no influence on decision making in the organization.
- Organizations with a **role culture** (represented by the Greek god Apollo) are based on formalized rules and regulations.
  - ○ Employees have clearly defined roles and operate within set rules and guidelines.
  - ○ Official positions of responsibility and formal company policies are core to decision making.
  - ○ This culture best suits bureaucratic organizations with tall hierarchical structures (see Chapter 2.2), such as typical public sector organizations.
- A **task culture** (represented by the Greek god Athena) exists when teams of individuals with a particular skill set and expertise are set up to tackle specific problems.
  - ○ Individuals focus on achieving specific problems or projects.
  - ○ Management needs to ensure the team consists of the right mix of skills, personalities, and leadership, often forming a matrix organizational structure (see Chapter 2.2). This is important to ensure the team is productive in completing the set tasks or projects.
- A **person culture** (represented by the Greek god Dionysus) exists when people see themselves or their skills as being more important than the organization.
  - ○ In such cultures, the organization only exists in order for people to work.
  - ○ It is a collection of individuals with similar qualifications, training and expertise, all working in the same organization, for example accountants, lawyers, and private doctors in a health clinic.

EXPERT TIP

Do not assume that only one type of corporate culture exists in an organization. Sub-cultures are likely to exist in different departments or divisions of the organization.

Cultural clashes when organizations change, including but not limited to, when organizations grow and merge and when leadership styles change (AO3)

- The **cultural norm** of an organization is the dominant corporate culture that exists within it.
- A **culture gap** exists when there is a difference between the desired culture of an organization and the actual culture that exists. This can often lead to culture clashes.
- Team norms are established by the dynamics and diversity of the people who make up each team, and the leader or manager. Members of the team interact with one another based on the established cultural norm.

- **Culture clash** might also exist if the beliefs and values of employees differ from those of senior leaders.

- **Cultural quotient** (CQ) refers to the ability and willingness of workers to understand other cultures in order to avoid cultural misunderstandings and to close culture gaps. A low degree of CQ can also cause culture clashes.

- Consequences of culture clashes include lower staff morale, lower productivity, conflict in the workplace, higher labour turnover, and reduced profitability.

- Irish academic and author Charles Handy (see Chapter 2.2) suggests that there is a direct link between a firm's organizational structure and its corporate culture – tall structures tend to be more bureaucratic, whereas flatter structures are generally more democratic.

- Culture clashes often happen when there is a merger, acquisition, or takeover (see Chapter 1.5), resulting in a new senior management team or board of directors.

- Therefore, an understanding and awareness of organizational culture is vital to managing change as a business grows and evolves.

- Different leadership styles within an organization can cause inconsistencies and confusion. Similarly, weak leadership is a cause of culture clash, as workers lack clear direction and purpose.

- Radical changes such as mergers and acquisitions (M&As) or hostile takeovers are likely to disrupt existing corporate cultures, creating uncertainties and causing anxiety for employees.

- Hence, culture clashes are a major reason why many M&As and takeovers fail to succeed.

- Miscommunications in the workplace are more likely to happen as a firm grows in size. Different languages being used by workers can create sub-cultures and cause further barriers to effective communication.

- As firms grow or evolve, a new vision and mission statement may be created, but could be met with resistance to change from the workforce. Again, this can cause some conflict within the organization.

- Charles Handy argued that organizations with a person culture have individuals who see themselves as unique and superior to the organization. Such people can therefore exert major influence on organizational culture, especially when there is a change in leadership or management in the organization.

- Organizational cultures can and do change over time. As a firm grows or evolves, or as the external business environment changes, markets become more competitive, which may necessitate managers to change the way in which things are done within the organization. To survive, it may be necessary to introduce new ideas and practices, ensuring people are able to adapt.

KEY CONCEPTS

Investigate how **change** and **creativity** have influenced the corporate culture for an organization of your choice.

2.6 Communication

SL/HL content	Depth of teaching
Formal and informal methods of communication for an organization in a given situation	AO3
Barriers to communication	AO2

Diploma Programme Business management guide (May 2022)

Formal and informal methods of communication for an organization in a given situation (AO3)

- **Communication** is the transfer of information from one party to another.

- Managers spend a significant proportion of their time communicating with internal and external stakeholders. Hence, effective communication is essential for businesses to be successful.

- Effective communication enables managers and workers to have a better understanding of and control over what they do.

- It is important for managers to understand different forms of communication (such as verbal, non-verbal, and written), irrespective of whether they are used formally or informally.

- Conflict resolution and negotiation skills (see Chapter 2.7) are important aspects of communication in business management, as disputes and disagreements are an inevitable part of any business.

- New communication technologies, such as the widespread use of emails, instant messaging services, corporate websites, video conferencing, and artificial intelligence (see Chapter 5.9), have had a significant impact on communications in business organizations.

- Cultural differences can impact communication, so it is important for managers to be aware of and sensitive to these differences, in order to communicate effectively with stakeholders from different and diverse backgrounds and cultures.

- Methods of communication can be categorized as formal or informal.

Formal methods of communication

- **Formal communication** refers to the flow and exchange of official information through authorized and predefined channels. Communication follows approved hierarchical structures and chains of command.

- This type of communication conforms to the prescribed professional standards and practices of the organization.

Examples of formal methods of communication include the following:

- *Meetings.* These are official gatherings of individual staff members to discuss work-related matters, and to make formal decisions. Meetings can be held in person (face to face) or virtually (online). A meeting agenda is used to outline the matters to be discussed.

- *Minutes.* These are official written records of the discussions in meetings, including decisions made and actions to be taken. They are usually produced by an assistant or assigned person at the meeting, and distributed to attendees for approval (to authenticate the document).

- *Emails.* Electronic mail is a form of written communication used to convey information quickly and efficiently using devices connected to the internet or computer networks, with the option to include attachments (such as documents, images, and videos). Emails are widely used in the business world for sending and receiving messages and sharing files and documents.

- *Memos.* A memorandum (or memo) is a type of short written communication used to convey information quickly and succinctly within an organization. They are used for internal communications only, often for sending reminders or announcements.

- *Letters.* As a type of formal written communication, letters are used to convey information to internal stakeholders (such as letters of appointments to a position in the firm) and external parties (such as customers, creditors, or suppliers). They are used for official correspondence, such as business proposals, customer complaints, or letters of resignation.

- *Reports.* These are detailed documents written in formal language. They are used to inform, persuade, or make policy recommendations. They are structured with a typical format, including an executive summary, an introduction, the main body containing the main findings and analysis, plus a conclusion.

- *Presentations.* These are oral and visual communication channels used to inform and/or persuade an audience. Unlike meetings, which involve discussion, presentations are predominantly a one-way communication, delivered in person or remotely by the presenter.

- *Press releases.* A press release is a written or recorded form of communication that is sent to members of the news media for publication or broadcast. The purpose is to provide information about a specific event, issue, or announcement (such as a product launch or an official response to a crisis). Press releases are often used to stimulate the interest of journalists and to encourage them to uncover and share the message contained in the release.

- *Contracts.* These are legally binding agreements between two or more parties, such as the terms and conditions of a business arrangement, sale and purchase agreement, or employment contracts.

■ Table 2.17 The main reasons to implement formal communication in the workplace

The main reasons to implement formal communication in the workplace	
It clearly defines and establishes authority.	It reduces the likelihood of mistakes and errors.
It can create discipline and consistency in communications within the workplace.	It can improve work co-ordination within and across different departments.
It tends to be more credible when sending important messages.	It improves overall efficiency by significantly reducing any ambiguities.

◼ Informal methods of communication

- Informal methods of communication refer to the unofficial and unstructured ways of sharing information within a business organization.

- Such communications do not follow formalized channels or protocols, but typically take place in private between people who have established a social relationship.

Examples of informal methods of communication include the following:

- *Gossip.* This refers to informally sharing information or communicating rumours, often in a private or discreet manner. It is often, but not always, the spreading of unverified information, but can also be a useful way to disseminate information quickly. However, rumours and gossip can have a significant impact on perceptions and decision making in the workplace. Hence, such informal communications can be harmful to people and the organization if not handled appropriately.

- *Small talk.* This refers to the exchange of casual or trivial conversations, typically as part of polite social interactions, such as asking about someone's day. It can be an effective way to build social relationships at work (getting to know someone) and to connect with other work colleagues who do not necessarily work in the same department. Such informal communications can help to establish a friendly or comfortable working atmosphere, but can disrupt productivity if not managed carefully.

- *Body language.* This form of non-verbal communication includes facial expressions, gestures, posture, and tone of voice. It can be an effective way to convey feeling or intent, but can also be misinterpreted or misused in certain situations.

■ **Table 2.18** The main reasons to embrace informal communication in the workplace

The main reasons to embrace informal communication in the workplace	
Employees can be more flexible and responsive to changing situations.	There is greater focus on individuals rather than hierarchical rankings.
It can be advantageous for encouraging supportive relationships in the workplace.	It can create a positive culture that encourages creativity, inclusion, and open communication.
There are more opportunities for communicating about different topics and issues across different areas of the business.	It provides the social and cultural contexts that help people connect with one another at work, including in formal work processes.

Barriers to communication (AO2)

- The phrase *barriers to communication* refers to any obstacle to effective communication in the workplace or the business world. It is often referred to as 'noise', as the barriers act to block or distort the message being communicated.

- Communication difficulties tend to exist more in larger organizations, but can certainly affect smaller businesses too.

- Barriers to communication include language, physical, psychological, technological, and organizational barriers:

  o *Language barriers.* The spoken and written language can make it problematic for people to communicate effectively with each other. For example, customers may speak a different language, accents and tones might cause misinterpretations, and jargon (or technical language) can make it challenging for people to understand the message being conveyed.

  o *Physical barriers.* Tangible hurdles can include physical distance (including different time zones) and poor infrastructure. These obstacles make it difficult for people to communicate with each other in person or online.

  o *Psychological barriers.* Intangible hurdles (or emotional barriers) can also exist, such as feelings of fear, anger, resentment, bias, or mistrust. These obstacles can also prevent people from communicating openly and effectively with one another.

  o *Technological barriers.* Poor internet connectivity and the use of outdated capital equipment can make it difficult for different stakeholders (such as workers, managers, suppliers, and customers) to communicate effectively through digital channels. Information overload from overexposure to online content can also create difficulties for effective communication.

  o *Organizational barriers.* These are internal obstacles created within the organization, such as rigid hierarchical structures (see Chapter 2.2), bureaucracy, or the lack of formal communication channels. These obstacles can prevent information from flowing freely and efficiently within the organization.

EXAM PRACTICE QUESTIONS

1 Define the term *formal communication*.   [2]

2 Explain **two** ways in which technology impacts communication within
   a business.   [4]

3 Explain how effective communication can lead to improved productivity in an
   organization.   [4]

2.7 Industrial/employee relations (HL only)

HL content	Depth of teaching
Sources of conflict in the workplace	AO2
Approaches to conflict in the workplace by employees: collective bargaining, work-to-rule, and strike action	AO3
Approaches to conflict in the workplace by employers: collective bargaining, threats of redundancies, changes of contract, closure and lock-outs	AO3
The following approaches to conflict resolution: conciliation and arbitration, employee participation and industrial democracy, no-strike agreement, and single-union agreement	AO3

Diploma Programme *Business management guide* (May 2022)

Sources of conflict in the workplace (AO2)

- Conflict occurs when the needs and wants of employees (or any stakeholder group) are ignored or unmet.

- Incompatible opinions and values within an organization (different perspectives or points of view) are a major source of conflict, as this causes disagreements between different stakeholders.

- Miscommunications, misunderstandings, and internal politics (workplace politics) worsen working conditions, reduce staff morale, and lower productivity.

- Grievance exists when workers have a cause for complaint in the workplace, especially regarding unfair treatment. It is a perceived injustice which also causes conflict.

- Unmanaged conflict can become a problem for businesses, resulting in demoralized staff, higher staff absenteeism, increased labour turnover, and industrial unrest (industrial action).

- Industrial action refers to the methods used by employees to achieve their objectives. It is often associated with conflict between the interests of the employer and employees.

- Conflict itself is not necessarily a negative thing, as it raises and addresses real problems in the organization. It is the way in which conflict arises and how it is managed that can create problems.

Approaches to conflict in the workplace by employees (AO3)

- **Employee representatives** are individuals or organizations (such as trade unions) that act as the collective voice of the workforce. They are usually elected by their colleagues (fellow employees).

- ○ Employee representatives are used as it is not practical for most businesses to negotiate with all their employees.
- ○ They have a duty to make the views of employees known to the management, regarding, for example, training and development needs, better terms and conditions of employment, and improved pay.
- ○ They strive to build trust and improve relations with employers.
- ○ They represent employees during times of legal disputes and conflict, for example with cases of unfair dismissal, or large-scale redundancies (job losses).
- ○ Employers can benefit from recognizing employee representatives due to the inclusive style of management, which may improve the commitment and performance of the employees.
- Examples of methods of industrial action taken by employees include collective bargaining, work-to-rule, and strike action.
- The outcome of the negotiation and collective bargaining process depends on the methods used and the relative bargaining strengths of the employee and employer representatives.

Collective bargaining

- Collective bargaining is the process by which employer and employee representatives negotiate on the terms and conditions of employment.
- Negotiations usually involve discussions regarding pay (wages and salaries), hours of work, and working conditions.
- Collective bargaining is important to individual workers, as they have little, if any, negotiation power on an individual basis.
- Negotiations and collective bargaining allow employees to put some pressure on the management team to listen to their requests or demands.
- The purpose of collective bargaining is to achieve a mutually beneficial outcome, thereby preventing conflicts from escalating beyond control.

Work-to-rule

- Work-to-rule occurs when workers adhere to every single rule, policy and procedure of the organization, with the intention of purposely disrupting production and reducing output.
- Employees strictly observe the rules and clauses of their employment contract, such as following all health and safety regulations very precisely. The intention is to get the employer to renegotiate, rather than to serve the purpose of the rules and regulations of the organization.
- Workers withdraw any goodwill by refraining from tasks and activities which might be customary, but not required by rule or in their job description, for example answering the telephone during a lunch break or leaving work slightly later than contracted in order to complete a task.

Strike action

- Strike action is an extreme method of industrial action, as it involves employees refusing to work, which prevents the organization from continuing to operate.
- It is usually used as a last resort when the other methods of negotiation between employee representatives and employers have failed to resolve a conflict.

- However, those involved in strike action are not being paid (as they refuse to work). Hence, strike action is usually only a temporary method used by employees.
- In many countries, there are legal issues regarding strike action. For example, trade unions have to give advanced warning to employers prior to taking such extreme measures.
- Strike action is a potential cause of a crisis for businesses (see Chapter 5.7).

Approaches to conflict in the workplace by employers (AO3)

- **Employer representatives** are the individuals or organizations that represent the senior management team in the collective bargaining process. They negotiate on behalf of employers in the process.
  - In some situations, the employer is legally obliged to consult or inform employees about developments in the business, for example in the case of relocation decisions, redundancies (job losses), or the threat of a hostile takeover from a rival business.
  - Employers typically use members of their senior management team in the process, although some may choose to use specialist management consultancy firms to represent their interests.
- The methods to manage conflict in the workplace used by employers include collective bargaining, threats of redundancies, changes of contract, closure and lock-outs.

Collective bargaining

- Collective bargaining is the process by which pay and conditions of employment are settled by negotiations between representatives of employees and their employers.
- Negotiations and collective bargaining are important for the employer because they can help to prevent disruptive industrial action such as strike action.
- Industrial action is detrimental for employers, due to the subsequent consequences, which include lower levels of goodwill, employee loyalty, productivity, and profitability.

Threats of redundancies

- **Redundancy** occurs when a business can no longer afford to hire a certain number or group of workers, or because a job ceases to exist, perhaps due to seasonal or technological factors, or a lack of available work.
- Redundancies can be voluntary or compulsory. Voluntary redundancies are often associated with generous compensation packages (severance pay). Involuntary redundancies happen as a last resort, often causing low staff morale and instability in the organization. Prolonged industrial disputes can lead to the threat of redundancies, as businesses start to incur losses.
- It can be challenging for a business to decide which workers to make involuntarily redundant. This needs to be done objectively, by, for example, basing it on a last-in-first-out system (number of years of service with the organization).

Changes of contract

- As the threat of redundancies can cause negative media attention, employers may choose to change employment contracts for employees who cause industrial unrest.
- This needs to be completed legally – changing employment contracts (for example, changing the terms and conditions of pay and working conditions) only when the time comes to renew the contracts.
- In extreme cases, the employer has the legal right not to renew the employment contracts of employees deemed to be counterproductive to the organization.

Closure and lock-outs

- Closure is an extreme method used by employers to deal with workers taking industrial action by stopping all business operations. This means there is no work for the staff, forcing them to renegotiate.
- Closure also means that workers do not receive any pay. If prolonged, closures can also result in job losses. Both consequences can weaken the bargaining strength of employees, driving them to compromise in the negotiation process.
- Lock-outs occur when employers temporarily prevent employees from working during an industrial dispute. Typically, security guards are hired, or locks are changed to prevent employees from entering the premises.
- Lock-outs eventually put financial pressure on workers as they are not paid during the period that they are prevented from working.
- However, closures and lock-outs can be disadvantageous to the industry, because such hostile actions can damage the organization's corporate image (see Chapter 2.5).

Approaches to conflict resolution (AO3)

- Conflict not only damages working relationships, but also the reputation of the organization. It acts as a barrier to effective communication and hinders productivity.
- Reducing or minimizing conflict in the workplace is in the best interest of all stakeholders in an organization.
- Methods of conflict resolution include (i) conciliation and arbitration, (ii) employee participation and industrial democracy, (iii) no-strike agreements, and (iv) single-union agreements.

Conciliation and arbitration

- Conciliation involves two parties in a dispute, such as employee and employer representatives, agreeing to use the services of an independent mediator (called the conciliator) to help in the negotiation process, in order to resolve their differences.
- Arbitration goes one step further, as it involves an independent arbitrator deciding on an appropriate outcome. Both parties agree to be legally bound by the final decision of the autonomous arbitrator.
- During conciliation and arbitration, both parties are kept separate to avoid the tense moments which can further intensify conflict. The conciliator communicates back and forth between the two sides and steers the discussions towards a settlement that both parties can agree on.
- Conciliation can help to prevent high legal fees if the case is taken to the courts. It is a simpler process than arbitration. Indeed, the threat of the high legal fees associated with a court trial means conciliation and arbitration have a high success rate.

- If one of the parties does not agree to the terms and conditions advised by the conciliator, it can take the case to arbitration.
- Both conciliation and arbitration can take up a lot of management time and financial resources.

Employee participation and industrial democracy

- Industrial democracy is the practice of involving and empowering people in the workplace. This includes giving employees opportunities to share responsibilities and empowering them with decision-making authority.
- Industrial democracy occurs through employee participation, meaning workers are involved in the decision-making process and are given responsibilities and autonomy to complete their jobs.
- Examples of employee participation include the following:
  - *Works council.* Employer and employee representatives meet to discuss company-wide issues, for example health and safety at work or organizational change. Pay negotiations are left to trade unions, not works councils.
  - *Teamworking opportunities.* People tend to respond positively to working with others, as this helps to satisfy their social or belonging needs (see Chapter 2.4).
  - *Employee share-ownership schemes.* Awarding employees with shares in the company is a common way to develop their sense of purpose and motivation.
- Motivation theorists such as Maslow and Herzberg (see Chapter 2.4) argue that industrial democracy helps to increase productivity, because workers are more involved, and thus feel valued.
- Employers also benefit from a more participative culture, so are less likely to experience industrial unrest. Employers benefit from lower rates of absenteeism and labour turnover.

No-strike agreement

- A no-strike agreement is a contractual agreement whereby a trade union pledges not to use strike action as a form of industrial action, as long as the employer meets their obligations as set out in the agreement.
- If workers choose to strike during the period of the agreement, employers have the legal right to discipline and/or fire (dismiss) the employees.
- The agreement typically involves both parties (employer and employees) agreeing to a process of arbitration in the event of the negotiation process collapsing, rather than employees resorting to strike action.

Single-union agreement

- A trade union (or labour union) is established to protect the interests of its members, for example to negotiate with employers for improved pay and better conditions at work. The unions are financed by the membership fees.
- Workers can belong to more than one trade union. Not all workers in the same organization belong to the same labour union.
- A single-union agreement means employers negotiate with just one labour union which represents all employees in the organization. This helps to simplify the collective bargaining process and to speed up decision making.

KEY CONCEPT

Discuss how **ethical** considerations can influence employer–employee relations in the workplace.

BUSINESS MANAGEMENT TOOLKIT

Discuss how Hofstede's cultural dimensions (HL only) can influence employer–employee relations in business organizations.

EXAM PRACTICE QUESTION

In May 2023, the British Medical Association (BMA) stated that pay negotiations with the government ended with an unsatisfactory offer for senior doctors and medical consultants in England. The BMA claimed that take-home pay has fallen by 35% since 2008 due to inflation. The government urged the BMA to consider the impact of the proposed strike action on patients. Junior doctors in England were also in pay talks with the government, while junior doctors in Scotland had already voted in favour of a three-day strike.

a   Define the term *strike action*.   [2]

b   In the context of the case study, explain one reason for and one reason against using strike action as a form of industrial action taken by employees.   [4]

3 Finance and accounts

3.1 Introduction to finance

SL/HL content	Depth of teaching
Role of finance for businesses: capital expenditure and revenue expenditure	AO2

Diploma Programme *Business management guide* (May 2022)

Role of finance for businesses (AO2)

- Finance is needed for starting up a new business, for its day-to-day operations, and/ or to fund an existing firm's growth, for example the purchase or rent of premises, machinery, capital equipment, and motor vehicles.

- Businesses need finance to pay for their ongoing costs, including for the purchasing of raw materials, components, and stock (inventory). They need to pay wages to their employees and pay their utility bills, such as water, gas, telephone, and electricity.

- Established businesses may need additional sources of finance to grow.

- All businesses have to spend money as part of their ordinary trading activities and daily operations.

- The need for finance, or the types of expenditure, can be categorized as **capital expenditure** and **revenue expenditure**.

- Capital refers to the money invested into a business that is used to purchase a range of productive assets, such as tools, machinery, and stock (inventory).

- Non-current assets are the assets of a business that are expected to last for more than 12 months and are used to generate revenue for the business.

- Capital expenditure is the long-term investment expenditure of a business for the purpose of supporting it to succeed and grow.

- Large sums of money are required for capital expenditure, as these represent long-term investments in the productive capacity of the organization.

- Capital expenditure is recorded on an organization's statement of financial position (or balance sheet) as it refers to the purchase of non-current assets.

- Revenue expenditure is the finance spent on the day-to-day or routine running of a business. It does not include the purchase of longer-term assets.

- The funds required for revenue expenditure are not as significant as those needed for capital expenditure, but must be made available immediately or at short notice to keep the business functional.

- Revenue expenditure is recorded on an organization's statement of profit or loss (or profit and loss account) as it refers to its trading costs and expenses.

- A successful business manages its revenue expenditure carefully. Spending too much of its limited funds on revenue expenditure means it can be challenging for the business to fund capital expenditure (long-term investments in the organization).

- At the same time, businesses need to have good cash flow and liquidity (see Chapter 3.7) in order to function. Avoiding a cash-flow crisis will enable a business to continue funding its revenue expenditures.

- Furthermore, uncontrolled spending on expenses, be it revenue or capital expenditure, can erode the profits of the business.

Key terms

Capital expenditure is spending on non-current assets. Examples include expenditure on buildings, capital equipment, tools, and vehicles.

Revenue expenditure is spending on a firm's daily or routine operations. Examples include expenditure on rent, raw materials, utility bills, and remuneration for employees.

■ **Table 3.1** Summary of revenue and capital expenditure

	Capital expenditure	Revenue expenditure
Meaning	Spending on non-current assets that will be used by the firm for at least the next 12 months.	Spending on items that are used up in a relatively short period of time, and within 12 months.
Examples	Expenditure on the purchase of property, capital equipment, motor vehicles, and computers.	Spending on raw materials, component parts, wages, salaries, insurance, utility bills, and fuel.
Where recorded	Statement of financial position (balance sheet).	Statement of profit or loss (profit and loss account).
Impact on profits	This type of spending has no immediate effect on profits. However, capital expenditure is essential if a firm is to generate long-term profits.	Revenue expenditure is essential to production but, if not controlled, can have an immediate and damaging effect on a business's profits.

> **KEY CONCEPT**
>
> With reference to the concepts of **change** and **sustainability**, discuss the importance of the role of finance for business organizations.

3.2 Sources of finance

SL/HL content	Depth of teaching
The following internal sources of finance: personal funds (for sole traders), retained profit, and sale of assets	AO2
The following external sources of finance: share capital, loan capital, overdrafts, trade credit, crowdfunding, leasing, microfinance providers, and business angels	AO2
The appropriateness of short- or long-term sources of finance for a given situation	AO3

Diploma Programme *Business management guide* (May 2022)

Internal sources of finance (AO2)

- The term **sources of finance** refers to where a business gets its money from to fund its daily operations (revenue expenditure) and investments (capital expenditure).

- Internal sources of finance come from within the business, using its own resources, for example personal funds (for sole traders), retained profits, and the sale of assets.

- Unlike external sources of finance, internal sources do not incur any interest charges. However, businesses are able to raise more finance through external sources.

■ Personal funds

- Sole traders and partnerships are likely to have their own personal funds from their savings which can be used to fund the start-up of their business.

- Sole proprietors and partners who do not invest (or risk) any of their personal funds are highly unlikely to secure finance from commercial banks and other lenders.

- The main drawback is the very limited funds that owners are usually able to use in order to fund their businesses.

▤ Retained profit

- Retained profit refers to the surplus funds that are reinvested in an established business, rather than the financial surplus being distributed to shareholders in the form of dividends.

- Retained profit is shown at the bottom of a firm's profit and loss account (see Chapter 3.4) and is listed as 'retained earnings'.

- It acts as an internal source of finance for a business because the funds belong to the owners of the organization, so it is part of an organization's equity, as recorded in the statement of profit or loss.

▤ Sale of assets

- Businesses can sell some of their non-current assets in order to raise finance.

- This option provides the business with an opportunity to dispose of non-current assets that are no longer needed (perhaps because they are old or obsolete). For example, a supermarket chain might sell its old fleet of delivery vehicles in order to raise cash towards the purchase of newer ones.

- However, the sale of non-current assets can compromise the firm's ability to raise working capital (see Chapter 3.7) if there are insufficient resources required for production.

External sources of finance (AO2)

- External finance comes from outside the organization, for example via external stakeholders (see Chapter 1.4).

- It is used when a business is unable to generate sufficient finance from its internal sources (the cheaper of the two categories of sources of finance).

- There are two main kinds of external sources of finance: share capital and loan capital. The latter incurs interest charges.

▤ Share capital

- Share capital is a long-term, external source of finance for a limited liability company (see Chapter 1.2), obtained by selling shares in the company to individual and institutional investors.

- An **initial public offering** (IPO) occurs when shares in a limited liability company are sold for the very first time on a stock exchange (or stock market).

- Only publicly held companies (see Chapter 1.2) are allowed to trade their shares on a stock exchange.

- The value of share capital is based on the value of the shares when they were first sold, not the current market price of the shares on the stock exchange.

- As an alternative to loan capital (which involves debt and incurs interest repayments), a limited liability company can raise finance by selling additional share capital. This process is called a **share issue**. However, this method does dilute ownership and control for existing shareholders.

- If some shareholders decide to sell their shares, this is done via a stock market without the company being directly involved – the original share capital is not affected; only the share ownership changes hands between the seller of the shares and the buyer (the new share owner).

Figure 3.1 The Frankfurt Stock Exchange, Germany

Loan capital

- Loan capital refers to borrowing funds from a financier (lender) such as a commercial bank.
- Examples include mortgages, bank loans, and overdrafts (see the next section of text).
- A loan agreement is for a set period of time, such as one, five, or twenty years. It is usually repaid in instalments over time for the duration of the loan agreement period.
- The lender charges interest on the loan amount. The interest rate can be fixed or variable.
- Two common forms of loan capital are mortgages and debentures:
  - A mortgage is a long-term source of loan capital which involves the financier demanding the borrower has **collateral** (a non-current asset, such as property, that provides financial security in case the borrower fails to repay the loan).
  - A debenture (or corporate bond) is a source of long-term loan capital, secured against a specific asset. Debenture holders do not have any ownership or voting rights, but usually receive some interest on their investment and are paid (if applicable) before a company's shareholders receive any dividends.

Overdrafts

- An overdraft is a financial service that allows a business to withdraw more money than exists in its bank account. It is, essentially, a type of short-term loan.
- The loan period is negotiable, but tends to be short term because the interest charges on overdrafts are usually very high.
- Overdrafts enable a business to have emergency access to finance during times of short-term liquidity problems (see Chapter 3.7) when cash flow is poor.
- It is a very common type of borrowing for small businesses and is used frequently.

Trade credit

- Trade credit is a very common source of external finance that enables a business to obtain goods or services from a supplier without having to pay for these immediately.
- The usual trade credit period is between one and two months (30–60 days). Some suppliers offer a price discount to customers who pay their invoices earlier.

- Examples of trade credit include credit cards and hire purchase:
  - ○ Credit cards and store cards provide interest-free credit if the full outstanding balance (the amount owed) is paid on time.
  - ○ Hire purchase (HP) involves paying for non-current assets (such as vehicles and expensive machinery or capital equipment) in regular instalments over a pre-agreed period. The finance company (lender) retains ownership of the non-current asset until the business pays the final instalment, at which point the business legally becomes the owner of the asset.

■ **Figure 3.2** Credit cards can provide interest-free credit if the full amount owed is paid on time

Crowdfunding

- **Crowdfunding** is an external source of finance that involves a business collecting relatively small amounts of money from a large number of supporters or donors (who make up the 'crowd').
- This is usually done through online platforms, such as Indiegogo, to raise awareness and gain backing from potential supporters.
- Crowdfunding is particularly popular with small and medium-sized businesses, because commercial banks may not be so willing to lend money to relatively small firms.
- The main advantage of using crowdfunding is that it can be an interest- and repayment-free source of finance. If the business offers rewards to its supporters, such as interest or a share of any profits made, these must be honoured.
- The main drawback is that each investor is likely to only contribute a relatively small amount to any business, so this limits the amount of finance it can raise.

Leasing

- Leasing is a common way for businesses to finance non-current assets without the necessary capital expenditure.
- A leasing contract signed by the lessee commits the borrower to pay a monthly fee for a fixed period of time so that they can use the asset.
- The asset is not the legal property of the business (it belongs to the lessor). This also means that it is the leasing company that takes responsibility for the maintenance of the non-current asset.

● For example, schools might lease computers, laptops, and photocopiers for teachers instead of buying them outright (which would be very expensive). The lessor of these assets is responsible for maintaining the machinery.

EXPERT TIP

Note the difference between hire purchase (HP) and leasing. With HP, ownership of the asset is transferred to the business after the final instalment is paid at the end of the trade credit period. With leasing (or hiring), ownership is not transferred at any point in the duration of the leasing contract.

■ Microfinance providers

● Microfinance providers are a type of banking service provided to unemployed or low-income earners who would otherwise struggle to gain external finance, for example by offering savings, insurance, loans, and remittance transfers.

● Microfinance gives low-income earners the opportunity to become self-sufficient by providing small loans, savings and other basic financial services.

● Microfinance providers charge interest on the loans, although the rates are generally lower than those offered by commercial banks.

■ **Table 3.2** Advantages and disadvantages of microfinance providers

Advantages of microfinance providers	Disadvantages of microfinance providers
• Helps those who are unemployed or on low incomes to become financially independent.	• Critics of microfinance condemn the system for earning profits from the poor, regarding it as being unethical.
• Empowers entrepreneurs of small businesses.	• Microfinance is small scale, so is insufficient to transform communities and societies.
• As around half of the world's population live on less than $2 a day, microfinance provides poverty relief.	• Microcredit loans can prove to be too expensive for some borrowers, as it is difficult for them to earn enough profit to sustain the loan repayments.
• Generates social benefits, e.g. health, education, clean water, and job creation.	
• Helps to build and encourage a culture of economic independence and responsibility.	

■ Business angels

● Business angels are wealthy individuals who invest in high-risk business projects, start-ups, or fast-expanding businesses with significant growth and profit potential.

● Business angels take huge risks, because they invest their own personal funds, so if the project fails they lose all the money they have invested.

● To compensate for the high risks, business angels often demand rights to partial ownership and control of the company. Therefore, this dilutes the owner's control, but does bring in much-needed knowledge, experience, and expertise.

● Finance raised from business angels can be useful for businesses that are unable to raise funds from commercial bank loans or through the stock market.

● They can provide a vital source of finance for small businesses that do not have access to conventional providers of finance, such as commercial banks.

The appropriateness of short- or long-term sources of finance for a given situation (AO3)

- Businesses need sufficient access to sources of finance in order to meet current and future needs. Definitions of short-, medium- and long-term finance vary from country to country, but generally:
  - Short term is up to one year, including, for example, overdrafts, trade credit, and crowdfunding.
  - Long term is more than one year, including, for example, share capital, bank loans, and leasing.
- The important thing for a business is to match the type of finance to its use – short-term finance, such as overdrafts, should be used to provide finance for daily operations and to cope with fluctuations in cash flow (see Chapter 3.7). By contrast, long-term finance is used to fund business growth and expansion.

The appropriateness of different sources of finance depends on the situation faced by a business. For example:

- The sale of assets would be appropriate if a business is upgrading obsolete (outdated) non-current assets, or if it has a major liquidity problem.
- The issuing of shares is only available (suitable) for limited liability companies; it is not appropriate for sole traders and partnerships.
- If the owners of a business are unwilling to allow others to have a significant stake in their business, then business angels are not appropriate.
- Loan capital is less appropriate for businesses with liquidity issues or with a very high gearing ratio, which includes firms that are already heavily indebted with borrowed funds (see Chapter 3.6).
- Crowdfunding is suitable for innovative start-up businesses in order to fund new business projects or ideas. In general, it is not a suitable source of finance for raising large amounts of capital, as the risks are very high, given that most start-up businesses fail.

■ **Table 3.3** Summary of the appropriateness of internal sources of finance

Source of finance	Advantages	Disadvantages
Personal funds	• There are no interest or administrative charges imposed.	• These are unlikely to be sufficient to fund most business operations.
Retained profit	• It can be used to pay for goods outright, without the need to borrow. • Unlike bank loans, retained profits do not have to be repaid.	• There are unlikely to be enough funds to allow the business to grow sufficiently. • Shareholders might demand higher dividend payouts.
Sale of assets	• Gets rid of outdated and unused non-current assets. • Can provide much needed finance during liquidity crises.	• May not fetch much money due to assets being secondhand. • The business may still need to replace the non-current assets.

■ **Table 3.4** Summary of the advantages and disadvantages of external sources of finance

Source of finance	Advantages	Disadvantages
Share capital	• Share capital reduces or removes the need to pay high interest on loans (debt). • A large amount of finance can be raised by issuing shares.	• Converting to a limited liability company can be complex, time consuming, and costly. • Dilution of ownership exposes a business to takeover bids.
Loan capital	• Helps to fund the purchase of non-current assets. • Accessible to most businesses.	• Loan capital incurs interest charges. • It increases the debts of the business.
Overdraft	• A quick and common source for dealing with liquidity problems.	• Very high interest rates are charged on the debts.
Trade credit	• Enables firms to buy now and pay later. • It is usually offered interest free during the credit period.	• Giving customers trade credit can increase **bad debts**. • It can encourage **overtrading**, causing high inventory costs.
Crowdfunding	• Access to a very large pool of potential investors. • Can be a cost-effective way to finance a project.	• Crowdfunding projects have a high risk of failure. • Project owners have a lack of control, as they are reliant on the 'crowd'.
Leasing	• Gives access to non-current assets without the need for capital expenditure. • The lessor is responsible for maintenance costs. • Upgrades are easily arranged.	• In the long run, leasing is more expensive than buying. • The lessor can impose quantitative limits on usage, e.g. a limit on the mileage for leased vehicles.
Microfinance	• Gives those who are typically excluded from banking services access to financial services. • Can help to lift people out of poverty in low-income countries.	• Usually involves high interest rates. • The funds are only minimal so may not be sufficient.
Business angels	• Useful for smaller firms that cannot raise finance via the stock market or commercial bank loans. • Benefits from the expertise and advice of the investors.	• Often involves dilution of control and ownership of the business. • Not an easily accessible source of funds for most businesses.

Key terms

Bad debts are the funds that cannot be recovered from a firm's debtors. As the money is no longer recoverable, it is written off as a loss or expense.

Overtrading exists when a business expands too quickly without sufficient sources of finance in place to sustain its operations.

3.3 Costs and revenues

SL/HL content	Depth of teaching
The following types of cost, using examples: fixed, variable, direct, and indirect/overhead	AO2
Total revenue and revenue streams, using examples	AO2

Diploma Programme *Business management guide* (May 2022)

Types of cost, using examples (AO2)

Costs, or costs of production, refer to the payments that a business must make as part of its operations. Examples include rent for hiring premises, wages for employees, the purchase of raw materials, and utility bills for gas, electricity, and telephone charges. The different types of business costs are explained below.

Fixed costs

- Fixed costs are costs of production that do not change with the level of output, meaning they are costs that have to be paid even if there is no output.
- Examples include rent on commercial property, the leasing costs of equipment and machinery, and salaries paid to senior managers.
- Diagrammatically, total fixed costs (TFC) are drawn as a horizontal line, starting on the y-axis at the value of fixed costs.

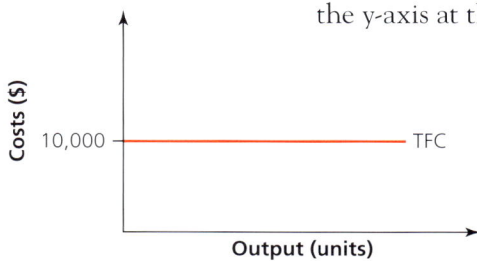

■ **Figure 3.3** Fixed costs of $10,000 for a business

> **EXPERT TIP**
>
> It is incorrect to assume that fixed costs do not change. For example, marketing costs can and do change over time, but not because of the organization's level of output.

Variable costs

- Variable costs are costs of production that change according to the level of output, meaning that variable costs increase when there is a greater level of output or production.
- Examples include the costs of purchasing raw materials and the wages paid to employees.
- Diagrammatically, total variable costs (TVC) are drawn as an upwards-sloping line starting at the origin, because no output means no variable costs to pay.
- The total costs of production (TC) are made up of total fixed costs (TFC) and total variable costs (TVC):

$$TC = TFC + TVC$$

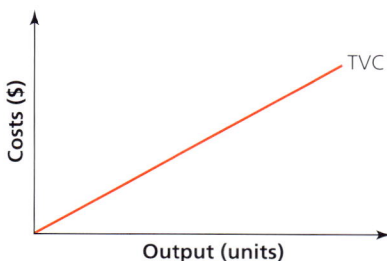

■ **Figure 3.4** Variable costs of a business

> **EXPERT TIP**
>
> What might be a variable cost for one business might not necessarily be so for another. For example, the cost of fuel is a variable cost for taxi firms, but not for a clothes retailer or cinema operator. It is important to consider costs in the context of the business being studied.

EXAM PRACTICE QUESTION

Calculate the following costs to 2 d.p. (where appropriate) from the data below:

Output	Total variable cost ($)	Total costs ($)
10	2,000	4,545
15	2,850	5,395

a Fixed cost of production. [2]

b Average fixed cost at 10 units and 15 units of output. [2]

c Average variable cost at 10 units and 15 units of output. [2]

d Average cost at 10 units and 15 units of output. [2]

▪ Direct costs

● Direct costs are costs that can be clearly and specifically identified with the output of a certain product or project.

● Direct costs can therefore include variable costs of production, such as raw material costs.

● However, direct costs can also include fixed costs, such as the cost of motor insurance for taxi operators.

● For Higher Level students, note that direct costs can be allocated to a particular cost or profit centre (see Chapter 3.9).

▪ Indirect (overhead) costs

● Indirect costs (or overheads) are recurring costs that cannot be clearly identified with the production or sale of a particular good or service.

● Examples include rent, legal fees, salaries of administrative staff, accounting fees, telephone bills, insurance, and electricity costs that can be linked to all departments within a business.

● For Higher Level students, please note that indirect costs cannot be easily or objectively allocated to a particular cost or profit centre (see Chapter 3.9).

Total revenue and revenue streams, using examples (AO2)

● Sales revenue or sales turnover refers to the income made from the sale of goods and services.

● Total revenue (TR) is calculated by multiplying the quantity sold by the unit price:

Total sales revenue = Price × Quantity sold

or

$$TR = P \times Q$$

● For example, if a cinema sells 1,200 tickets for a movie, at an average price of $11, then its total revenue from the screening is $11 × 1,200 = $13,200.

EXPERT TIP

Do not confuse revenue with profit. Profit is the positive difference between total revenue and total costs:

Profit = TR – TC

Only after all costs of production have been paid from a firm's total revenues can it declare a profit or loss.

Revenue streams

Most businesses have more than one source of revenue. These various sources of income are known as **revenue streams**. Table 3.5 shows examples of various revenue streams for different businesses.

■ **Table 3.5** Examples of revenue streams for selected businesses

McDonald's	Apple	Virgin Group
Fast food sales from restaurants	Computer accessories	Virgin Atlantic (airline carrier)
Franchise license fees	iTunes	Virgin Megastores (retail)
Royalties from franchisees	Laptops	Virgin Money (finance)
Rents paid by franchisees	Smartphones	Virgin Radio (entertainment)

KEY CONCEPT

Examine how **change** has impacted on the costs and revenues for an organization of your choice.

EXAM PRACTICE QUESTIONS

1 Complete the cost, revenue, and profit data in the table below. All figures are in US dollars ($). [4]

	October	November	December	January
Sales revenue	5,800	6,000	8,800	
Variable costs	3,480		5,280	2,580
Fixed costs	1,500	1,500		1,500
Total costs		5,100	6,780	
Profit				220

2 The table below refers to the costs and revenues of YT Toys Ltd when operating at 5,000 units of output per month:

Item	Costs and revenue ($)
Price	$20
Raw materials per unit	$8
Rent	$7,000
Salaries	$8,000

   a Calculate the total cost of producing 5,000 units. [2]
   b Calculate the profit made by YT Toys Ltd if all its output is sold. [2]

3.4 Final accounts

SL/HL content	Depth of teaching
The purpose of accounts to different stakeholders	AO2
Final accounts: Profit and loss account	AO2, AO4
Final accounts: Balance sheet	AO2, AO4
Different types of intangible assets	AO2
HL content	**Depth of teaching**
Depreciation using the following methods: straight-line method and units of production method (HL only)	AO2, AO4
Appropriateness of each depreciation method (HL only)	AO3

Diploma Programme *Business management guide* (May 2022)

The purpose of accounts to different stakeholders (AO2)

- **Final accounts** are financial statements produced for a specific trading period, usually per tax year. They comprise the profit and loss account and the balance sheet.
  - The profit and loss account shows the financial performance of the business (its revenues and costs) at the end of a specific trading period, usually a fiscal year.
  - The balance sheet shows the financial position of a business (its assets, liabilities, and equity) on a specific date.
- These financial statements are important, because they show directors, owners (or shareholders), and other key stakeholder groups the financial performance of the business during the accounting period.
- The final accounts of a business enable managers to have important quantitative data to support decision making.
- For external stakeholders, the purpose of accounts is to help them to make rational judgements about the business. For example, accounts mean that commercial banks and other lenders can assess the extent to which the business can afford debt (borrowing).
- It is important for shareholders to hold directors accountable for their use of the company's finances and to assess how safe their investment is; in other words, the final accounts indicate the firm's ability to survive in the short term.
- Potential shareholders and investors will be interested in a firm's financial records, as this may affect their willingness to invest in the company. They can use the final accounts to measure the firm's profitability and liquidity position.

Final accounts: Profit and loss account (AO2, AO4)

- The **profit and loss account** shows the profit (or loss) for a business after all costs have been deducted from its revenues, per time period (see Table 3.6).
- **Sales revenue** refers to the money a business earns from selling its goods and services to customers.

- **Cost of sale (COS)** refers to the direct costs of production. It can include the cost of raw materials, component parts, packaging, and direct labour costs. The formula for calculating COS is:

    Cost of sales = Opening stock + Purchases – Closing stock

- **Gross profit** is the amount of profit from a firm's ordinary trading activities. It is calculated by taking away the value of COS from the sales revenue:

    Gross profit = Sales revenue – Cost of sales

- **Expenses** are the indirect costs of production, for example rent, insurance, and management salaries. Interest and tax are not included in this section of the final accounts because they are expenses that are beyond the control of the business, making historical benchmarking (comparisons) difficult or meaningless.

- Note that costs and expenses (or any other deductions) are shown in brackets in the final accounts.

- **Profit before interest and tax** shows the value of profit before deducting interest repayments on bank loans (the rate being determined by the central bank) and taxation on profits (the rate being determined by the central government).

- **Profit after interest and tax** shows the value of profit a business has at its disposal after all costs are deducted (including interest and tax payments). The profit can then be distributed between shareholders and/or retained for use within the business.

- **Dividends** are the payments that a company makes to its shareholders from its profit after interest and tax. The amount distributed to shareholders is determined by the director.

- **Retained profit** is the value of profit that remains after all costs are paid and shareholders have been compensated. It is an important internal source of finance (see Chapter 3.2) that can be used for maintenance, investments, financing business growth, or kept as reserve finance.

■ **Table 3.6** Prescribed format for the statement of profit or loss (for a profit-making entity)

Statement of profit or loss for (*Company Name*), for the year ended (*Date*)

	$m
Sales revenue	800
Cost of sales	(300)
Gross profit	500
Expenses	(200)
Profit before interest and tax	300
Interest	(25)
Profit before tax	275
Tax	(50)
Profit for period	225
Dividends	(100)
Retained profit	125

Adapted from the Diploma Programme *Business management guide* (May 2022), page 59

Note the following differences between the P&L account for non-profit and for-profit business entities.

For-profit entities	Non-profit entities
Gross profit	Gross surplus
Profit before interest and tax	Surplus before interest and tax
Profit before tax	Surplus before tax
Profit for period	Surplus for period
Retained profit	Retained surplus

EXPERT TIP

The board of directors decides how much dividends are paid out to shareholders if the company declares a profit. The amount of funds that remain (retained profits) can then be used as an internal source of finance.

EXAM PRACTICE QUESTIONS

1 Malanow Ski Company has opening stock valued at $45,000, a closing stock value of $35,000, and has purchased stock during the year costing $65,000. Calculate the company's cost of sales (COS). [2]

2 Construct a profit and loss account from the data for Axner Insurance Company for the year ending 31 March 2023. [4]

	$
Cost of sales	430,000
Dividends	65,000
Expenses	80,000
Gross profit	270,000
Interest	25,000
Retained profit	70,000
Sales revenue	700,000
Tax	30,000

Final accounts: Balance sheet (AO2, AO4)

- The **balance sheet** shows the value of an organization's assets and liabilities at a particular point in time (see Table 3.7).
- **Assets** are the items of value that a business owns, for example property, equipment, stock, and cash.
- **Liabilities** are the debts a business owes to others, including money owed to banks or trade creditors.
- **Non-current assets** are long-term assets (expected to last more than 12 months from the balance sheet date).
  - These are used to produce goods and services, and include property, plant, and equipment.
  - The value of most non-current assets depreciates over time (meaning their value drops), so deducting accumulated depreciation gives the net value of non-current assets.

- **Current assets** are the short-term and liquid assets of a business that are intended to be used up within a year of the balance sheet date. They consist of cash, debtors, and stock.
  - ○ *Cash.* This is the money a business has at its premises and in its bank account, making it easily accessible.
  - ○ *Debtors.* These are customers who have received goods or services, but have yet to pay for them. The typical credit period given to customers is 30–60 days.
  - ○ *Stock.* Inventory of goods for sale within a relatively short period of time.
- **Current liabilities** are short-term debts that need to be repaid within 12 months of the balance sheet date. They comprise bank overdrafts, trade creditors, and short-term loans.
  - ○ *Bank overdrafts.* An overdraft is a banking service that enables customers to overdraw on their bank account, meaning they can take out more money than exists in the account. Overdrafts are used for very short-term purposes and are typically repaid within a few months in order to avoid high interest charges.
  - ○ *Trade creditors.* Suppliers may offer trade credit (the option to buy now but pay later), which needs to be repaid typically within 30–60 days.
  - ○ *Short-term loans.* These are advances (lending) from financial institutions, such as commercial banks or credit unions, that need to be repaid within 12 months.
- The difference between a firm's current assets and its current liabilities is called **working capital** (or **net current assets**). This is the amount of money available for the day-to-day running of the business. It is needed to fund business activity, for example to pay wages, purchase raw materials, and settle utility bills.
- **Net assets** is the term that refers to the overall value of a firm's assets after all its liabilities are accounted for. The formula for calculating this is:

  Net assets = Total assets − Total liabilities

- The value of net assets on a balance sheet must balance with the value of the organization's **equity** (or **shareholders' equity**). This refers to the firm's internal sources of finance, made up of share capital and retained profit. It is used to determine the net worth of a business organization.
- **Share capital** is the value of equity in a company funded by shareholders. This value can increase over time if the business issues (sells) more shares as a source of finance (see Chapter 3.2).
- **Retained earnings** refers to the amount of money that remains after all costs have been paid (including interest and tax) and allocating a proportion of the profits to shareholders (in the form of dividends). It is recorded in both the profit and loss account and the balance sheet (as a source of equity).

■ **Table 3.7** The prescribed format for the balance sheet (statement of financial position) for a profit-making entity

Statement of financial position for (*Company Name*) as of (*Date*)

	$m	$m
Non-current assets		
Property, plant, and equipment	500	
Accumulated depreciation	(20)	
Non-current assets		480
Current assets		
Cash	10	
Debtors	12	
Stock	35	
Current assets		57
Total assets		537
Current liabilities		
Bank overdraft	5	
Trade creditors	15	
Other short-term loans	22	
Current liabilities		42
Non-current liabilities		
Borrowings (long-term)	300	
Non-current liabilities		300
Total liabilities		342
Net assets		195
Equity		
Share capital	110	
Retained earnings	85	
Total equity		195

Adapted from the Diploma Programme *Business management guide* (May 2022), page 61

EXAM PRACTICE QUESTION

Construct a balance sheet for Lietz Watch Company from the data below, presented on 31 December 2023. [4]

	$ million
Accumulated depreciation	30
Bank overdraft	1
Borrowings (long term)	100
Cash	25
Debtors	20
Other short-term loans	30
Property, plant, and equipment	200
Retained earnings	34
Share capital	50
Stock	15
Trade creditors	15

Different types of intangible assets (AO2)

- An **intangible asset** is a non-physical asset that adds value to an organization, for example customer goodwill and intellectual property rights (patents, copyrights, and trademarks).

■ **Figure 3.5** 'Slide to unlock' is a patented technology

- **Goodwill** refers to the established reputation and networks of a business, enabling it to be worth more than the market value of its quantifiable assets. It helps to attract and retain workers and to establish new investors. The value of goodwill is only realized when the business is actually sold.

- A **patent** is the exclusive right granted to an organization by the government to make use of an invention or process for a particular period of time. It gives the inventor an incentive to invest time and money to conduct research and development. Patents give the business a unique selling point (USP) for a given time period.

- **Copyrights**, as a form of intellectual property right, give the owner or holder the legal rights to a creative piece of work, for example a book, some music, or a movie. It provides legal protection against competitors using the published works of the owner.

- **Trademarks** are the legal protection for an organization's registered symbol (logo), word (brand), or phrase (slogan). Some large multinational companies, such as Apple, Coca-Cola, and Toyota, have brand values worth billions of dollars.

Depreciation using the following methods: straight-line method and units of production method (AO2), and Appropriateness of each depreciation method (AO3) (HL only)

- Although depreciation reduces the value of non-current assets, there is no actual cash outflow from the business. Instead, it is recorded on the profit and loss account as an expense, thereby reducing profit for the year.

- It is important to calculate depreciation, as managers, shareholders, lenders, the government, and potential investors all want to know how much the business is actually worth. If it is not considered, profits become overstated until the time comes for the non-current assets to be replaced.

- Wear and tear (continued usage over time) is the major cause of the fall in the value of non-current assets such as vehicles and machinery. As the asset has been used, it does not perform as well. Used assets tend to fetch a lower market value.

- In many cases, the asset has a **residual value** (or **scrap value**) when being replaced. However, the scrap value at the end of the asset's useful life is difficult to assess.

- Non-current assets can also become obsolete (outdated), as newer models and better technologies become available over time. In such cases, the scrap value of the asset could be zero.

> **Key term**
>
> **Depreciation** is the decline in the value of a non-current asset over time, mainly due to its continued usage (wear and tear) and newer models or better technologies being available.

Straight-line method

- The **straight-line method** of calculating depreciation reduces the value of non-current assets by equal amounts each year (see Figure 3.6).

- It is calculated using the formula:

$$\text{Annual depreciation} = \frac{\text{Purchase cost} - \text{Residual value}}{\text{Lifespan}}$$

- The main advantage of straight-line depreciation is the simplicity of the method to calculate depreciation.

- The main weakness is that most non-current assets, such as vehicles or computer hardware, depreciate significantly more in the early part of their life. Writing off the same amount of money each year can create misleading figures for the book value of the non-current assets.

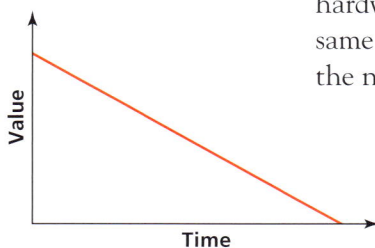

■ **Figure 3.6** The straight-line depreciation method

EXAM PRACTICE QUESTION

Tse and Li Solicitors recently purchased a new computer system for $120,000. It has an estimated useful life of four years, with an estimated residual value of $20,000. Calculate the amount of annual depreciation for the firm. [2]

Units of production method

- The **units of production method** of calculating depreciation is based on the actual usage of an asset. Typically, this is based on the number of units that the asset produces, or the number of hours that it is used.

- For example, a taxi or delivery vehicle will depreciate in value based on the mileage used, rather than the time (as in the case of the straight-line method).

- It is calculated by using the formula:

$$\text{Depreciation} = \text{Actual use (in units)} \times \text{Depreciation rate}$$

$$\text{Depreciation rate} = \frac{\text{Cost} - \text{Residual value}}{\text{Useful life (in units)}}$$

- The units of production method is the more accurate approach of calculating depreciation, because it takes into account the actual usage of the asset. However, it is less straightforward to calculate than the straight-line method.

WORKED EXAMPLE

Suppose a business purchases a machine for $100,000 and it is expected to produce 100,000 units over its useful life of five years, after which it is expected to be sold for $10,000.

What would the depreciation expense be if the business produces 20,000 units of output in the first year? To answer this question, the following steps are taken:

- Depreciation rate = ($100,000 − $10,000) / 100,000 = $0.90 per unit

- Depreciation expense = $0.90 × 20,000 = $18,000

■ **Figure 3.7** A taxi will depreciate in value based on the mileage used

EXPERT TIP

It will prove useful to learn and understand the formulae used to construct the final accounts. *Formulae in italics are HL only.*

What is being calculated	Formula
Cost of sales (COS)	Opening stock + Purchases − Closing stock
Depreciation – straight-line method (per year)	*(Purchase cost − Residual value) ÷ Lifespan of asset*
Depreciation – units of production method	*Actual use (in units) × Depreciation rate*
Depreciation rate	*(Cost − Residual value) ÷ Useful life (units)*
Expenses	Profit − Gross profit
Gross profit	Sales revenue − Cost of sales
Net assets	Non-current assets + Working capital − Non-current liabilities
Profit	Gross profit − Expenses
Equity (or shareholders' equity)	Total assets − Total liabilities
Retained profit	Profit after interest and tax − Dividends

KEY CONCEPT

Explore the role of **ethics** in the reporting of final accounts.

3.5 Profitability and liquidity ratio analysis

SL/HL content	Depth of teaching
The following profitability ratios: gross profit margin, profit margin, and return on capital employed (ROCE)	AO2, AO4
Possible strategies to improve these ratios	AO3
The following liquidity ratios: current ratio and acid-test (quick) ratio	AO2, AO4
Possible strategies to improve these ratios	AO3

Diploma Programme *Business management guide* (May 2022)

Profitability ratios (AO2, AO4), and Possible strategies to improve these ratios (AO3)

- **Ratio analysis** is a business management tool for analyzing and judging the financial performance and liquidity of an organization.
- It enables managers to make historical comparisons of the financial performance of a business in different time periods, and interfirm comparisons against industry benchmark indicators.
- **Profitability ratios** measure the ability of a business to generate profits and enable stakeholders to measure the return on their investments, such as the financial returns for shareholders.
- Profitability ratios express profits as a percentage of sales revenue. They can be calculated using the gross profit margin, profit margin, and return on capital employed (ROCE).

◼ Gross profit margin

> **Key term**
>
> **Gross profit margin (GPM)** is a profitability ratio that shows a firm's gross profit expressed as a percentage of its sales revenue.

- **Gross profit** is the difference between a firm's sales revenue and its cost of sales (COS).
- The formula for calculating the **gross profit margin (GPM)** is:

$$\text{Gross profit margin} = \frac{\text{Gross profit}}{\text{Sales revenue}} \times 100$$

- The higher the GPM, the more profitable the firm has been.
  - Methods a business can use to improve its GPM ratio include:
    - using improved promotional strategies to persuade more customers to buy its products
    - introducing new products with higher gross profit margins
    - cutting prices of products sold in highly competitive markets in order to attract more customers
    - sourcing suppliers with cheaper raw material prices, resulting in lower COS.

WORKED EXAMPLE

If sales revenue equals $10 million, COS equal $6 million, and expenses equal $3 million, the gross profit = $10m − $6m = $4m.

Hence, the GPM = ($4m ÷ $10m) × 100 = 40%.

◼ Profit margin

> **Key term**
>
> **Profit margin** measures a firm's overall profit (after all costs have been deducted), expressed as a percentage of its sales revenue.

- Profit is the financial surplus remaining after all costs, including expenses, have been fully paid.
- The **profit margin** ratio shows the percentage of sales revenue that is turned into overall profit. It is calculated using the formula:

$$\text{Profit margin} = \frac{\text{Profit before interest and tax}}{\text{Sales revenue}} \times 100$$

- The higher the profit margin, the greater the financial return as a percentage of the firm's sales revenue. It also indicates greater efficiency in managing the firm's expenses.

- To improve the profit margin, managers can strive to reduce excessive and unnecessary day-to-day expenses. In the long term, the business might even consider relocating to areas with lower rent charges, for example.

WORKED EXAMPLE

If sales revenue equals $10 million, COS equal $6 million, and expenses equal $3 million, then profit = $10m − $6m − $3m = $1m.

Hence, the profit margin ratio = $1m ÷ $10m = 10%.

EXAM PRACTICE QUESTION

Zinchenko's Kitchen has declared a gross profit of $3.5 million this year from its sales revenue of $5.5 million. The expenses were $1.5 million. Calculate the gross profit margin and profit margin for Zinchenko's Kitchen. [3]

Return on capital employed (ROCE)

- **Capital employed** is the sum of all funds invested in a business. It includes both debt and equity, so non-current liabilities + equity (as shown on the balance sheet).

- The **return on capital employed (ROCE)** is an important ratio that measures the financial performance of an organization compared to the amount of capital invested in the business.

Key term

The **return on capital employed (ROCE)** ratio measures a firm's profitability and efficiency in relation to its size (as measured by the firm's capital employed).

- It is calculated using the formula:

$$\text{Return on capital employed (ROCE)} = \frac{\text{Profit before interest and tax}}{\text{Capital employed}} \times 100$$

- The ROCE ratio can be improved by using any combination of strategies that involve:
  - increasing sales revenues, for example through promotional offers, reduced prices to entice customers, wider distribution networks or improved products
  - reducing costs, for example by taking greater advantage of economies of scale (see Chapter 1.5), improved quality management systems (see Chapter 5.3), or better stock control systems (see Chapter 5.6).

EXPERT TIP

Many students seem to think that profitability ratios are used to see how much profit a business earns. This can be done simply by looking at the profit and loss account. Ratios require the comparison of two numbers, such as comparing gross profit with sales revenues.

EXAM PRACTICE QUESTION

Tierney and Partners has a recorded gross profit of $100m, expenses of $10m, and capital employed of $300m. Calculate the firm's return on capital employed (ROCE). [2]

Liquidity ratios (AO2, AO4), and Possible strategies to improve these ratios (AO3)

Key term

Liquidity ratios are the financial ratios that look at a firm's ability to pay its short-term financial obligations (bills and debts).

- **Liquidity ratios** calculate the extent to which a business can pay off its short-term debts with its current assets.

- Managing liquidity is important to prevent a liquidity crisis (when a business is unable to pay its short-term debts).

- The two categories of liquidity ratios are the **current ratio** and the **acid test ratio**.

Current ratio

- The **current ratio** measures the value of a firm's liquid assets (cash, stocks, and debtors) in relation to its short-term liabilities (bank overdrafts, trade creditors, and short-term loans).

- It is calculated using the formula:

$$\text{Current ratio} = \frac{\text{Current assets}}{\text{Current liabilities}}$$

- As an absolute minimum, the current ratio must be 1:1, meaning that the firm has enough liquid assets to pay off its current liabilities (short-term debts). The ideal current ratio will depend on the size of the business and the specific industry in which it operates.

- To improve the current ratio, a business can:

  - attract more customers and encourage them to pay by cash

  - deposit cash that is not being used imminently into higher interest bank accounts

  - use its cash balance to pay off short-term debts

  - negotiate with suppliers for an extended trade credit period to improve its liquidity position

  - fund short-term debts with non-current liabilities, which allows the business to repay debts spread over a longer period of time.

WORKED EXAMPLE

If a firm's current assets equal $15 million and its current liabilities equal $7.5 million, then the current ratio = $15 million ÷ $7.5 million = 2:1.

This means that for every $1 of current liabilities, the firm has $2 in liquid assets.

EXPERT TIP

A higher current ratio is not always a good thing. A business can have too much stock, which ties up working capital. It can hold too much cash, which should be used to fund business activity instead. It might also have too many debtors, which again harms working capital.

Acid test (quick) ratio

- The **acid test ratio** (or **quick ratio**) is similar to the current ratio except that stock (inventory) is excluded from the calculation of current assets.

- It is a suitable measure of liquidity for businesses with stocks that are not always easily converted into cash, or for products that have a long working capital cycle (see Chapter 3.7).

- The following formula is used to calculate the quick ratio:

$$\text{Acid test (quick) ratio} = \frac{\text{Current assets} - \text{Stock}}{\text{Current liabilities}}$$

- An acid test ratio of less than 1:1 means the firm has a liquidity problem, as there are insufficient funds from its current assets to pay off short-term debts.

- To improve the acid test ratio, a business can:

  - use the same methods that improve the current ratio

  - improve its stock control management system (see Chapter 5.6). This is because when the value of a firm's stock (inventories) falls, the acid test ratio increases.

WORKED EXAMPLE

If current assets equal $15.6 million, current liabilities equal $11.2 million and stock equals $1.8 million, the acid test ratio = ($15.6 million − $1.8 million) ÷ $11.2 million = 1.23:1.

This figure means the business has $1.23 of liquid assets (without having to sell any of its stock) for every $1 of current liabilities it incurs.

EXAM PRACTICE QUESTION

Romero Accessories has the following financial data: bank overdrafts = $55,000, cash = $150,000, debtors = $65,000, short-term loans = $25,000, stocks = $145,000, and trade creditors = $80,000.

a   Calculate the firm's current ratio.   [2]

b   Calculate the firm's acid test ratio.   [2]

3.6 Debt/equity and other efficiency ratio analysis (HL only)

HL content	Depth of teaching
The following further efficiency ratios: stock turnover, debtor days, creditor days, and gearing ratio	AO2, AO4
Possible strategies to improve these ratios	AO3
Insolvency versus bankruptcy	AO2

Diploma Programme *Business management guide* (May 2022)

Efficiency ratios (AO2, AO4), and Possible strategies to improve these ratios (AO3)

- **Efficiency ratios** are used to measure how well an organization's resources are used to earn income from the available capital.

- Examples of efficiency ratios include stock turnover (or inventory turnover), debtor days, creditor days, and gearing.

- These ratios are used by managers to help improve the organization's operations, for example by reducing the time taken to collect cash from customers, or speeding up the time to convert stock into cash.

- There is a positive correlation between efficiency ratios and profitability ratios (see Chapter 3.5) – when businesses are efficient with their resources, they tend to be more profitable.

Stock turnover

- The **stock turnover ratio** is used to calculate how many times a firm's inventory needs to be replaced in a given time period (typically a year), or how quickly its stock is sold and replaced.

- It is calculated using one of two formulae:

$$\text{Stock turnover (number of times)} = \frac{\text{Cost of sales}}{\text{Average stock}}$$

or

$$\text{Stock turnover (number of days)} = \frac{\text{Average stock}}{\text{Cost of sales}} \times 365$$

> **Key term**
>
> The **stock turnover ratio** measures the number of days it takes a business to sell its stock or the number of times the business replenishes its stock during a given period of time.

where
$$\text{Average stock} = \frac{\text{Opening stock} + \text{Closing stock}}{2}$$

- Stock turnover varies for businesses operating in different industries. For example, supermarkets will have a higher inventory turnover rate than high-end jewellers or manufacturers of luxury sports cars.

- Businesses that sell perishable products rely on a short working capital cycle, so need to have a high stock turnover rate. By contrast, those selling products that are durable and with a large profit margin can afford for their stock turnover to be lower.

- Stock turnover is a less relevant financial ratio to service providers such as tuition colleges, insurance companies, tour operators, and hairdressers, because they hold few, if any, tangible products for sale.

- Methods to improve the stock turnover ratio include:
  - disposing of obsolete stock to reduce the firm's level of stock and the costs of holding inventory
  - offering a narrower range of products so there is better stock control and less stockpiling
  - implementing a just-in-time stock control system (see Chapter 5.3) as stocks of raw materials and component parts are ordered only when needed – there is no need to hold any amount of inventory.

WORKED EXAMPLE

Suppose a business has $10,000 of average inventory and cost of sales of $100,000. This means the firm has sold its stock 10 times over.

Alternatively, it takes an average of 36.5 days for the firm to sell its average inventory holding.

EXAM PRACTICE QUESTION

Wenger Co. has cost of sales (COS) valued at $525,000. It started the year with stock worth $250,000 and at the end of the year had closing stock valued at $50,000. Calculate the company's stock turnover ratio. [2]

◼ Debtor days

- The **debtor days ratio** calculates the average debt collection period of a business – the time taken to collect money from its customers who have bought goods and services on credit.

- It measures how efficient an organization is with credit control.

- The debtor days ratio is calculated by using the formula:

$$\text{Debtor days ratio (number of days)} = \frac{\text{Debtors}}{\text{Total sales revenue}} \times 365$$

- In general, the shorter the debtor days ratio, the better it is for the business. A higher ratio suggests that sales revenue has grown faster than cash receipts from customers, meaning a higher proportion of customers pay using trade credit.

- Methods to improve the debtor days ratio include:
  - encouraging customers to pay by cash, for example by offering a cash discount
  - reducing the credit period offered to clients
  - tighter credit control, for example only offering credit to customers with a good track record of paying their invoices on time.

Allbright Co. has sold 100,000 units of output at a price of $15 each. It has debtors to the value of $300,000. Calculate the firm's debtor days ratio. [2]

Creditor days

> **Key term**
>
> The **creditor days ratio** measures the average number of days a business takes to repay its creditors.

- The **creditor days ratio** calculates the length of time taken, on average, for a business to pay its suppliers and other trade creditors. It is calculated by using the following formula:

$$\text{Creditor days ratio (number of days)} = \frac{\text{Creditors}}{\text{Cost of sales}} \times 365$$

- In general, a business that delays paying its bills and short-term debts can maximize its cash outflow (assuming there are no interest charges for late payments or loss of goodwill from suppliers and other creditors).

- When the value of creditors rises, the ratio also rises. This suggests that customers are spending more using trade credit, or the timing of payments to suppliers and other creditors has been delayed, meaning it takes longer to pay creditors.

- For a business, the creditor payment period (creditor days ratio) should ideally be longer than the debt collection period (as measured by the debtor days ratio). This would improve the organization's net cash flows, at least in the short term.

- Trade credit is typically offered for 30–60 days, so a creditor days ratio in this region is generally acceptable. However, this varies between industries and countries.

- Methods to improve the creditor days ratio include:
  - negotiating extended credit periods with suppliers and other trade creditors
  - seeking alternative suppliers that offer better trade credit terms and conditions
  - paying for stock and other items of expenditure with cash, rather than using trade credit.

Baryani Inc has sold stock valued at a cost of $202,000. The company owes $24,900 to trade creditors. Calculate the firm's creditor days ratio. [2]

Gearing ratio

> **Key term**
>
> The **gearing ratio** reveals the degree to which a business is financed by loan capital, by comparing debt finance and the total capital employed.

- The **gearing ratio** is a measure of efficiency and financial risk to help managers interpret the extent to which the firm's capital employed has been financed by debt finance (borrowed funds).

- Gearing involves the use of long-term borrowings and other forms of non-current liabilities, for example external sources of long-term finance (such as debentures and mortgages), to fund business activity and expansion.

- The gearing ratio is calculated by using the formula:

$$\text{Gearing ratio} = \frac{\text{Non-current liabilities}}{\text{Capital employed}} \times 100$$

Where

$$\text{Capital employed} = \text{Non-current liabilities} + \text{Equity}$$

- A highly geared organization is generally vulnerable to increases in interest rates, as the repayment on existing loans intensifies. It is also at greater risk during a recession as sales revenue declines rapidly, yet repayment of its non-current liabilities still exists.

- Firms with a high gearing ratio are highly dependent on borrowing and long-term debt, so are seen as being risky investments.
- Conversely, businesses with a lower gearing ratio have greater dependency on internal funding, so are less exposed to fluctuations in interest rates. A low gearing ratio suggests that the firm is financially stable, so there is a low risk of it facing liquidity issues.
- Methods to reduce a firm's gearing ratio include:
  - paying off some non-current liabilities (loan capital), such as the repayment of a mortgage or debentures (see Chapter 3.2)
  - improving working capital (see Chapter 3.7), such as improved inventory control or faster collection of payments owed by debtors. This would help the business to generate cash, which can be used to repay or pay off debts
  - using more internal sources of finance, such as retained profits or share capital, to fund business growth and expansion.

EXPERT TIP

High gearing does not necessarily mean unaffordable gearing, especially if interest rates are low and there is high market growth potential. A business might have a high, but affordable, gearing ratio, with the loans being used to fund its expansion plans. Hence, it can actually lead to improved profitability in the long term.

EXAM PRACTICE QUESTIONS

1 Jayner Co. has an existing bank loan of $10 million. It has share capital of $15m and retained profit of $5m. Calculate the firm's gearing ratio. [3]

2 **a** Calculate the gearing ratio for the two firms below. [2]

   b From the limited data shown, outline which company represents higher risk for potential investors. [2]

	Jakub Bakery	Kiwior Bakery
Capital employed	$250,000	$260,000
Non-current liabilities	$80,000	$90,000
Mortgage	$35,000	$27,000

Insolvency versus bankruptcy (AO2)

- **Insolvency** refers to the financial condition of being unable to pay existing debts as scheduled, or when they are due. This can be a regular but temporary state faced by businesses. Examples include when a business faces a cash flow crisis or the loss of a major business contract.
- **Bankruptcy** is a last resort and a legal declaration and process for dealing with prolonged insolvency issues. It involves the liquidation of assets in order to raise cash to pay off creditors and lenders. In most cases, bankruptcy is likely to damage the reputation and creditworthiness of the owner(s) of the failed business.
- A business is technically insolvent for a prolonged period before it actually files for bankruptcy. Some other key differences between insolvency and bankruptcy are shown in Table 3.8.

■ **Table 3.8** The main differences between insolvency and bankruptcy

Insolvency	Bankruptcy
A financial condition, often temporary.	A legal process that deals with insolvency.
Can lead to business failure, i.e. bankruptcy.	Collapse (closure) of the business.
Creditors can take action to recover the debt.	Creditors have limited influence on the outcome.
Creditworthiness is not necessarily damaged.	Likely to damage creditworthiness.
No legal consequences with insolvency.	Legal consequences come with bankruptcy.

EXPERT TIP

Make sure you review Chapter 3.4 when revising ratio analysis (Chapters 3.5 and 3.6). Quite often in the exams, students are asked to calculate ratios from figures given in the balance sheet and profit and loss account.

KEY CONCEPT

Discuss how **creativity** can impact the operational efficiency of business organizations.

3.7 Cash flow

SL/HL content	Depth of teaching
The difference between profit and cash flow	AO2
Working capital	AO2, AO4
Liquidity position	AO2
Cash flow forecasts	AO2, AO4
The relationship between investment, profit, and cash flow	AO2
Strategies for dealing with cash flow problems	AO3

Diploma Programme *Business management guide* (May 2022)

The difference between profit and cash flow (AO2)

- Cash flow is an indication of how well a business is doing in terms of whether it is able to pay its bills and other costs.
- Net cash flow is the difference between cash inflow (cash received from the sale of goods and services) and cash outflow (cash used to pay for the operational costs of the business).
- Profit is the revenue remaining from the sale of goods and services after all costs are paid.
- A contribution to profit is earned when a sale is made. For example, a business earns $460 from the sale of a product sold at $1,000, for which the direct costs were $540. However, the cash is not necessarily received immediately, as some customers might pay by trade credit (see Chapter 3.2).
- It is possible for cash flow to be negative when a business earns a profit on the sale of a product, while cash flow can be positive even if a business makes a loss.
- A profitable business can still go bankrupt (see Chapter 3.6) if it has negative cash flow, for example if it does not have the cash to pay for its operational costs and bills. Hence, small businesses need to focus on cash flow more than profit, at least in the short term.

- A business often borrows money (such as overdrafts and bank loans) to survive, until sufficient cash comes into the organization.

- In the short term, a business must have adequate cash to run its operations whether it is profitable or not. In the long term, a business must be profitable while managing its cash flow.

Working capital (AO2, AO4)

- Working capital (net current assets) is the money that a business has available for its operational activities and to meet its short-term obligations, for example the money it has to buy raw materials, settle invoices, pay for its marketing, or pay wages to its workers.

- Without working capital, the business is unable to operate or trade.

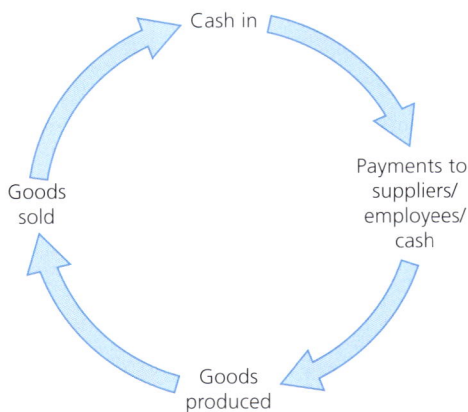

■ **Figure 3.8** The working capital cycle

- It is shown on a firm's balance sheet (see Chapter 3.4) as the value of net current assets – current assets minus current liabilities.

- The working capital cycle refers to the time lag between a firm paying for the operational and production costs of a good or service and actually receiving the cash from the sale of the product (see Figure 3.8).

- Businesses that receive cash regularly from the sale of goods and services have short working capital cycles, as is the case for supermarkets and cafés. Those with long production schedules, for which customers pay in instalments and/or by credit, have longer working capital cycles. Hence, it is more challenging for these to manage cash flows.

Liquidity position (AO2)

- Liquidity refers to how much cash a business has that is readily available, or the level of ease with which the business can sell an asset and convert this into cash without losing significant value.

- Liquid assets are shown on a firm's balance sheet as 'current assets'. These consist of cash itself (held at the bank or in the business itself), debtors, and stock (inventory).

- High liquidity means that an asset can be sold quickly for cash at the expected market value (market price). Low liquidity means that it takes a long time to sell the asset, especially if the business is unwilling to reduce the selling price.

- Liquidity is important, as it shows the ability of a business to meet its financial obligations and unexpected costs – liquidity indicates the financial security of an organization.

- Ratio analysis (the current ratio and acid test ratio) can be used to measure the liquidity position of a business (see Chapter 3.5). The higher these ratios, the better a firm's liquidity position (or financial health), as it shows the business is in a stronger position to meet its financial obligations.

EXAM PRACTICE QUESTION

Suppose a business has current assets to the value of $3 million and current liabilities of $2 million. Comment on the firm's liquidity position. [2]

Cash flow forecasts (AO2, AO4)

- Cash flow is the movement of money into and out of a business.
- Cash flow forecasting refers to the prediction of cash coming in and moving out of a business over a given period of time, for example the next 6 or 12 months.
- Monitoring a firm's cash flow is important to avoid liquidity problems (periods when there are cash shortages), so the business has enough money to continue its daily operations.
- Cash inflow mainly comes from the sale of goods and services.
- Cash outflow occurs when a business pays for its items of expenditure, including, for example, raw materials, staff wages, utility bills, insurance, and rent.
- **Net cash flow** is the difference between cash inflows and cash outflows per time period:

    Net cash flow = Cash inflow − Cash outflow

- There is positive cash flow if the cash inflows exceed the cash outflows for a given time period. Negative net cash flow means cash outflows exceed the cash inflows.
- Cash flow problems can arise due to internal reasons (poor cash flow management) or external factors (such as seasonal demand).
- Being able to predict how cash will flow into and out of the business can help its financial management and decision making.
- The **closing balance** in a cash flow forecast is the amount of cash at the close of a trading period, usually at the end of the month. This figure becomes the 'opening balance' in the subsequent time period.
- The **opening balance** in a cash flow forecast is the amount of cash at the beginning of a trading period, usually at the start of each month. It is equal to the value of the closing balance in the previous time period.

EXAM PRACTICE QUESTIONS

1 Tartinelli Inc. has the following financial information: opening balance = $70,000, cash outflows = $80,000, and cash inflows = $120,000. Calculate the closing balance for the firm. [2]

2 Shield Sports Equipment has produced a cash flow forecast which predicts a closing year-end balance of $150,000. The company later discovers that a payment of $17,000 was not processed from the sales figure, and that an invoice for $13,000 is yet to be paid. Calculate the closing balance for the firm. [2]

3 Study the financial information below and answer the questions that follow.

    Kaergaard & Co. cash flow statement (excerpts):

    Opening balance: $35,500
    Cash inflow: $195,000
    Cash outflow: $150,000

    a Calculate the net cash flow for Kaergaard & Co. [2]
    b Calculate the closing balance for Kaergaard & Co. [2]

Cash flow forecasting formulae

Net cash flow = Cash inflow − Cash outflow

Closing balance = Opening balance + Net cash flow

Opening balance = Closing balance in preceding month

The relationship between investment, profit, and cash flow (AO2)

- Investment refers to the capital expenditure (see Chapter 3.1) of a business – the spending on non-current assets such as premises, equipment, and machinery.
- Survival and sustainability mean that entrepreneurs must invest in their business for longer-term profitability. The lack of investment and inability to adapt to change has forced many businesses to collapse, including HMV, Blockbuster, and Kodak.
- By contrast, successful investments lead to improved cash flow and profitability.
- Investment decisions are made on the assumption that profit will be generated in the future.
- However, investment expenditure clearly leads to cash outflow, at least in the short term.
- The benefits of an investment project are likely to be reaped over several years (see Chapter 3.8).
- Assets purchased for an investment project may be sold at the end of their useful life, minus their depreciated value (see Chapter 3.4). This can generate much-needed cash inflow.

Strategies for dealing with cash flow problems (AO3)

- The strategies used to deal with cash flow problems depend on the causes of the problems, such as:
  - sales revenue being lower than expected
  - costs of production being higher than budgeted
  - unexpected costs that arise
  - customers who buy on credit (see Chapter 3.2) and are slow to pay their invoices
  - customers who buy on credit and fail to pay (bad debts)
  - overstocking of items that do not sell well.
- Hence, to solve cash flow problems, a business can (i) reduce its cash outflows, (ii) improve its cash inflows, and/or (iii) look for additional finance.

■ Reduce cash outflows

- The business can seek to improve trade credit from its suppliers (see Chapter 3.2), by, for example, paying on credit rather than paying cash in advance.
- It can offer price discounts to customers who make early payment of invoices.
- The business can reduce the duration of credit offered to its own customers (although this might reduce the demand from some customers).
- It can reduce delivery costs by negotiating a bulk-buying deal with suppliers (although this could lead to higher costs of stock control).
- The business can lease rather than buy assets such as equipment, machinery, and building. For example, the firm might sell its headquarters but immediately lease it back on a long-term basis.
- It can hold lower levels of stock (inventory) to free up cash.
- It can renegotiate rents or even consider relocation to cheaper premises.
- The business can negotiate with suppliers for longer trade credit periods or look for cheaper local suppliers.

▥ Improve cash inflows

- The business can strive to improve its marketing mix (see Chapter 4.5) in order to increase brand awareness, sales revenue, and customer loyalty.
- Businesses can consider raising the prices of products that have a high degree of brand loyalty (products with price inelastic demand – see Chapter 4.5).
- Alternatively, a business can lower the prices of products that face fierce competition (products with price elastic demand – see Chapter 4.5).
- The business can improve its product portfolio management (see Chapter 4.5) by stocking more of the best-selling products and reducing or removing stocks of products that do not sell well.

▥ Look for additional finance

- The business can use an overdraft or loan capital (see Chapter 3.2) during times of negative cash flow or when the closing balance is negative. However, this would incur interest charges.
- The business can seek growth opportunities – for example, a sole trader might form a partnership to benefit from an additional source of finance and shared skills and responsibilities with the partner(s).
- It can sell non-current assets to raise income, for example unused or obsolete equipment, furniture, and machinery. In extreme cases of liquidity problems, the business might even sell non-current assets such as vehicles, premises, or subsidiary companies.

EXPERT TIP

When tackling cash flow forecasts, be sure to look out for negative cash flow figures and/or negative closing balances. Business management is about decision making and problem solving – if there aren't any problems for the business in question, then cash flow forecasts would not be required.

EXAM PRACTICE QUESTIONS

a Complete the three-month cash flow forecast for Raliba & Co.: [4]

	July ($)	August ($)	September ($)
Opening balance	0	(50)	0
Cash inflows			
Sales revenue	1,500		1,900
Bank overdraft	0	100	
Total cash inflow		1,700	1,900
Cash outflows			
Materials	350	400	450
Wages	200	200	
Rent	900	900	900
Utility bills	100	150	200
Cash outflow			1,870
Net cash flow			
Closing balance	(50)		

b Explain **two** causes of cash flow problems. [4]

c Explain **two** ways that Raliba & Co. might resolve its cash flow problems. [4]

3.8 Investment appraisal

SL/HL content	Depth of teaching
Investment opportunities using payback period and average rate of return (ARR)	AO3, AO4
HL content	**Depth of teaching**
Investment opportunities using NPV (HL only)	AO3, AO4

Diploma Programme *Business management guide* (May 2022)

Investment opportunities using payback period (AO3, AO4)

- **Investment** refers to the business expenditure on non-current assets with the potential to generate future financial benefits, for example the purchase of a new factory or upgrading of computer systems.
- **Investment appraisal** is a quantitative decision-making tool used to assess whether the capital expenditure of a firm is justifiable in terms of whether it will be financially worthwhile.
- The **payback period (PBP)** method of investment appraisal measures the estimated time it will take for an investment project to earn enough profit to recover the initial cost of the investment.
- The PBP allows a firm to see whether it will recover the cost of a non-current asset (such as a fleet of commercial vehicles, photocopier machines, or computer networks) before it needs to be replaced.
- If the annual net cash flows from an investment project are known, the formula used to calculate the payback period is:

$$\text{Payback period} = \frac{\text{Cost of the investment}}{\text{Annual net cash flow}}$$

- The larger the annual contribution (or annual net cash flow), the faster the payback period.
- An investment project is generally considered desirable if the PBP is relatively short (which depends on industry norms and the firm's maximum desired PBP).
- The PBP method is suitable for firms that:
  - focus on time as a priority for investment decisions
  - regard liquidity to be of more importance than profitability
  - want a quick return on their investment.

> **Key term**
>
> The **payback period (PBP)** is the estimated length of time it takes for a business to recover the initial cost of an investment project.

■ **Table 3.9** Advantages and disadvantages of payback period

Advantages of payback period	Disadvantages of payback period
• It is the simplest and quickest method of investment appraisal to calculate. • It is easy for managers to interpret and understand the results. • The depreciation of non-current assets does not directly affect the PBP, but can be easily included in the calculation. • It helps managers choose investment projects with a short PBP so as to reduce risks.	• It ignores the timing of the net cash flows, despite the future value of cash being lower. • It is not generally suitable for long-term projects, i.e. those with a long PBP. • Time, rather than profitability, is the focus of attention which could be unrealistic for most private sector firms. • It does not consider the useful life of the non-current asset after its payback period.

EXAM PRACTICE QUESTIONS

1 Nimes Construction Co. is considering investing €1,155,000 in new industrial machinery. The annual net cash flows arising from the investment are €330,000. Calculate the project's payback period. [2]

2 WordsWorth Book Publishers is considering an investment of $220,000 in new printing equipment that is expected to generate the following net cash flows over the next five years:

Year	Net cash flow
1	$30,000
2	$40,000
3	$60,000
4	$70,000
5	$60,000

The management at WordsWorth Book Publishers wants a quick recovery of the investment cost due to the highly competitive nature of the industry.

a Define the term *payback period*. [2]

b Calculate the payback period for WordsWorth Book Publishers and comment on your findings. [4]

Investment opportunities using average rate of return (ARR) (AO3, AO4)

- The **average rate of return (ARR)** measures the predicted annual profit generated from an investment project, expressed as a percentage of the initial investment cost.

- The ARR is compared to the firm's desired rate of return in order to determine whether to accept or reject an investment proposal. This is often based on the prevailing interest rate in the economy and/or the predicted ARR for other proposed investment projects.

- It is calculated using the formula:

$$\text{ARR} = \frac{\text{Average annual profit}}{\text{Initial investment}}$$

- The higher the value of the ARR, the more financially attractive an investment project tends to be on financial grounds.

- The higher the interest rate, the less attractive the ARR tends to be, as it is safer to just leave cash in a commercial bank instead of being burdened with risks, especially for firms that need to borrow money to fund their investment projects.

Key term

The **average rate of return (ARR)** is an investment appraisal technique that calculates the average annual profit of an investment project, expressed as a percentage of the initial amount invested in the project.

■ **Table 3.10** Advantages and disadvantages of average rate of return

Advantages of ARR	Disadvantages of ARR
• The ARR is simple to understand and straightforward to calculate.	• Unlike the net present value method, the ARR ignores the timings of net cash flows.
• Unlike the payback period, the ARR focuses on profitability rather than time.	• Unlike the PBP, the ARR focuses on profits rather than cash flow in order to break even quickly and to generate cash to invest in other projects.
• The firm can use the ARR to evaluate its financial performance.	
• As the ARR is expressed as a percentage, it can be useful to compare the attractiveness of a range of different investment projects.	• The figures are predictions only, so tend to be less accurate the longer the investment project under consideration is.

EXAM PRACTICE QUESTIONS

1 The management at Chandelier World is investigating the feasibility of replacing its old precision-cutting machinery. The new machinery would cost $460,000 and increase the firm's annual revenue by $150,000, but raise operating costs by $60,000 a year. The estimated useful life of the new machinery is 12 years with no scrap (secondhand) value. The management wants an average rate of return (ARR) of 15% on all its capital investments.

    a Calculate the average rate of return (ARR) of the new machinery for Chandelier World. [2]

    b Comment on whether Chandelier World should purchase the new machinery. [2]

2 Villano Watch Company is deciding whether to upgrade its computerized invoicing system for $155,000. The annual expected gains (or annual contributions) from doing so over the system's expected useful life cycle of five years is shown below.

Year	Annual contribution
1	$30,000
2	$40,000
3	$50,000
4	$40,000
5	$30,000

    a Calculate the average rate of return. [2]

    b Comment on whether Villano Watch Company should invest in the computerized invoicing system. [4]

Investment opportunities using net present value (NPV) (HL only) (AO3, AO4)

- **Net present value (NPV)** is the difference between the total present values of future net cash flow and the initial cost of the investment project.
- It is calculated by taking away the cost of the investment project from the sum of the present values for the duration of the project.
- If the annual interest rate is 10%, then the present value of receiving $1,000 in one year's time is $909.10. This means $909.10 invested today, earning 10% return, would be valued at $1,000 in one year's time. The **discount rate** is therefore 0.9091.
- The higher the discount rate, the lower the NPV, because of the higher opportunity cost of receiving cash in the distant future.

Key terms

Net present value (NPV) is an investment appraisal technique that calculates the real value of an investment project by discounting the value of future cash flows. Once the initial cost of the investment project is deducted from the total discounted cash flow, the NPV is found.

A **discount rate** is a number used to reduce the value of a sum of money received in the future in order to determine its present value. This is the opposite of a compound interest rate.

- The NPV shows the value of the total financial return on an investment project expressed in today's value, identified in monetary terms.
- The NPV looks at the opportunity cost of money, as cash received in the future is worth less than it is worth today.
- In general, the higher the interest rate, the lower the present (current) value of money that is received in the future.
- If the NPV figure is positive, then the investment project is feasible on financial grounds. This is because the higher the NPV, the more attractive the investment project.
- The longer the investment project under consideration is, the longer it takes for net cash flows to materialize, so the lower the future value (net worth) of the project tends to be.

■ **Table 3.11** Advantages and disadvantages of net present value

Advantages of NPV	Disadvantages of NPV
• It considers future net cash flows (earnings) expressed in today's value, making the calculations more realistic.	• The NPV can be tedious to calculate, especially as so many variables can alter the final net cash flow figures.
• It is more accurate than the ARR as the NPV method discounts the future values of net cash flows (money is worth less in the future).	• It can be difficult or subjective to decide on an accurate discount rate if the economy's inflation and interest rates fluctuate considerably.
• Managers can compare the effects of different discount rates on their investments.	• It is difficult to accurately forecast net cash flows in the distant future.

EXPERT TIP

Should NPV appear in the final examinations, a discount table will be provided to HL students in the exam paper – see page 66 of the Diploma Programme *Business management guide* (May 2022).

EXAM PRACTICE QUESTION

Chucharek Parlour is considering the purchase of five industrial massage chairs for a per unit price of $13,000. The estimated net cash flows during the useful life cycle of five years from the investment are shown below, along with the discount rates at 5% for the duration of the investment.

Year	Net cash flow	Discount rate
1	$15,000	0.9524
2	$20,000	0.9070
3	$30,000	0.8638
4	$20,000	0.8227
5	$20,000	0.7835

a Calculate the payback period of the investment project. [2]

b Calculate the average rate of return from the investment project. [2]

c Outline why the net present value method of investment appraisal discounts future net cash flows. [2]

d Calculate the net present value of the investment project. [3]

e Explain whether the purchase of the industrial massage chairs represents a feasible investment for Chucharek Parlour. [4]

KEY CONCEPT

Discuss the importance of **ethics** and **sustainability** for investment decisions.

EXPERT TIP

This unit only considers the quantitative tools used in investment appraisal. In reality, qualitative techniques are also used to determine whether an investment project is worthwhile, and whether the investment decision is in line with the organization's vision or mission, business objectives, corporate culture, market trends, and external factors, such as forecasts about the economy.

3.9 Budgets (HL only)

HL content	Depth of teaching
The difference between cost and profit centres	AO2
The roles of cost and profit centres	AO2
Constructing a budget	AO2, AO4
Variances	AO2, AO4
The importance of budgets and variances in decision making	AO2

Diploma Programme *Business management guide* (May 2022)

The difference between cost and profit centres (AO2)

- A **cost centre** is a department or division within an organization that is responsible and held accountable for its own costs.
  - The cost centre does not generate any direct revenue but adds to the cost of running the business.
  - Examples include the following departments: personnel (human resources), research and development (R&D), marketing, technical support, and customer service.
- A **profit centre** is a department or division within an organization that is responsible and held accountable for both its own costs and revenues, and hence the resulting profits.
  - An example is multiple chain businesses, with each branch or store of the organization responsible for its own profits or losses.
  - As with cost centres, the managers of profit centres are held accountable for their financial performance. Typically, managers of profit centres are responsible for achieving a target level of profit.

The roles of cost and profit centres (AO2)

- *Monitoring and control.* Cost and profit centres help businesses to control each aspect of their operations. This is particularly the case for large and expanding businesses. Thus, it becomes easier and more accurate to monitor the organization's performance by using variance analysis of each centre.
- *Motivational.* Empowering, entrusting and delegating responsibility to cost and profit centres can be highly motivating for employees.
- *Enhancing decision making.* The speed and the quality of decision making improves, because managers of cost and profit centres are empowered to make autonomous decisions.

- *Accountability.* Using cost and profit centres helps to make managers accountable for their specific responsibilities, including the ability to control costs and/or revenues.

- *Strategic planning.* Profit centres can be used for strategic planning and resource allocation if there is sufficient data generated about which centres incur the most costs and/or contribute the most revenue to the organization.

However, there are limitations of establishing cost and profit centres. These include the following:

- Centres can create unhealthy and destructive competition between the various departments, hindering the organization's ability to reach its targets.

- Distributing the firm's fixed costs to cost and profit centres is somewhat of a subjective and arbitrary task, so can lead to arguments between employees. For example, how should rents and utility bills be split between the various centres?

Constructing a budget (AO2, AO4)

- A budget is a plan of the costs and revenues with the purpose of achieving the objectives of a business in a given time period, usually one year.

- A budget usually includes all the trading activities of a business and its predicted level of sales revenue and costs (see Table 3.12 for the IB's prescribed format for constructing a budget).

- Budgets are used widely in almost all organizations, irrespective of their size or which sector they operate in. For example, theme parks such as Disneyland and Universal Studios set budgets for their sales (from admission tickets), catering (in their food outlets), and retail shops (for merchandise).

- Constructing a budget is relatively straightforward, as it simply requires managers to identify all sources of revenue and items of expenditure. For example:

  o Revenue can come from sales revenue (selling goods and services) and interest earned from cash balances at the bank.

  o Cost items include expenditure on salaries and wages for employees, materials from suppliers, rent, advertising, and electricity.

■ **Table 3.12** IB prescribed format for a budget for both profit and non-profit business entities

All figures in $'000	Budgeted figure
Revenue	
Sales revenue	500
Interest earned	10
Total revenues	**510**
Costs	
Salaries and wages	120
Materials	65
Rent	25
Advertising	10
Electricity	15
Total costs	**235**
Excess of revenues over (under) costs	**275**

Variances (AO2, AO4)

- A **variance** exists when the actual outcome differs from the budgeted figure. For example, a variance would occur if sales were planned to be 5,000 units, but actual sales were only 4,500 units.

- Variances are measured for a specified time period, such as per month, quarter, or year, by comparing the actual result with the budgeted figure (see Tables 3.13 and 3.14).

- Variances are classified as either **favourable variances** (if they cause higher than expected profits) or **adverse variances** (if they result in a fall in profits).

■ **Table 3.13** Examples of variances for Tomiyasu Garments Co.

Variable	Budget	Actual	Variance
Sales of product A (units)	1,000	1,110	Favourable variance of 110 units
Sales of product B (kg)	50,000	45,000	Adverse variance of 5,000 kg
Raw material costs ($)	45,000	51,000	Adverse variance of $6,000
Wages ($)	$110,000	$107,000	Favourable variance of $3,000

■ **Table 3.14** IB prescribed format for constructing budgets and calculating variances

Budget for (name of business) for the period ended 20XX

All figures in $'000	Budgeted figure	Actual figure	Variance
Revenue			
Sales revenue	500	480	20(A)
Interest earned	10	14	4(F)
Total revenues	510	494	16(A)
Costs			
Salaries and wages	120	135	15(A)
Materials	65	68	3(A)
Rent	25	25	0
Advertising	10	8	2(F)
Electricity	15	20	5(A)
Total costs	235	256	21(A)
Excess of revenues over (under) costs	275	238	37(A)

[F] = Favourable variance

[A] = Adverse variance

Adapted from the Diploma Programme *Business management guide* (May 2022)

- Budgetary control is important for effective financial management. Variance analysis can help managers to get early warning signs of potential financial problems. For example, if sales of a particular product are below budget, managers can respond by reducing output or increasing marketing expenditure in an attempt to increase sales.

- Variance analysis also allows businesses to examine whether budgets and targets are being adhered to. Hence, variance analysis acts as an additional financial control mechanism.

- The budgeting process and variance analysis help to ensure that no department or individual budget holder spends more than the business expects, thereby preventing any unpleasant surprises.

EXAM PRACTICE QUESTIONS

1 Calculate the variance for the following items for Anita Maria Caterers Co.:
   a Cost of materials: budgeted = $10,000 but actual = $11,500   [1]
   b Cost of labour: budgeted = $3,700 but actual = $3,200   [1]
   c Sales of cakes: budgeted = $26,000 but actual = $24,800   [1]

2 Cleo Williamson runs a successful hair salon business. Her latest monthly budget is shown in the table below.
   a Explain why Cleo Williamson uses budgets.   [2]
   b Complete the missing figures for the hair salon business.   [4]

Variable	Budgeted ($)	Actual outcome ($)	Variance ($)
Wages		4,400	400 adverse
Salaries	6,500	6,500	0
Stock	1,700	1,800	
Revenue	16,550		340 favourable
Direct costs	3,600	3,450	

   c Suggest why a favourable variance might be investigated by Cleo Williamson.   [2]

The importance of budgets and variances in decision making (AO2)

- Budgets and variance analysis are important in strategic planning because they ensure that the financial implications of business decisions are fully considered.

- By empowering budget holders, the process can allow the board of directors to concentrate on core business issues (strategic planning) and only to get involved if significant variances or problems occur.

- Budgets enable a business to turn its strategy into practice. This is because all business operations need to be funded by the money allocated to various budgets of the organization.

- The budgeting process and variance analysis help to provide a benchmark against which a manager's success (or lack of) can be measured and rewarded. For example, a sales manager who exceeds an agreed sales budget might receive an annual performance bonus or qualify for the company's share ownership scheme (see Chapter 2.4).

- The effectiveness and appropriateness of leadership in the organization become questionable if budgets are ignored or not adhered to.

- Budgets and variance analysis enable senior managers and other key stakeholders to measure the degree of success or failure of the firm's business strategy.

EXPERT TIP

Budgets and variance analysis do not, on their own, ensure successful strategic planning and implementation. Although they are useful management tools for monitoring business operations, they are based on assumptions and predictions that may prove to be inaccurate. There are many external influences that can cause a divergence between actual and planned outcomes.

BUSINESS MANAGEMENT TOOLKIT

Discuss how different aspects of Hofstede's cultural dimensions (HL only) can influence the budgeting process in business organizations.

4 Marketing

4.1 Introduction to marketing

SL/HL content	Depth of teaching
Market orientation versus product orientation	AO2
Market share	AO2, AO4
The importance of market share and market leadership (HL only)	AO3
Market growth	AO2, AO4

Diploma Programme *Business management guide* (May 2022)

Market orientation versus product orientation (AO2)

- **Marketing** is the management process of anticipating, identifying, and satisfying the needs and desires of customers. This is typically done in a profitable way.
- The marketing department of an organization aims to provide the right products, suitably priced, distributed conveniently for customers to purchase, and promoted effectively to attract customers.
- Businesses can take two alternative approaches to their marketing: market orientation versus product orientation.

Product orientation

- **Product orientation** is an inward-looking marketing approach that focuses on making products that a business knows how to make or has been making for a long time, rather than focusing on the needs and wants of potential customers.
- This is the approach used by technologically advanced and highly innovative manufacturers of high-tech goods.
- Product-orientated businesses focus on creativity and innovation which can give them a unique selling proposition and competitive advantages.
- Product orientation can succeed when businesses have a strong market reputation, such as in the case of Coca-Cola, Google, Lego, Nike, Ray-Ban, Rolex, and Samsung, or in markets where the pace of change is very slow.
- Product-orientated businesses are focused on issues relating to internal production processes. This can lead to such businesses losing their market if competitors are instead highly focused on customer needs. For example, Apple missed out on the sale of large-screen smartphones (phablets) due to its product-orientated approach, allowing Samsung to dominate the market.

Market orientation

- By contrast, **market orientation** is an outward-looking marketing approach that focuses on meeting the specific wants and needs of customers and potential customers, meaning firms focus on marketing products they can sell, rather than what they can make well.

- Market-orientated businesses conduct market research to find out what their customers want, and then focus their energies on making and improving these products in line with customer feedback and preferences.
- Businesses that take this approach use promotions and advertising to keep customers informed of changes and developments in the products they offer.
- Market orientation forces organizations to be more flexible (by focusing on changing consumer needs and wants), thereby lowering the risks of business failure.
- As market-orientated firms are able to align their products with the expectations and demands of customers, there is a higher likelihood of success.
- Whether a business opts for market or product orientation depends on numerous factors:
  - *Nature of the product.* Market orientation is more suitable for mass-produced goods, but product orientation is more suitable for innovative and high-end quality products.
  - *Organizational culture.* Pioneering firms such as Apple and 3M focus on product orientation, whereas retailers such as Walmart and Zara focus on meeting the needs and wants of their customers.
  - *Number of competitors.* An industry with few competitors means a product-orientated approach could be suitable.
  - *Research and development (R&D).* Businesses with no budget or minimal budget for R&D are far more likely to use market orientation, whereas those with large R&D expenditure (such as pharmaceutical companies) can use product orientation.

Market share (AO2, AO4)

> **Key term**
>
> **Market share** refers to an organization's portion of the total value of sales revenue in a particular industry.

- **Market share** is a measure of a particular business's relative size, based on its sales revenue expressed as a percentage of the total sales revenue in the industry.
- Market share is calculated by using the formula:

$$\text{Market share} = \frac{\text{Firm's sales revenue (\$)}}{\text{Total industry's sales revenue (\$)}} \times 100$$

- This allows a business to compare itself to the size of its competitors in terms of sales revenue.
- Data about market share help to reveal the extent to which a market is competitive by adding the market share values of the largest few firms in the industry. For example, if the top three supermarket chains in a country account for 75 per cent of the market share, then it can be concluded that the industry is not highly competitive.
- As a common marketing and business objective, most firms strive to increase their market share.

EXAM PRACTICE QUESTION

Kowloon Pots has a market share of 16.4 per cent in the garden pots market in Hong Kong. The market is worth $1,400,000 per year. Calculate the annual sales revenue of Kowloon Pots. [2]

The importance of market share and market leadership (HL only) (AO3)

- Being able to compare the relative size of businesses enables managers to take appropriate actions to remain competitive.

- Having a larger market share is beneficial to a business, as it can mean better brand loyalty, better economies of scale (due to larger-scale operations), better access to customer data and insights, and more profit. In addition, their customers are less sensitive to higher prices being charged.

- **Market leadership** refers to an organization's position as the leading business in a particular market due to its dominant market share.

- Market leaders also enjoy a good corporate image, which can help to attract more investors and better-skilled employees, due to the perceived or associated reputation of firms with large market share. In addition, retailers and distributors are more likely to stock the products of market leaders, further helping to improve their sales and profits.

- However, changes in the external business environment (see STEEPLE analysis in the Business management toolkit chapter) can change the fortunes of a firm without much warning, including those which are market leaders. Chapter 5.7 outlines examples of crises that can threaten the survival of even large and well-established businesses. Still, it is the larger firms that have the best chance of survival in these instances.

> **Key term**
>
> **Market leaders** are the firms with the largest market share in a particular industry.

Market growth (AO2, AO4)

- New businesses tend to aim for break even and survival, whereas established businesses might aim for greater market share and market growth.

- **Market growth** is a common business objective that refers to the increase in the size and value of a market over time. It can be calculated by the size of the organization's customer base, sales revenue, and market share.

- Market growth strategies (see Chapter 1.5) include mergers and acquisitions (M&As), takeovers, joint ventures, strategic alliances, and franchising.

- Additionally, market growth can be achieved through the methods in the Ansoff matrix (market penetration, market development, product development, and diversification), which can be used to increase sales revenue and market share.

- Examples of products or markets that have seen market growth in recent times include the market for electric vehicles (EVs), online streaming services (such as Netflix, Disney+, Hulu, and Spotify), virtual reality (VR), cloud computing (see Chapter 5.9), cybersecurity services (also covered in Chapter 5.9), and online education services.

- Market research (see Chapter 4.4) is important for understanding the changing needs and preferences of customers, allowing businesses to determine growing and shrinking markets. This can help businesses to sell the goods and/or services that appeal to customers in growing markets and to divest from markets that are in decline.

- Market growth is often used as an indicator of an organization's level of success. Overall, it is a key indicator of the past performance as well as the potential of the market to prosper in a sustainable way. However, past performance is not indicative of the future, and organizations need to be aware of the dynamic nature of business, which is continually evolving and subject to change caused by both internal and external factors.

EXAM PRACTICE QUESTION

The data below show the number of IB World Schools across the world that offer IB DP Business Management and Economics.

Year	Number of IB World Schools	
	Business Management	**Economics**
2020	1,136	1,089
2021	1,367	1,223
2022	1,468	1,384

Calculate the market growth for both subjects between 2020 and 2022. Express your answers to 2 d.p. [3]

KEY CONCEPT

Examine how the concepts of **change** and **ethics** have impacted the marketing strategies for an organization of your choice.

4.2 Marketing planning

SL/HL content	Depth of teaching
The role of marketing planning	AO2
Segmentation, targeting (target market), and positioning (position maps)	AO2, AO4
The difference between niche market and mass market	AO2
The importance of having a unique selling point/proposition (USP)	AO2
How organizations can differentiate themselves and their products from competitors	AO3

Diploma Programme *Business management guide* (May 2022)

The role of marketing planning (AO2)

- **Marketing planning** refers to the systematic process of researching and analyzing potential markets and devising appropriate marketing strategies to achieve an organization's marketing objectives.

- The main role of marketing planning is to identify and meet the needs and preferences of customers and the target audience. Therefore, the plan allows marketing managers to make more informed decisions about their marketing strategies to increase sales revenue.

- Market research (see Chapter 4.4) is an essential part of marketing planning, because it allows the business to have a better understanding of its customers and the market in which it competes.

- The marketing plan allows marketers to have a unified purpose and sense of direction – the marketing plan provides a written guide for a business to follow in marketing its products.

- As the marketing plan is one part of the organization's overall business plan, managers can align marketing goals and strategies with the overall aims and objectives of the organization.

- The operations department uses sales forecasts (see Chapter 4.3) to create a production schedule. The finance department uses the forecasts to create budgets (see Chapter 3.9). The human resources department uses sales forecasts for workforce planning (see Chapter 2.1).

- Marketing planning also enables the business to engage in meaningful marketing communications, including advertising, promotional, and public relations campaigns.

Segmentation, targeting (target market), and positioning (position maps) (AO2, AO4)

- A **market segment** is a distinct group of customers with similar characteristics and similar needs or wants. It is a sub-group within a larger market, made up of customers with similar characteristics, for example age, gender, income, ethnic group, or religion.

- A **target market** is a particular market segment that a business can focus its marketing effort on.

■ Market segmentation

- As it can be expensive to create a different marketing mix for different market segments, businesses often resort to targeting specific segments.

- Once a market is segmented, particular sub-groups can then be targeted using an appropriate marketing mix and strategies to achieve the firm's marketing objectives. For example, Samsung's marketing aimed at young people in their 20s will be somewhat different to their strategies targeted at older customers in their 50s or 60s.

- Market segmentation allows businesses to gain greater knowledge about their customers. This knowledge is likely to create more cost-effective and successful marketing. Hence, without market segmentation, a firm's marketing mix might be inappropriate for its potential market.

- Organizations choose to segment their market in order to create distinct consumer profiles in several ways, based on socio-economic, psychographic, demographic, and geographic factors.
  - ○ *Socio-economic segmentation.* This seeks to classify consumers according to their income, profession, or education. Businesses can then devise different marketing mixes targeted at each market segment.
  - ○ *Psychographic segmentation.* This focuses on personality traits, lifestyles, and attitudes, for example customers who like to buy organic produce.
  - ○ *Demographic segmentation.* This focuses on population structures such as age, gender, ethnicity, marital status, language, family size, and religion.
  - ○ *Geographic segmentation.* This is based on the physical location of the customer and includes consideration of the natural environment and climate of the location. It is useful when target markets have different preferences based on where they are located.

- Market segmentation can be useful in identifying new business opportunities, such as finding an unfilled niche in the market.

- However, market segmentation only generates a limited number of groupings, with potential stereotyping of customers. Some customers may not fit neatly into these categories.

- Ultimately, the purpose of market segmentation and targeting is to allow firms to generate greater sales and higher profits. Being more customer focused enables businesses to improve the cost effectiveness of their marketing, while increasing sales, market share, and profits.

> **Key term**
>
> **Market segmentation** is the process of splitting a market into distinct consumer groups to better understand their needs.

Targeting

- The process of market segmentation is followed by **targeting**. This enables a business to devise a different and more appropriate marketing mix for each market segment.

- Market segmentation acknowledges the fact that customers are different in ways such as demographic factors based on characteristics including religion, gender, or marital status. Hence, there are likely to be several market segments within any given market.

- Segmentation enables businesses to gain a better understanding of consumer profiles in each segment. This is crucial for devising a more effective and targeted marketing mix.

- Consumer profiles typically include a person's age, gender, marital status, education, income level, and spending patterns. Knowledge of consumer profiles is an important consideration when devising the marketing mix so that businesses can target these groups more effectively.

- Targeting enables a business to fine-tune its marketing strategy by devising an appropriate product, price, place, and promotional mix for each market segment. This offers more opportunities for higher sales and growth for the business.

- It can also be cost-effective if targeting leads to an efficient use of the organization's resources in conducting successful and justified marketing activities.

Positioning (position maps)

- A **position map** helps a business to show the position of its products in a market, relative to its rivals in the industry (see Figure 4.1).

- Having a clearer idea of customer perceptions, and hence a firm's position in the market, helps the business to improve its marketing strategies. In turn, this can help to increase sales revenue, market share, and profits.

- Different categories of products can be seen in a position map that uses price and quality as the benchmark variables:

  - A **premium product** is shown in a position map as one perceived by customers to be of high quality but at a high price, for example Cartier watches, Porsche cars, or Häagen-Dazs ice creams.

  - A **cowboy product** in a position map is one that is perceived by customers to offer low quality but at a high price. While such products can maximize sales in the short term, they are not sustainable.

  - A **bargain product** in a position map is one that is perceived to offer high quality but at a low price. This short-term tactic can help to boost sales and gain brand awareness, but is also not sustainable.

  - An **economy brand** in a position map is one that offers low quality but also at a low price, for example supermarket own-branded products such as cleaning products, drinks, and canned foods.

- If a firm finds its position on a position map differs from what the business envisaged or strived for, it needs to **reposition** the product or brand by appealing to a different market segment or by executing an improved marketing mix.

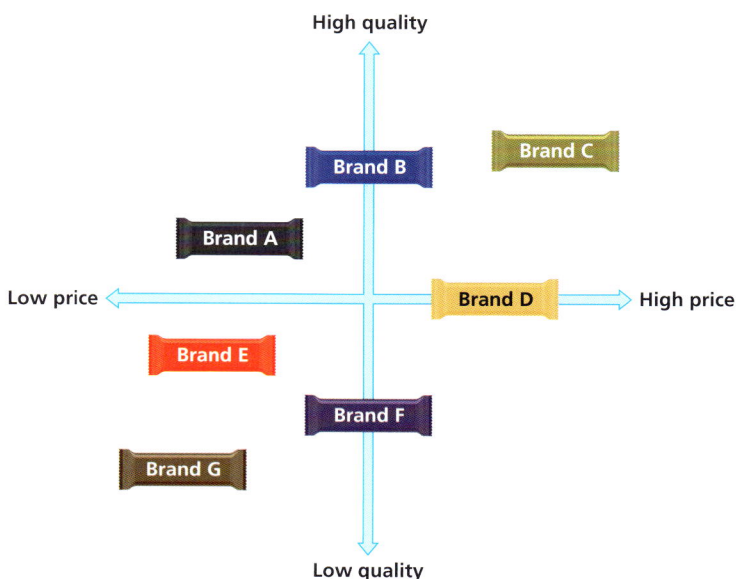

■ **Figure 4.1** Example of a position map in the chocolate industry

The difference between niche market and mass market (AO2)

- Niche markets are small and focused, so there are opportunities for high profit margins because premium prices can be charged.
- A niche market is a group of customers with a distinctive set of traits who have rather unique needs or preferences, such as, for example, organic foods, customized products, eco-tourism, or the market for private tutors of ab initio Italian in Taiwan.
- Niche marketing enables small firms to operate profitably, as large organizations do not tend to cater for these markets due to the small market size and limited opportunities to exploit economies of scale.
- There are few barriers to entry in most niche markets. However, this also means there is a high risk of new businesses entering the industry, which increases direct competition.
- Mass markets are those which provide goods and services that appeal to an extensive number of customers. Therefore, marketers use a single, broad marketing message targeted at the general public rather than a specific target audience.
- In mass markets, producers sell standardized products to large consumer markets, so profit margins are lower on each unit sold.
- Mass marketing helps a business to enjoy economies of scale by catering for a large number of customers, leading to larger profits from increased sales.
- It can create brand awareness and brand recognition among a wide and general target audience of customers.

Key terms

Niche marketing is a marketing strategy based on identifying and serving a relatively small and specific target market.

Mass marketing is a marketing strategy aimed at all consumers in a market without trying to differentiate them into separate market segments.

The importance of having a unique selling point/proposition (USP) (AO2)

- A unique selling point (USP) (also known as a **unique selling proposition**) can be an important source of competitive advantage for a business. For example, Apple's USP has been its distinctive and highly innovative products.
- Businesses with a USP focus on marketing the exclusive features, attributes, or benefits of the product.
- Having a USP makes a business exclusive and differentiates it from competitors in the market. This helps to improve brand awareness (recognition) and brand loyalty, so gives the business a strategic advantage over its rivals.
- A firm's USP is used as part of its marketing strategy to communicate the distinctive value of a good or service to customers.
- Having a USP can be important for the long-term success of a business, as it helps it to establish and maintain a strong market position, as well as having competitive advantages.

Key term

A **unique selling point (USP)** is any positive feature or aspect of a business, brand, or product that makes it distinctive (stand out) from those offered by competitors.

How organizations can differentiate themselves and their products from competitors (AO3)

- Product differentiation creates a perception among customers that the firm's product is different or unique, so generates better value relative to those of its competitors.
- Market research and market segmentation data enable a firm to differentiate its products.

Key term

Differentiation is the process of making a business or its products distinct from others in the same market.

131

- Firms try to differentiate their products by altering some or all aspects of their marketing mix (see Chapter 4.5). For example:
  - ○ *Product.* Adding new features, designs, colours, and sizes, or focusing on product quality.
  - ○ *Price.* Differentiated pricing for different products and market segments.
  - ○ *Place.* Using e-commerce for the convenience of customers.
  - ○ *Promotion.* Using logos, slogans, and branding, or promoting a USP such as sustainable business practices.
  - ○ *People.* Offering personalized customer service and exceptional after-sales support.
  - ○ *Process.* Implementing new technologies or processes that competitors do not offer.
  - ○ *Physical evidence.* Using tangible representation of the business or products, such as packaging, to create a more memorable and positive customer experience.

■ **Table 4.1** Advantages and disadvantages of differentiation

Advantages of differentiation	Disadvantages of differentiation
• Allows the firm to charge a higher price due to the uniqueness of the product.	• Can be a very expensive strategy.
• Creates brand awareness, brand recognition, and brand loyalty.	• Making products unique can mean that it is difficult to reap the benefits of economies of scale if the products are mass produced.
• Creates placement (or distribution) advantages as more retailers will want to have the product for sale.	• Can create confusion in the minds of consumers through excessive differentiation and advertising clutter.

KEY CONCEPT

Investigate how the concepts of **creativity** and **ethics** have impacted the marketing planning for a product, brand, or business organization of your choice.

4.3 Sales forecasting (HL only)

HL content	Depth of teaching
The benefits and limitations of sales forecasting	AO2, AO4

Diploma Programme *Business management guide* (May 2022)

The benefits and limitations of sales forecasting (AO2, AO4)

Key term

Sales forecasting is a quantitative technique used to predict the level of sales revenue that a firm expects to earn over a certain period of time.

- **Sales forecasting** is necessary to help an organization successfully plan for its business functions:
  - ○ If sales are predicted to increase for the foreseeable future, the human resources department may need to recruit more workers.
  - ○ Cash flow forecasts will also rely on sales forecasting data. Profit forecasts will depend on the level of sales expected over a certain period of time.
  - ○ Production schedules will be based on the expected level of sales. Stock (inventory) control will depend on the forecasted level of sales.
- Hence, sales forecasting drives many other aspects of strategic planning in a business. Managers want to understand market trends and the underlying reasons for these.

- It is an important tool that enables a business to identify opportunities and threats in advance.
- Sales forecasts are generally based on recent sales trends, market analyses of the industry, and the state of the economy (such as a recession or economic boom).
- Forecasts are often presented in the form of time series data. This aspect of sales forecasting predicts sales revenue by using the underlying trend from a series of actual sales data recorded at regular times in the past.
- Sales forecasting enables managers to extrapolate (or deduce) the sales trend. Extrapolation assumes that sales patterns are stable and past data are indicative of the near future.

The benefits of sales forecasting

- Sales forecasting techniques (such as extrapolation – see simple linear regression in the Business management toolkit) help managers to identify trends by smoothing out seasonal, cyclical, or random variations in the data set.
- It is a useful planning tool to help managers reduce uncertainties and risks in the future.
- Identifying a trend enables the business to extrapolate or predict future sales revenues as a basis for strategic and financial planning.
- Sales forecasting can enable managers to allocate more realistic budgets for the different functional areas of a business.

The limitations of sales forecasting

- Only sales forecasts for a relatively short period of time are likely to be accurate, so the usefulness of the tool can be questioned.
- The key assumption of sales forecasting techniques is that what happened in the past is likely to continue in the future. This can prove to be unrealistic, especially in an environment where change is inevitable, so extrapolated results can be somewhat overly simplistic.
- To be of value, sales forecast data must be based on reliable data and information, although these are not necessarily easy or cheap to collect.
- Sales forecasts can be accurate for predicting the sales of single products, but tend to be less accurate for large multinational companies that sell a broad range of products.
- Sales forecasting is not suitable for all types of businesses, for example it doesn't work so well for product-orientated industries with very dynamic customer preferences such as the fast fashion and high-tech industries.
- Qualitative factors that affect sales revenues are not easy to incorporate in sales forecasting techniques. Hence, this can cause the results to be less accurate in predicting sales in the future.
- Variations of sales are also likely to occur in reality. These can be categorized as seasonal variations, cyclical variations, and random variations.

Seasonal variations

Key term

Seasonal variations are the expected periodic fluctuations in sales revenues over a given time period, such as peak trading periods during certain times of the year.

- Seasonal variations are deviations in the values of sales data around the trend line, repeated on a regular basis.
- These variations are caused by environmental or cultural factors which cause different people to have different levels of demand at different times of the year.
- To calculate the seasonal variation, managers find the numerical difference between the observed data values and the values on the trend line. The variations can be expressed in absolute dollar terms or as a percentage of the deviation from the trend.

- Calculations of seasonal variations are used to adjust the predicted sales revenue from the trend over a one-year period in order to generate a more accurate prediction of quarterly sales.
- Many products face seasonal fluctuations in demand, for example umbrellas, ice creams, Easter eggs, Christmas trees, school uniforms, and IB examiners.

Cyclical variations

> **Key term**
>
> **Cyclical variations** refer to the recurrent fluctuations in sales revenues linked to the business cycle.

- **Cyclical variations** are generally attributed to fluctuations in the business cycle (the sequence of booms and slumps in the economy). For example, a thriving economy (with a high rate of economic growth) will cause sales forecasts to be revised upwards. In contrast, a prolonged recession (when economic activity is low and mass-scale job losses occur in the economy) means sales forecasts need to be revised downwards.
- Unlike seasonal fluctuations which occur at predictable intervals during the year, cyclical variations can last more than a month, a quarter, or even a year. For example, many countries took over five years to get over the global financial crisis of 2008. Similarly, countries across the globe are still recovering from the COVID-19 pandemic.
- To make the predicted sales forecasts more accurate, the sales figures need to be adjusted using statistical techniques such as standard deviation (see descriptive statistics in the Business management toolkit).

Random variations

> **Key term**
>
> **Random variations** are unpredictable and erratic fluctuations in sales revenues, caused by irregular and unexpected factors.

- **Random variations** are caused by irregular, unintended, or unforeseen factors, for example a natural disaster, prolonged periods of inclement weather, the outbreak of a war, the spread of a highly infectious disease, a corporate scandal, or a public relations crisis due to a major product recall.
- Random variations can occur at any time. This causes unusual and irregular fluctuations in actual sales revenue figures.
- As random variations are erratic and unpredictable, there is no specific formula that can be used to isolate and identify the deviations.

> **KEY CONCEPT**
>
> Are there **ethical** dilemmas in the choice of data that are used to make sales forecasts?

4.4 Market research

SL/HL content	Depth of teaching
Why and how organizations carry out market research	AO2
The following methods/techniques of primary market research: surveys, interviews, focus groups, and observations	AO2
The following methods/techniques of secondary market research: market analyses, academic journals, government publications, media articles, and online content	AO2
The difference between qualitative and quantitative research	AO2
The following methods of sampling: quota, random, and convenience	AO2

Diploma Programme *Business management guide* (May 2022)

Market research
is the systematic
process of
collecting,
collating,
analyzing, and
interpreting data
and information
about existing
and potential
consumers,
competitors, and
markets. It is used
by businesses
to aid their
marketing planning
and marketing
strategies.

**Primary market
research** (or **field
research**) is the
systematic process
of collecting,
recording,
analyzing, and
interpreting
new data and
information about
a specific issue
of direct interest
to the business,
for example
through the use
of questionnaires,
interviews, focus
groups, and
observations.

**Secondary market
research** (or
desk research)
is the collection,
collation, and
interpretation of
existing data and
information from
previously available
sources, such as
market analyses,
academic journals,
government
publications, media
articles, and online
content.

Why and how organizations carry out market research (AO2)

Reasons why businesses conduct **market research** include the desire to:

- determine customer preferences about a product, for example design, colour, size, smell, or taste
- discover the likelihood of customers buying their products
- assess customer sensitivity to different price levels
- discover and learn about new market trends
- reduce the risks of marketing activities such as new product launches and pricing decisions
- investigate various market demographics and their potential different reactions, preferences and behavioural variations, depending on, for example, age, gender, religion, marital status, location, and income level
- explain sales patterns and variances (see Chapter 3.9).

In general terms, organizations can carry out market research in one of two ways:

- **Primary research** is market research that does not already exist about a product, business, or issue. Features of primary research include the following:
  - The collection of firsthand data for a specific purpose.
  - It often represents a limited or skewed perspective.
  - Hence, there is a need to select a sample that is representative and statistically significant, to ensure the results are reliable.
  - It often provides in-depth qualitative data and information.
  - Primary sources are not always objective sources, as they are often based on people's opinions and the judgement of the researchers.
  - It is relatively expensive to gather the data and information compared with secondary market research.

- **Secondary research** is market research of data and information that already exists. Features of secondary research include the following:
  - Reusing secondhand data and information already collected by someone else for a different purpose.
  - It generally draws findings from large, representative samples.
  - Some secondary sources involve a cost, for example subscription and/or association fees.
  - The internet has revolutionized how secondary market research is obtained, by offering convenience, speed, and an immense range of online content.

■ Table 4.2 Advantages and disadvantages of primary market research

Advantages of primary research	Disadvantages of primary research
• It provides bespoke, specialist market research data, which are up-to-date and specific to the requirements of the business. • It can give businesses a competitive edge by gathering new data and information about customer purchasing patterns and habits, in order to anticipate changes in their spending behaviour.	• Relatively higher costs of conducting primary market research compared with secondary market research. • The monotonous task of conducting primary research, such as carrying out lengthy interviews or a tedious number of questionnaires.

- Enables firms to focus on more effective and targeted marketing approaches, rather than an expensive and less effective mass-marketing approach.
- It can provide detailed and informative qualitative findings to inform a firm's marketing and corporate strategies.
- New technologies allow online surveys to be conducted more quickly, easily, and cheaply.
- Allows access to a wide range of sources.

- The time-consuming process of collecting, collating, and interpreting primary data.
- Decision making can be delayed due to the lengthy time involved in designing, conducting, collating, and interpreting primary research.
- Imperfections in primary market research techniques (such as biased questions or a statistically invalid sample size) lead to unrepresentative and misleading market research findings.

Table 4.3 Advantages and disadvantages of secondary market research

Advantages of secondary research	Disadvantages of secondary research
• Relatively quicker and cheaper to collect than primary research. • Often available free of charge, e.g. company websites, government statistics, and online news media sources. • Ease of access to data sources, especially with online sources such as Wikipedia and online search engines such as Google.	• Data and information have to be adapted to the firm's particular needs. • Data and information can become out of date very quickly. • Rival firms also have access to the same secondary data sources. • There may be biases in the data and research that are not apparent to the user.

EXPERT TIP

Organizations can use internal sources of secondary data, that is, data previously published by the firm itself, such as company reports, historic sales figures, and profit levels. This varies from external secondary market research data (published by other organizations such as market analyses, reports and academic journals), which is what students tend to write about.

Methods/techniques of primary market research (AO2)

Primary market research can be conducted using several methods, including surveys, interviews, focus groups, and observations.

Surveys

- Surveys are a method of gathering both qualitative and quantitative information from a sample of individuals for market research purposes.
- They are the most common method of primary research.
- There needs to be a large enough sample of consumers to provide statistically valid and representative data.
- They are often used to gain customer feedback from people who have recently purchased a good or service, for example from hotel guests, restaurant diners, or car drivers.
- Questionnaires are used to ask consumers or potential consumers for their opinions and preferences about a particular good or service.
- A combination of closed questions ('Yes/No', or 'Agree/Disagree') and open-ended questions ('Tell us about …' or 'What is your opinion concerning …') can be asked.
- Variations include postal surveys, personal surveys, self-completed surveys, telephone surveys, and online surveys.

- They can be an expensive and time-consuming method of market research.
- They can suffer from selection or interviewer bias and/or poorly worded questions, thus generating unrepresentative results.
- Furthermore, many people are reluctant to fill out questionnaires, or they do so in a hurry without giving much thought to the questions or their responses.

Interviews

- Interviews are conducted by an interviewer who asks respondents (interviewees) a series of questions. Interview questions tend to be more detailed than those asked in surveys.
- They can be conducted face-to-face, online, or on the telephone.
- Like questionnaires, they can be specifically designed to meet the needs of the organization.
- They help to determine the interviewee's opinions and beliefs.
- Questions that are difficult to understand can be explained to interviewees. This can help to resolve the issue of cultural and linguistic bias that surveys can suffer from.
- As it usually involves only a small number of customers, the results might not reflect the views of the market in which the business is interested.
- There is also potential interviewer bias, which could distort the results or analysis of answers.
- Interviews can be time consuming and costly to conduct.

Focus groups

- Focus groups are a small cluster of consumers who meet together with a researcher for market research purposes.
- They involve groups brought together on one or more occasions, where consumer panels are asked to answer and discuss questions about a specific good or service.
- They enable detailed investigation of the psychology of customers – their opinions and attitudes, and what motivates them as consumers of the product.
- As part of the target market, focus groups are used to identify the wants and needs of different market segments.
- Using focus groups can be costly, as participants are usually provided with financial incentives such as gifts and free samples.

Observations

- Observations involve researchers watching and recording customer behaviour, for example identifying which supermarket aisles customers spend most of their time in.
- Unlike surveys and interviews, observations are not dependant on the willingness and ability of research subjects (those selected for market research) to respond accurately.
- The information collected from observations tends to be more objective and accurate as there is no interviewer bias.
- However, analyzing the results from observations is labour intensive and time consuming.

Methods/techniques of secondary market research (AO2)

Secondary market research can be conducted using several methods, including market analyses, academic journals, government publications, media articles, and online content.

■ Market analyses

- Market analysis refers to the collection of data and information about market characteristics of a particular good, service or industry, including information regarding market size, market growth potential, and information on competitors.

- It is a quick and relatively cheap way of examining and assessing the potential of a new good or service.

- New businesses often rely on market analysis reports to prepare their business plans.

- Valuable sources for conducting market analysis include market research firms, annual company reports, websites of competitors, and trade journals or publications.

- It is often included as part of a firm's SWOT analysis (see the Business management toolkit section).

■ Academic journals

- These are formal scholarly journals related to a specific academic discipline such as business management, psychology, natural sciences, or economics.

- Journal articles are written by academics such as university lecturers and professors, the content of which is often peer-reviewed.

- They are typically written in a standard format: abstract, methodology, results and findings, discussion, conclusions, bibliography, and appendix. Citations and footnotes are also used.

- The intended audience is the research community, for example professionals and academics, such as university students and professors.

- They often serve as a critique of existing research or an introduction of new research presented for academic scrutiny.

- Academic journals are generally objective as they are not usually written for the benefit of any single business.

- Examples include *Academy of Management Journal*, *Cambridge Journal of Economics*, and *Journal of International Management*.

EXPERT TIP

Many students confuse academic (or scholarly) journals with business magazines and other popular business media (for example, *Bloomberg Businessweek* or *Forbes' Fortune* magazine). Remember, the authors of academic journals are academics rather than professional journalists.

■ Government publications

- Government publications refers to official documentation and information released by local, national and international governments or treaty organizations (such as the European Union or United Nations).

- These documents vary widely in purpose and content. Unlike academic journals, there is no standardized format for government publications.

- Governments produce a huge volume of publications on a broad variety of issues, thus providing researchers with a rich choice of data and information.
- Examples include population statistics, unemployment figures, inflation rates (consumer price levels), economic growth rate, the annual government budget, and import–export data.
- Government publications are a major source of information in virtually every field of research.
- Most government publications are available to the general public and are usually accessible free of charge.
- However, many researchers underuse government publications because the documents tend to be difficult to find.

■ Media articles

- Media articles are documents or articles that appear in print or online media.
- Examples include the following:
  - Newspapers, both in published format and online versions, providing a vast range of market research information, for example *The International Tribune*, *The Times of India*, *The Wall Street Journal*, and *USA Today*.
  - News magazines, including *TIME*, *Businessweek*, *The Economist* and *Forbes' Fortune*.
  - Trade journals, for example *Advertising Age* (for the marketing sector), *The Grocer* (for supermarkets), and *Computer Weekly* (for those working in ICT).
- Users of media articles need to be conscious of potential bias from the authors of the articles.

■ Online content

- Online content is provided via the internet and can provide access to a broad range of resources. The sources include company websites, blogs, social media platforms, videos and documentaries, and any other information that can be found online.
- Due to the ease of access to a huge volume of information that is widely available, users of online content need to critically evaluate the reliability of such information.
- Access to online content is usually straightforward, with plenty of non-subscription websites available (for example, bbc.co.uk) and the spread of news via social media and social networks (for example, Twitter and Facebook).

The difference between qualitative and quantitative research (AO2)

- **Qualitative research** is based on opinions, feelings, and perspectives, such as why consumers prefer a certain brand of product. It generates in-depth, non-numerical information. The results of qualitative research are usually descriptive rather than predictive.
- **Quantitative research** is based on facts and figures – numerical patterns, correlations and results, such as how many people prefer a particular brand over its rivals. The results of quantitative research are usually predictive rather than descriptive.

■ **Table 4.4** Features of qualitative and quantitative research

Qualitative research	Quantitative research
• Involves an in-depth investigation into the motivations and reasons behind consumer behaviour. • Based on opinions and perspectives. • Often uses primary research to find out about consumers' tastes, opinions, and buying habits. • Can be conducted using market research techniques such as focus groups, questionnaires, and interviews. • Can provide a wealth of information despite the low number of respondents. • Provides far more detailed and honest information regarding the motivation, attitudes or habits of consumers.	• Relies on a large number of responses to get numerical results. • Uses closed questions, categorical selections, and/or scaled rankings for responses in order to gather and calculate results easily. • Quicker and easier to collect, collate, and interpret than qualitative responses. • Tries to establish correlations, i.e. whether there is a relationship between two or more variables. • Quantitative analyses help to make decision making more objective. • Quantitative analyses alone do not reveal the 'whole picture' without qualitative input.

Methods of sampling (AO2)

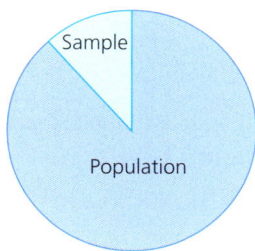

■ **Figure 4.2** The difference between sample and population

- **Population** is a statistical term that refers to all potential customers of a particular market, or all the people that fulfil some chosen criteria, for market research purposes.
- **Sampling** is the practice of selecting a small group of customers from the population of a certain market for the purpose of market research (see Figure 4.2).
- Sampling seeks to create a group of respondents for market research who are regarded to have representative views of the target market.
- Sampling is used as it is impractical, too expensive, and unnecessary to include the entire market population for research purposes.
- Sampling methods include quota, random, and convenience.

▓ Quota sampling

- A quota refers to a predetermined allocation of specific sub-groups of the population for sampling, for example 25 females and 35 males in a sample size of 60 people.
- It involves selecting a certain number of people from different market segments with shared characteristics, for example age, gender, religion, ethnicity, or income level.
- The assembled quota sample has the same proportions of individuals as the entire population (of the market for the product) regarding known characteristics.
- The purpose is to gather representative data from sub-groups to get around the issues of random sampling.
- It is suitable when researchers want to investigate a trait or a characteristic of a certain sub-group, or to observe relationships between sub-groups.
- Researchers need to determine in advance the specific characteristics on which they will base the quota sample. This is vital to ensure representative results from the research.
- Quota sampling is often used with convenience sampling, so the researcher has control over who is included in the sample.

Random sampling

- This method involves selecting individuals in such a way that everyone in the total population has an equal chance of being chosen.
- Research subjects are often randomly chosen by a computer using information stored in a database.
- Hence, there is no bias in the selection of respondents for market research, so the outcome of the research is likely to be more accurate.
- Random sampling is a simple, quick, and cheap method of sampling, especially as research subjects are readily available.
- However, the convenience of random sampling also means there is a high probability that the selected sample is unrepresentative of the population.

Convenience

- Samples are created using subjects who are easily accessible to the researcher.
- The selection of research subjects in convenience sampling is usually self-selected (because the research subjects are easily accessible) or unguided, meaning it is volunteers who choose to respond.
- However, the findings could be skewed and unrepresentative of the wider population.
- Generalizations and inferences are difficult to make, as the researchers are unlikely to use a sample that covers sufficient sub-groups within the population.

Irrespective of the sampling method used, the results from data collection can contain both **sampling** and **non-sampling errors**.

- Results are often presented using different formats:
  - Pie charts to show percentages – for example, the percentage of respondents who selected a certain choice in a survey.
  - Line graphs to show time–series data – for example, a firm's profit figures over the past five years.
  - Bar charts to show frequencies – for example, comparative sales figures of different companies.
  - Tables are also used to present numerical data in a tabular format.
- Qualitative results may be simplified by presenting the main findings in a summary using various formats, such as text, tables, or infographics.

Key terms

Sampling errors are the mistakes that arise from the sampling design, for example the sample size being too small, the selection of an unrepresentative sample, the use of inappropriate sampling methods, or having bias built into the research.

Non-sampling errors are market research mistakes that are not attributed to human errors, for example untruthful answers by respondents which distort the findings.

EXPERT TIP

When analyzing results from data collection shown in graphs and charts, it is important to check the data axes carefully. Don't assume that the examiner knows what you understand.

BUSINESS MANAGEMENT TOOLKIT

Discuss the role value of descriptive statistics in the market research process.

KEY CONCEPT

Discuss the role of **creativity** and **ethics** in conducting market research.

4.5 The seven Ps of the marketing mix: 1 Product

SL/HL content	Depth of teaching
The relationship between the product life cycle, product portfolio, and the marketing mix	AO2
Extension strategies	AO3
The relationship between the product life cycle, investment, profit, and cash flow	AO2
The following aspects of branding: awareness, development, loyalty, and value	AO2
The importance of branding	AO2

Diploma Programme *Business management guide* (May 2022)

The relationship between the product life cycle, product portfolio, and the marketing mix (AO2)

- The **product life cycle** (PLC) refers to a marketing theory that illustrates the different stages a typical product goes through from its launch to its eventual withdrawal from the market.

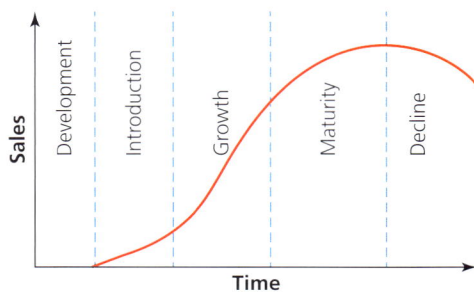

■ **Figure 4.3** The product life cycle

- The PLC diagram (see Figure 4.3) shows sales revenue on the y-axis and the timeline on the x-axis.
- The five typical stages of the PLC model are as follows:
  - *Research and development (R&D)*. The first stage of the PLC involves designing and developing a product before it is launched for sale.
  - *Introduction*. When the product is launched onto the market for sale. It usually requires significant investment in promotion and advertising to sustain sales.
  - *Growth*. When sales increase rapidly with the product becoming well known to the market.
  - *Maturity*. When sales revenue is at, or near, its maximum, with minimal or no more scope for growth, in other words when sales become saturated.
  - *Decline*. The last stage in a product's life cycle when sales continually decline. The product is eventually withdrawn from the market.

KEY CONCEPT

Examine how **change** (such as changing technology and fashion) have impacted the product life cycle in an industry of your choice.

Managing the marketing mix for a product varies according to the stage of the product in its life cycle. Examples are shown in Table 4.5.

■ **Table 4.5** The relationship between the product life cycle and the marketing mix

PLC stage	Marketing mix
R&D	• Expenditure on market research to refine the product for commercial launch. • Pricing, distribution, and promotional ideas are discussed prior to launch.
Introduction (launch)	• Marketing efforts to raise brand and product awareness, e.g. sales promotion campaigns. • Advertising expenditure is high in an attempt to boost sales. • Limited distribution channels, so sales are generally low. • Possibly high prices if there is limited competition, and to recoup R&D costs, or low prices to gain market share. • Spending on branding in order to differentiate the product from rival ones.
Growth	• Brand awareness and loyalty develop, so sales increase. • Marketing efforts continue to build brand preference and customer loyalty. • Stabilizing prices to ensure market growth and value for money. • Sales promotion and other marketing campaigns to get potential customers to switch from rival products and brands.
Maturity	• Marketing efforts focus on holding the market position to maximize profits. • Product differentiation is vital to lengthening this stage in the PLC. • Promotion is widespread. • Price competition can become intense. • Possible extension strategies are used to prolong the life of the product, e.g. new features and benefits, other forms of differentiation, or entering new markets.
Decline	• Lower prices, possibly aiming to be the lowest cost provider. • Decision made either to continue with marketing efforts to sell the product (for as long as possible) or to pull it (if losses are incurred).

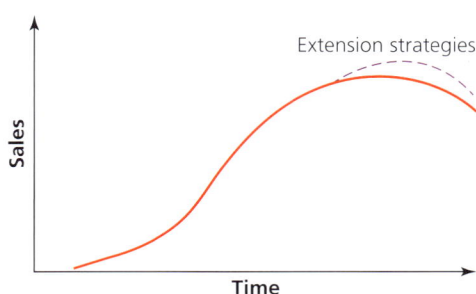

■ **Figure 4.4** Extension strategies and the product life cycle

Extension strategies (AO3)

- **Extension strategies** are marketing techniques used to prolong a product's life cycle (see Figure 4.4).
- Examples include cutting prices, product enhancements (such as 'special editions'), redesigning or repackaging the product, short-term promotions, and exporting the product to overseas markets.
- Extension strategies are used when a product is in a saturated market, or as it enters the decline stage of the product life cycle.
- The extent to which product extension strategies are used depends on the relative costs and benefits (revenues) from implementing the plans.

The relationship between the product life cycle, investment, profit, and cash flow (AO2)

■ **Table 4.6** The relationship between the product life cycle, investment, profit, and cash flow

PLC stage	Investment	Profit	Cash flow
R&D	Very high R&D costs	Loss	Negative
Introduction	Very high marketing costs	Loss, but smaller	Negative, but improving
Growth	High marketing costs	High	Positive
Maturity	Lower	Profit peaks	Positive
Decline	Little, if any	Profit falls	Declines/negative

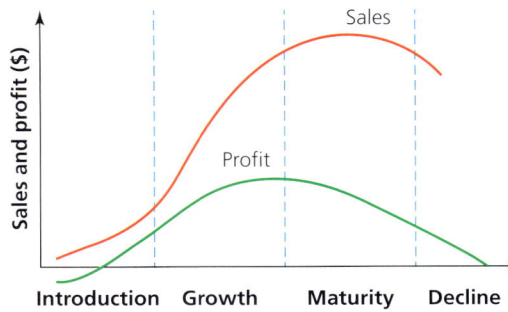

Figure 4.5 The relationship between the PLC and profit

Aspects of branding (AO2)

- Branding refers to a unique name or identity for a business, for example Apple, McDonald's, LEGO, and Toyota.
- The role of branding for a business includes:
  - creating a legal identity for its goods and services
  - acting as a source of product differentiation
  - building brand awareness and recognition of the brand or product
  - encouraging brand loyalty (customer loyalty)
  - creating a particular corporate image.
- An effective brand helps to give the business a major competitive edge.
- Aspects of branding include brand awareness, brand development, brand loyalty, and brand value.

Awareness

- **Brand awareness** refers to the extent to which people recognize and remember a particular brand name or branded product.
- It is largely about gaining new customers and adding value for the business.
- Promotional strategies such as above-the-line (ATL) promotion and free samples are used as part of a brand awareness strategy.
- Familiarity with a brand can lead to a higher sales volume of a good or service.
- Businesses often use family branding to raise brand awareness. This type of branding involves selling different products under the same brand name, as seen with Apple, Kellogg's, and Heinz.

> **EXPERT TIP**
>
> Branding can be a vital part of the marketing mix, with research showing that customers are largely affected by brand perception and not just prices. However, in some cases, customers prefer lower prices over the brand. It is important to write your answers in the context of the business in question.

Development

- **Brand development** is an aspect of an organization's marketing strategy that focuses on what a brand stands for. It is also about communicating the value of a brand to customers and other stakeholders.
- Different people are attracted to a brand for different reasons, so brand development is concerned with establishing the relevant valuable aspects of the brand to different customers.

- It is about delivering a consistent brand image that gives the business a competitive edge over its rivals. An example is McDonald's use of its brand name for its products – McNuggets, McMuffin, McCafé, and McFlurry.
- Product endorsements and sponsorship deals are common methods of brand development.
- The market is often flooded with a large number of rival brands, thus offering customers an array of choice. Brand development is about connecting with customers to build lasting relationships and to gain their loyalty.
- Brand development shapes people's perceptions of a brand, which ultimately determines its success or failure.
- Nevertheless, brand development can be extremely expensive and there is no guarantee that it will succeed. Popular brands of the past include Kodak, Compaq, Sony Ericsson, Toys R Us, and Woolworths.

Loyalty

- **Brand loyalty** happens when customers repeatedly purchase their favourite brand, rather than switching to a rival brand.
- It is the result of successful brand development and marketing strategies so that consumers develop and maintain preference for a particular brand.
- While brand awareness is generally about gaining new customers, brand loyalty is about retaining those customers and getting them to make repurchases.
- Branding becomes relatively more important than price once loyalty is developed.
- Customers purchase their preferred brand regardless of price or convenience. For example, according to Coca-Cola's website, its customers enjoy 1.9 billion servings of its products each day.
- Customer loyalty programmes (rewards programmes) are often used as part of an organization's promotional strategy to foster brand loyalty. These programmes provide incentives for customers to make repeat purchases for additional benefits such as price discounts.

■ **Table 4.7** Benefits of brand loyalty

Benefits of brand loyalty

- It makes customers less price sensitive, so higher prices can be charged, allowing the firm to earn higher sales revenue.
- It encourages repeat customers and prevents customers from switching to rival brands.
- Loyal customers are likely to recommend products that they like to their family and friends.
- It can lead to an increase in the value of the business as brands are intangible assets (see Chapter 3.4).
- It increases the chances of success when launching new products under the same brand name.

Value

- There is no universally accepted definition or measure of brand value, although the most commonly used considers the estimated future earnings attributable to the brand.
- In its simplest form, the term **brand value** refers to what a brand is worth to the business and its shareholders.
- Brand value adds to the benefits provided by a good or service. For example, customers buy a Ferrari or Porsche for more than just the ability to drive a car.

- A firm's brand can go up or down in value based on a range of factors, such as its earning potential, market share, and corporate reputation.
- Brand awareness, brand development, and brand loyalty are all dimensions of brand value.
- However, measuring the value of a brand is difficult and somewhat subjective.

The importance of branding (AO2)

- Branding creates a unique identity for a product, enabling it to be distinguished from rival products in the market.
- Branding can enable customers to know what to expect, irrespective of where they are in the world.
- An effective branding strategy encourages customer loyalty, for example repeat purchases.
- It enables businesses to charge higher prices, thereby improving their profit margins.
- Brands add value so customers get more than just the good or service they buy – there is an emotional value attached to purchasing certain brands.

4.5 The seven Ps of the marketing mix: 2 Price

SL/HL content	Depth of teaching
The appropriateness of the following pricing methods:	AO3
• Cost-plus (mark-up) pricing	
• Penetration pricing	
• Loss leader	
• Predatory pricing	
• Premium pricing	
• Dynamic pricing (HL only)	
• Competitive pricing (HL only)	
• Contribution pricing (HL only)	
• Price elasticity of demand (HL only)	

Diploma Programme *Business management guide* (May 2022)

The appropriateness of the following pricing methods (AO3)

- **Pricing methods** are the various ways that a business determines the prices of its goods and services.
- Managers consider a range of factors when setting prices, such as the cost, competitor prices, and varying market conditions.

Cost-plus (mark-up) pricing

- **Cost-plus pricing** (also known as **mark-up pricing**) involves adding a profit element to the costs of production, meaning that the price is set above the cost by a predetermined amount.
- The **mark-up** (or the **profit margin**) can be expressed as a percentage figure (for example, 60 per cent added on top of the cost of production) or an absolute amount (for example, $20 above costs).

- Hence:

    Price = Cost of production + Profit margin

■ **Table 4.8** Advantages and disadvantages of cost-plus pricing

Advantages of cost-plus pricing
• It is the simplest form of pricing method and is suitable for all products.
• It is straightforward to calculate.
• It helps to ensure the selling price covers all production costs in order to at least break even.

Disadvantages of cost-plus pricing
• It ignores the impact of lower prices that rival businesses may be charging.
• It does not focus on raising the potential level of demand, but the calculated price instead.

WORKED EXAMPLE

The cost of producing one unit of output for Bornton & Co. is $5. The firm uses a mark-up of 40%.

So, to determine the firm's selling price for the product, it will need to add 40% on top of its costs of production to ensure each unit sold earns a mark-up (contribution towards profit).

Hence, the selling price is: $5 × 1.4 = $7

WORKED EXAMPLE

Bornton & Co. sells a different product for $1.98, for which its costs of production are $1.20.

The following steps are used to calculate the percentage profit margin (mark-up) on the product:

$1.98 = $1.2x$

$x = $1.98 ÷ $1.2 = 65\%$

or

[($1.98 − $1.2) ÷ $1.2] × 100 = 65%

■ Penetration pricing

- **Penetration pricing** involves setting the price low enough to enter an industry and gain market share from existing firms (often advertised as a 'special introductory price offer').
- The low pricing method enables the firm to create brand awareness when launching a new good or service, or when entering a new market.
- It is a short-term to medium-term pricing method, as it can lead to losses or very low profit margins, so is not sustainable.

■ **Table 4.9** Advantages and disadvantages of penetration pricing

Advantages of penetration pricing
• Allows a business to enter a market and/or to launch a new product into an existing market, acquiring market share rapidly.
• Can discourage potential new competitors from entering due to the low prices and low profit margins.
• Lower prices can give a firm competitive advantages over their rivals.
• Appealing pricing can encourage word-of-mouth recommendations by customers.
• It can force the business to focus on cutting costs, raising productivity, and/or improving its efficiency in order to be able to charge low prices.

Disadvantages of penetration pricing

- If costs increase suddenly and/or rapidly, the firm could be operating at a loss.
- A firm that sets a low price might build a corporate image of low quality which it could find difficult to resolve when prices need to increase.
- Similarly, the firm may lose some customers who care more about quality than low prices.
- Customers may come to expect low prices, making it difficult for the business to raise prices at a later date.

> **EXPERT TIP**
>
> Try to avoid repeating the same point in the exams, as you will not get credit for doing so. For example, when asked to explain two reasons why penetration pricing is used by businesses, some candidates have stated 'to gain more customers' and 'to increase market share'. These points are not distinct.

Loss leader

- Loss-leader pricing involves setting the price of a good or service below its cost of production, in order to attract customers to buy the product along with other items that have higher profit margins.
- For example, a bakery might sell a particular product at just $0.50 each, rather than the normal price of $2, in order to encourage customers to buy other goods at the bakery.
- Essentially, the use of loss leaders is a form of sales promotion.
- In order to limit its losses, the firm is likely to impose a rule on the maximum number of purchases (per customer per visit) of the loss-leader product.
- It is a short-term pricing method used for a single product, as making a loss is not sustainable.
- As customers may get used to products being loss leaders, businesses such as supermarkets may introduce different loss leaders every so often.

■ **Table 4.10** Advantages and disadvantages of loss-leader pricing

Advantages of loss-leader pricing

- Using loss leaders can help to gain customer loyalty as people generally like bargains.
- Increased sales revenue from customers buying other goods while purchasing the loss leader in the retail store.
- Loss leaders are an effective way to get rid of older stock or merchandise.

Disadvantages of loss-leader pricing

- Customers may become accustomed to and expect loss-leader products, which can prove to be expensive and unsustainable for some businesses.
- The firm makes a loss on these products and there is no guarantee that customers will purchase other products in addition to the loss leaders.
- Firms need to ensure there are sufficient stocks of the loss leader; this creates problems of stockpiling (see Chapter 5.6), yet it may be necessary to prevent customer dissatisfaction.

Predatory pricing

- **Predatory pricing** involves charging a low price, even below costs of production at times, in order to harm the sales of rival firms and to restrict competition.
- It is used by a business that is threatened by the potential entry of a new competitor.
- In extreme cases, existing firms with large market power may start a price war (when firms continually reduce their prices), forcing less established firms to leave the industry.

■ **Table 4.11** Advantages and disadvantages of predatory pricing

Advantages of predatory pricing

- Lower prices can encourage customers to switch to buying the products of a business.
- Sales revenue will increase following the price reductions if customers are price sensitive.
- Low prices can act as a barrier to entry for firms considering entering the industry.

Disadvantages of predatory pricing

- Predatory pricing is illegal in some countries, e.g. competition law in the European Union (EU) prohibits firms from selling products at a loss deliberately to force their rivals out of business.
- Lower prices can trigger quality concerns about the good or service.
- It can encourage or force competitors to retaliate, thereby initiating a price war.
- Predatory pricing can lead to increased market power, which is anti-competitive.
- It is an unsustainable pricing method in the long term.

◼ Premium pricing

- **Premium pricing** (sometimes referred to as **prestige pricing**) is a pricing method that sets a high price, one that is substantially above the market average. It is used to convey the quality, luxury, and superiority of the product or the brand.
- Due to the prestige associated with the product, this pricing method is sustainable.
- Examples of brands that use premium pricing include Ferrari, Gucci, Rolex, and Rolls-Royce.
- It is suitable when customers for the firm's product are not sensitive to price changes, perhaps due to a strong degree of brand loyalty.

■ **Table 4.12** Advantages and disadvantages of premium pricing

Advantages of premium pricing

- The premium price enables the firm to earn higher profit margins.
- Premium prices on the products sold by a business can increase the brand value of the firm.
- Many premium-priced products can become status symbols, with the brands enjoying free word-of-mouth marketing from the owners (customers).

Disadvantages of premium pricing

- Limited customer base as the product is exclusive so not everyone is able to afford it.
- There are high costs of research and development to produce premium quality products.
- There are high marketing costs in order to create brand awareness of premium-priced products, and to convince customers to purchase such products.
- Premium pricing is not suitable for most products, especially in markets that have a high degree of competition.

■ **Figure 4.6** Theme parks use dynamic pricing

◼ Dynamic pricing (HL only)

- **Dynamic pricing** (also known as **surge pricing**) is a pricing method based on different time periods, to reflect changes in the level of demand. The price surges when demand is extremely high and drops when demand is low.
- Product prices are continuously changing to reflect changes in real-time demand and supply conditions.

- Examples of businesses that use dynamic question include:
  - taxi ridesharing operators that charge higher prices during peak times of the day
  - theatres and cinema operators that may charge lower prices during less busy days of the week
  - amusement parks (theme parks) that charge different entrance prices during different times of the year
  - airline carriers that charge higher prices during holiday seasons, such as school holidays in the summer.
- Dynamic pricing relies on management information systems, big data, and sophisticated algorithms (see Chapter 5.9) to track and measure levels of demand in real time and then to adjust prices accordingly.

■ **Table 4.13** Advantages and disadvantages of dynamic pricing

Advantages of dynamic pricing

- The premium prices charged during peak periods enable the firm to earn higher profit margins.
- By contrast, the discounted prices during off-peak periods help the firm to make better use of its capacity.
- It can improve stock control (inventory management), such as offering discounted prices for overstocked products.

Disadvantages of dynamic pricing

- Customer dissatisfaction, as people purchase the same product (such as an airline ticket or hotel room) but at different prices, which means some will pay more than others – no one likes to be overcharged.
- It reduces the degree of customer loyalty, as customers continually search for the best deals and offers elsewhere.
- Even with the use of technology, dynamic pricing is time consuming, as a business needs to continually monitor market conditions of demand (customers) and supply (competitors), as well as management of its own resources (such as the number of employees).

■ Competitive pricing (HL only)

- Competitive pricing is a simple pricing method whereby a firm sets the price of its products in relation to the prices set by its rivals in the market.
- It is common in markets where customers can easily make a direct comparison between different products, such as in local supermarket stores.
- The rise in online shopping and popularity of price comparison websites have made it easier for customers to compare prices charged by different businesses. This can force businesses to be more competitive with the prices they charge.

■ **Table 4.14** Advantages and disadvantages of competitive pricing

Advantages of competitive pricing

- The benchmark price level ensures the firm's products are competitively priced, which helps to protect its market share.
- It is a low-risk strategy, especially for new businesses and those that operate in a highly competitive market.

Disadvantages of competitive pricing

- Undercutting the prices of a competitor can spark a price war, resulting in lower profit margins for all rivals.
- Price is not the only factor that determines competitiveness, so the business may need to also consider branding or quality, for example, despite these strategies raising costs of production.

◼ Contribution pricing (HL only)

- **Contribution pricing** involves setting a price that exceeds the variable cost per unit of producing the product. This means the sale of each product makes a positive contribution towards the payment of fixed costs. Once enough units have been sold to pay off all fixed costs, further sales will earn the business a profit.
- Contribution per unit (see Chapter 5.5) is calculated using the formula:

  Selling price – Average variable costs

WORKED EXAMPLE

Suppose a restaurant has the following data:

Average price of a meal = $25, average variable cost of a meal = $13, and total fixed costs = $6,000 per month.

- The unit contribution is $25 – $13 = $12.
- The break-even output (when all fixed and variable costs are covered) = $6,000 / $12 = 500 meals per month.
- If the business needs to reach break even earlier, it could consider raising the average price to $28. In this case, the break-even output would fall to 6,000 / (28 – 13) = 400 meals per month.

◼ **Table 4.15** Advantages and disadvantages of contribution pricing

Advantages of contribution pricing

- It is useful for a business to know how much contribution is earned on the sale of each item and therefore how many units it must sell in order to reach break even.
- It is a flexible pricing method, especially as the business can use existing data on prices, variable cost, and fixed costs.
- It is useful for a business that takes one-off, special orders, as it allows it to determine how much profit can be earned on the contract.

Disadvantages of contribution pricing

- Contribution does not equate to profit, e.g. while a higher selling price might enable a business to reach break even quicker, it does not mean customers will necessarily buy the product at higher prices.
- Allocating fixed costs between different products (see Chapter 3.9) can be somewhat subjective, which leads to inaccurate or uncompetitive prices being charged.

◼ Price elasticity of demand (HL only)

- **Price elasticity of demand** (PED) measures the extent to which demand for a product is responsive to changes in the price of the product.
- There is **price elastic demand** for a product if the change in price leads to a larger proportional change in the quantity demanded, for example if the price falls by 5 per cent and the quantity demanded subsequently expands by 10 per cent. Examples of price elastic products include the numerous types and brands of soft drinks and candy (confectionary).
- **Price inelastic demand** exists for a product if the change in price leads a smaller proportional change in the quantity demanded, for example if the price increases by 10 per cent but the quantity demanded only contracts by 5 per cent. Examples of price inelastic products include salt, electricity, petroleum, and nail clippers.

> **EXPERT TIP**
>
> Price elasticity of demand is calculated by using the formula:
>
> $$\frac{\text{Percentage change in quantity demanded}}{\text{Percentage change in price}}$$
>
> Or
>
> $$\text{PED} = \frac{\% \, \Delta QD}{\% \, \Delta P}$$
>
> It is essentially a fraction, with the numerator representing the percentage change in quantity demanded and the denominator representing the percentage change in price. So, if the fraction is <1, it means demand is price inelastic, as the numerator is smaller than the denominator, and vice versa.

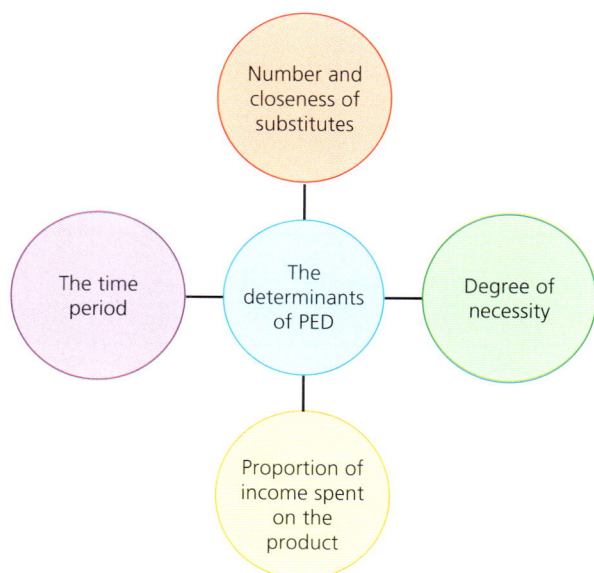

■ **Figure 4.7** The determinant of price elasticity of demand (PED)

- Determinants of price elasticity of demand (PED):
  - *Substitution.* The greater the number and availability of close substitutes, and the more competitive their prices are, so the higher the value of PED will tend to be. By contrast, products with few, if any, substitutes (such as private education and prescribed medicines) have price inelastic demand.
  - *Necessity.* Products that are regarded as essential (such as staple foods, fuel, and housing) tend to be price inelastic, as people will continue to purchase these even if prices rise. By contrast, the demand for luxury goods and services is relatively price elastic.
  - *Income.* The greater the proportion of consumers' income spent on a good or service, the more price elastic demand will be.
  - *Time.* People need time to find alternatives and adapt their habits, tastes, and preferences. Over time, they can adjust their demand based on more permanent price changes by switching to alternative products.

- Knowledge of the PED for a firm's products enables the business to determine the impact of price changes on quantity demanded and sales revenue (see Table 4.16). Recall from Chapter 3.3 that sales revenue is calculated by price multiplied by quantity sold (or P × Q).
- In general, price inelastic demand means a firm can increase sales revenue by raising its price, and the opposite applies to price elastic demand.
- Essentially, an understanding of PED should lead to improved pricing decisions.

■ **Table 4.16** The relationship between PED and total revenue

Price change	Price inelastic	Price elastic
Increase in price	Sales revenue increases	Sales revenue decreases
Reduction in price	Sales revenue decreases	Sales revenue increases

KEY CONCEPT

Examine how the concept of **ethics** has affected the pricing methods for a business organization of your choice.

4.5 The seven Ps of the marketing mix: 3 Promotion

SL/HL content	Depth of teaching
The following aspects of promotion: above the line promotion, below the line promotion, and through the line	AO2
Social media marketing as a promotional strategy	AO3

Diploma Programme *Business management guide* (May 2022)

Aspects of promotion (AO2)

- **Promotion** is the marketing process of raising customer awareness and interest in a product or brand in order to generate sales.
- Promotion, as part of the marketing mix, has a key role in creating brand awareness and brand loyalty.
- It is the communication aspect of the marketing mix.
- The objectives of promotion include:
  - building product and brand awareness
  - creating customer interest
  - providing product information
  - stimulating demand for the product
  - differentiating the product from rival products
  - reinforcing and developing the brand name.
- The three key aspects of promotion are above the line (ATL) promotion, below the line (BTL) promotion, and through the line (TTL) promotion.

Above the line promotion

- Above the line (ATL) promotion is paid-for marketing communication via independent media, for example advertising on television or in national newspapers.
- A third-party organization (such as YouTube, Google, a commercial radio station, or cinema) has responsibility for and control of the process.
- The key reason for using ATL promotion is the potentially huge reach to customers, as it has a very broad appeal and is largely untargeted. However, the main limitation is the high expense of ATL promotion.

■ **Table 4.17** Advantages and disadvantages of various ATL promotions

Medium	Advantages	Disadvantages
Cinema	• Captured audience of potential customers seated in the cinema. • Targeted marketing based on the type of movie being screened. • High impact from large screen and high-end sound system.	• The impact or message may be lost or forgotten after viewers have watched the movie. • A passive audience of people who may talk or consume food and drinks during the adverts.
Magazine	• Access to specific customer target groups, e.g. car magazines for motor enthusiasts. • Adverts have a longer shelf life as people don't tend to throw away magazines so quickly. • High readership rate.	• Glossy adverts in popular magazines are very expensive. • Planning is difficult as adverts are often placed six months prior to publication. • Advertising clutter can put off readers of magazines.
Newspaper	• Most newspapers can reach a large number of people within a specified geographical area. • Printed adverts can be referred to at a later date.	• Adverts compete for the attention of newspaper readers. • A relatively short life span as newspapers are usually just read once.
Online	• The opportunities for online advertising continue to grow rapidly around the world. • Reaches both a national and a global audience. • Highly accessible to customers.	• There are cheaper online methods, e.g. the firm's own website, blogs, or social media. • Online advertising clutter, such as pop-up adverts, means online adverts can be ignored.
Outdoor advertising	• Large billboard posters are highly visible and attract attention. • Constant reminders, as adverts are repeatedly seen by people, e.g. commuters and drivers. • Digital displays can have more appeal due to the use of moving images.	• Many outdoor adverts (such as billboards) are static. • They can be vulnerable to vandalism or damage from severe weather conditions. • Messages must be brief as large images are more effective than lots of text.
Radio	• People can multi-task while listening to the radio, e.g. drivers. • Ability to reach specific target groups, e.g. teenagers through to older people. • Morning and evening commuters offer huge marketing prospects.	• No visuals, so may not be as effective as audio-visual adverts. • People often regard the radio simply as background noise. • Radio adverts have far less of a national reach than TV adverts.
Television	• Impact of sight, sound, and motion to grab viewers' attention. • TV adverts can connect emotionally with viewers. • Broadcast times can target specific markets, e.g. children. • Huge potential to reach mass-market audience.	• Very expensive so is not suitable or affordable for smaller firms. • Viewers might 'channel hop', i.e. change channels during adverts. • It is usually effective only when the advert is seen several times. • Limited information as adverts are generally very short.

EXPERT TIP

Students often use the terms 'advertising' and 'promotion' interchangeably. While advertising is indeed a major part of promotion, the latter is much broader and includes far more than just advertising as outlined in this unit.

▣ Below the line promotion

- Below the line (BTL) promotion refers to promotional activities that the business has direct control over, for example direct mail and customer loyalty programmes.
- BTL promotion is aimed directly at the target audience, rather than a generic audience, as in the case of ATL promotion.
- Hence, BTL promotion does not use the mass media.
- It is suitable when the business has direct contact with customers, for example through direct marketing, point-of-sale (POS) displays, newsletters, and public relations.
- The results and effectiveness of BTL campaigns are easier for a business to measure.

■ **Table 4.18** Advantages and disadvantages of BTL promotions

Medium	Advantages	Disadvantages
Customer loyalty programmes	• These encourage brand loyalty and frequent repurchases. • The database of customer details can be used for direct marketing.	• Rewards systems, such as price discounts and free gifts, can be expensive to maintain. • Administrative costs can be high.
Direct mail	• Highly targeted as the business knows the target market groups. • Newsletters, brochures, and catalogues can help to keep customers informed and keen. • Encourages customers to directly purchase from the business.	• Administrative and postage costs can be high. • Low readership rate, as a lot of direct mail through the post is regarded as 'junk' mail. • Advertising clutter can make it difficult for an advert to stand out.
Email	• The internet provides wide opportunities for e-marketing. • Generally inexpensive. • Environmentally friendly (email marketing is paper-free). • Opt-in email subscription lists can generate good responses.	• Customers might regard emails as spam (unsolicited messages). • Legal issues need to be considered, e.g. data privacy laws. • Undelivered and/or unread emails due to spam filters.
Exhibitions and trade shows	• Captured audience of potential customers at the venue. • Opportunities for retail customers and consumers to see the product firsthand.	• Intense competition from rival exhibitors. • Limited opportunities to exhibit at trade shows throughout the year.
Merchandising	• Promotes impulse purchases. • Selling internal merchandise with the firm's logo or brand further promotes brand awareness. • Provides an extra revenue stream from the sale of merchandise.	• The production of the firm's own merchandise can be expensive. • Additional running costs are incurred, e.g. stock control. • Merchandise often contributes to visual clutter.
Point of sale (POS)	• Encourages impulse (unintended) purchases. • Highly visible promotion so ideal for marketing new products. • Easy to monitor the most popular product selection.	• Inventory (stock) control may be problematic. • May not catch the attention of customers due to so many POS displays.
Public relations (PR)	• Develops positive relationships with the media and the public. • Often perceived as a highly credible form of promotion. • Particularly cost effective when compared to the direct costs of other forms of BTL promotion.	• The news media often publishes or broadcasts an edited version of the marketing message. • There is no guarantee that journalists and the news media will run a story, despite efforts to put it together.

Sales promotion	• A range of incentives to entice customers, e.g. price discounts.	• It is only a short-term promotional tactic.
Sponsorship	• Marketing advantages of being associated with the person/organization sponsored. • Exclusive marketing exposure during sponsored events.	• Negative actions of the person/organization sponsored could compromise the firm's integrity and reputation. • Can be extremely expensive.

Key terms

Merchandising refers to the use of branded products (such as toys, cups, souvenirs, and clothing) linked to a business organization or its products (such as a theme park, blockbuster movie, theatre show, or music band).

Point of sale (POS) refers to the marketing of goods in stores where customers can purchase the goods. It is based on convenience (positioned in a way so they are easily accessible to customers, such as by supermarket checkouts) and prompts impulse buying.

Public relations (PR) refers to an organization's planned and sustained process of maintaining mutual understanding with the general public. The PR team tries to gain favourable publicity via the media and other channels, for example via educational programmes, news conferences, community activities, and sponsorship of local events.

BUSINESS MANAGEMENT TOOLKIT

Discuss the importance of descriptive statistics for effective below the line (BTL) promotion.

■ Through the line (TTL) promotion

- This refers to the combination of appropriate methods of ATL and BTL promotion, aimed at promoting different products to different market segments.

- It can include advertising, personal selling, public relations, direct marketing, and sales promotion, for example.

- TTL promotion enables a business to get a more holistic view of the market and reach out to its customers in as many appropriate ways as possible.

- For instance, a range of ATL and BTL methods can be used for advertising a new Hollywood blockbuster movie, for example TV, radio, newspapers, magazines, billboards, web pages and social media platforms.

- All elements of a TTL promotional strategy have two main purposes: to inform customers about the product and to persuade them to buy the product over rival products or brands.

- TTL promotion helps a business to achieve greater brand awareness and have more market presence.

- However, the main drawback of TTL promotion is the high cost involved in implementing both ATL and BTL promotional activities. Hence, only large and financially stable businesses can afford to use TTL promotional campaigns.

EXPERT TIP

When advising a business on an appropriate marketing mix, do remember to write in the context of the organization. Students have been known to write about 'buy one get one free' deals for the motor car industry and customer loyalty schemes for health care providers; more thought and care is needed to score well in the exams!

Social media marketing as a promotional strategy (AO3)

- Technology has changed the way in which businesses use promotional strategies, such as social media marketing (SMM).

- SMM is the use of online tools, platforms, and websites to promote products in a less formal way, for example on Facebook, Instagram, Pinterest, Reddit, Snapchat, TikTok, Twitter, WeChat, and YouTube.

- Social media entails content that can be uploaded, including videos, newsletters, blogs, and online discussion forums.

- SMM is also used as a form of direct marketing. The aim is to raise product and brand awareness by creating a marketing buzz around a product or service, for example the launch of a new movie.

- It can potentially have a global reach, enabling customers to view the business from a different perspective. For example, a company's Facebook site might include photos of staff social functions and outreach programmes in local communities.

- SMM can help a business to connect with its customers on a more personal and emotional level, making its products more appealing.

- SMM can often lead to the spread of information about a firm's goods or services from one internet user to another, possibly creating exponential growth in a marketing message. This is known as **viral marketing**.

- As consumers are the advocates of the promotional message, SMM and viral marketing can help to spread marketing messages wider and faster than traditional ATL or BTL methods.

- Social media networks encourage people to willingly share their opinions, ideas, feedback, photos, and videos, thereby providing many market research opportunities for businesses.

> **KEY CONCEPT**
>
> Investigate the impact of **change** and **creativity** on the promotional strategies for an organization of your choice.

4.5 The seven Ps of the marketing mix: 4 Place

SL/HL content	Depth of teaching
The importance of different types of distribution channels	AO3

Diploma Programme *Business management guide* (May 2022)

The importance of different types of distribution channels (AO3)

- **Place** (or **distribution**), in the marketing mix, is about making the good or service available to consumers (the end users).

- An effective distribution strategy ensures that customers are able to purchase the product easily, meaning the right product is distributed to the right consumers at the right time.

- Distribution is a crucial part of the marketing mix for all businesses – there is little purpose in having a great product sold at an attractive price if customers are unable to find a retailer nearby that sells it. The more readily available the product, the more likely it will sell well.
- Place is about the location of the consumer, not the business itself. Hence, a key function of place in the marketing mix is to provide convenience to consumers.
- It involves strategies the business uses to get its goods to the location of the customers, be it on a regional, national, or international basis.

EXPERT TIP

A common mistake made by students is to confuse place with location. **Place** refers to distribution in the marketing mix (where customers can purchase their products), while **location** is about the physical position of a business organization (where the business is situated). Place is vital to all businesses, but having a physical presence is not necessarily so.

- A distribution channel refers to the process or system of how to get the product to consumers, for example via retailers, wholesalers, or vending machines.
- If a manufacturer does not sell directly to the consumer, then intermediaries are used, including agents or distributors (see Figure 4.8).
- Channels of distribution can come in numerous forms:
  - A zero-channel network uses no intermediaries, which means the manufacturer sells directly to the customer, for example farmers who sell their agricultural produce straight to customers.
  - A one-channel network involves selling to retailers.
  - A two-channel network involves the goods going via wholesalers and retailers.
  - A three-channel network uses an agent (perhaps to sell the product overseas) who sells the goods to wholesalers on behalf of the producer.
- An intermediary, such as an agent or retailer, is a third-party business that offers distribution services between two trading parties.
- Distribution channels include direct distribution, retailers, wholesalers, mail order, and e-commerce.

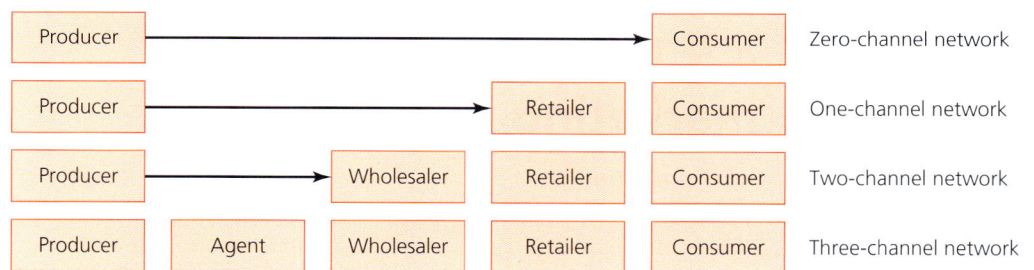

■ **Figure 4.8** Channels of distribution

■ Direct distribution

- Direct distribution (or a zero-channel network) involves the producer selling the good or service without using an intermediary, for example hairdressers or driving instructors.
- It involves the producer dealing directly with the consumers of its products.
- The internet has created an alternative channel for producers to sell direct to the consumer, for example via Amazon, eBay, Taobao, and iTunes.

■ Retailers

- Retailers are businesses that sell direct to customers, for example Walmart, Home Depot, Best Buy, 7-Eleven, and Tesco.
- Retailers are often multi-store outlets, offering choice and convenience for customers.
- 'People' in the marketing mix plays a huge part in the tertiary sector. This is because employees directly interact and engage with customers so can enhance customer relations, which ultimately leads to higher sales.
- A key drawback of using retailers is that retail stores often have to pay expensive rent (in addition to the costs of the store's decorations, furnishings, and staff salaries and wages). The higher costs mean that retailers end up charging higher prices for the manufacturer's products.

■ **Table 4.19** Types and characteristics of retailers

Types of retailers	Characteristics
Chain stores	• Two or more outlets. • Uses the same business name and model (standard business practices).
Department stores	• Multiple producers (departments) within the same retail building. • A large and wide range of goods available. • Convenience shopping for customers, all under one roof.
Discount stores	• A wide range of products available at discount prices. • May include some well-known branded products.
Supermarkets	• Large retail stores with all types of goods, usually groceries, and daily products, e.g. health and beauty products. • Sell fast-moving consumer goods (FMCGs) direct to customers.
Superstores	• Very large retail stores located in out-of-town areas (due to the amount of land needed). • Sell a wider variety of products, e.g. household electronic appliances and furniture.

EXPERT TIP

Students often confuse retailers with wholesalers and suppliers. Retailers sell directly to consumers, whereas wholesalers and suppliers usually sell to other businesses.

■ **Figure 4.9** Supermarkets are retail stores that sell directly to customers

■ Wholesalers

- Wholesalers buy large quantities of products direct from manufacturers and then sell these to customers in smaller quantities (a process known as 'breaking bulk').
- Retailers benefit from buying smaller quantities from wholesalers rather than significantly larger volumes if bought directly from manufacturers.
- Producers benefit from wholesalers due to lower transaction costs and fewer deliveries. Wholesalers also take care of the promotion, thereby reducing costs for the manufacturer.
- However, wholesalers might not stock the full range of a manufacturer's products.
- They might also not be conveniently located for some retailers, especially smaller ones.

Mail order

- Mail order is the use of the postal system to distribute goods.
- It traditionally relies on the use of catalogues and order forms, although the internet has reduced the reliance on hard copies of these items.
- It is a short distributional channel so helps to cut production costs and possibly prices for customers.

E-commerce

- E-commerce is the use of the internet to conduct business transactions.
- It has created an array of opportunities for both producers and retailers to sell to customers, especially during and since the national lockdowns caused by the COVID-19 pandemic.
- It is a relatively inexpensive distribution channel, providing customers with worldwide access, 24 hours a day, from the convenience of their home or office.
- With increased access to the internet and the global trend of greater use of mobile devices (such as smartphones and tablet computers), e-commerce creates a huge opportunity for businesses to use the internet as a distribution channel.

The appropriateness (and hence importance) of different distribution channels

When selecting a distribution channel for a particular product, the following need to be considered:

- *Type of product.* This relates to whether the product is a producer good or a consumer good (for example, aircraft or fast food), or technical (in which case specialist distributors and agents may be needed to explain how the product works). Perishable goods need to reach customers quickly and/or need to be widely available in retail outlets so they can be sold rapidly. A customized product made specifically for a client would be sold using direct distribution.
- *Frequency of purchase.* Whether the product is bought in mass markets on a daily basis (in which case retailers such as supermarkets might be suitable), or whether it is bought infrequently (such as mattresses, for example).
- *Product price.* An expensive product with an exclusive image, such as a Lamborghini car or a Rolex watch, will be sold in a limited number of retail outlets. By contrast, mass-market products such as Coca-Cola are sold in a wide range of retail outlets and other distribution channels.
- *Location of customers.* For example, e-commerce could be a viable distribution channel for customers located in rural areas or in overseas markets.
- *Availability of rival products.* Producers will usually compete with rivals head on by selling their products using the same distribution channels, thereby competing directly for customers.
- *Size of the market.* Mass-produced goods require a system of geographically widespread distributional channels, possibly including overseas markets.
- *Available finance.* The better the financial position of a business, the greater its distribution networks can be.
- *Degree of control expected.* The more intermediaries used, the less control a producer has over the marketing of its own products. Longer distribution channels can cause communication problems, so are costlier, whereas shorter channels enable prices to be lower.

- *Legal considerations.* There could be legal limitations for the sale of certain products, for example medicines, chemicals and fireworks.

EXAM PRACTICE QUESTION

Suggest a suitable channel of distribution for the following products:

a Aircraft [2]

b Music albums [2]

c Cinema tickets. [2]

4.5 The seven Ps of the marketing mix: 5 People, 6 Processes, 7 Physical evidence

SL/HL content	Depth of teaching
People: The importance of employee–customer relationships in marketing a service, and cultural variation in these relationships	AO3
Processes: The importance of delivery processes in marketing a service, and changes in these processes	AO3
Physical evidence: The importance of tangible physical evidence in marketing a service	AO3
Appropriate marketing mixes for particular products or businesses	AO3

Diploma Programme *Business management guide* (May 2022)

The seven Ps model in a service-based market (AO2)

- Bernard H Booms and Mary J Bitner (1981) added to the traditional four Ps of the marketing mix with an extra three Ps: people, processes, and physical evidence.

- The seven Ps model, also known as the **extended marketing mix**, is applicable to the marketing of services, whereas the traditional four Ps are used for the marketing of physical goods.

- Booms and Bitner argued that the marketing of intangible services needs to be different to that of tangible goods, because of the unique characteristics of services: intangibility, heterogeneity, and perishability.

- The marketing strategy for the provision of services must be effective as, arguably, satisfied customers are the best publicity for a firm's products.

People: The importance of employee–customer relationships in marketing a service, and cultural variation in these relationships (AO3)

- From the perspective of customers, when a service is being provided, the person delivering the service is not detached from the product itself. For example, a rude waiter will spoil even the best of meals served in an elegant restaurant.

- People deliver a physical service with a visible result, for example assistants, stylists, hairdressers, and nail technicians in a salon.

■ **Figure 4.10** The marketing mix (seven Ps)

- Successful organizations focus on the service element of the marketing mix by investing in their people (employees). This is done by training and developing workers to deliver outstanding customer service.
- The attitude and behaviour of an employee directly affects the experience of the customer, be it positive or negative. This has a direct impact on whether the customer is likely to return.
- McDonald's, for example, has its own university (called Hamburger University, in Illinois, USA) where staff are trained in various aspects of restaurant management and customer service, to ensure consistency across all their branches around the world.
- The development of social networks and social media has meant that the people element of the extended marketing mix has become ever more important. The news about poor customer care spreads much faster and wider than previously possible.

Processes: The importance of delivery processes in marketing a service and changes in these processes (AO3)

- Process refers to the operational aspects of a service, such as the procedures, protocols, timing, and sequencing of activities related to the service, for example queuing systems in a large sports stadium.
- Processes include queuing systems, payment systems (for example, the ability to pay by credit card or online bank transfer), and after-sales customer care.
- Processes ensure the same level of service delivery to every customer, even though the experience of each customer might be different. For example, all customers in a restaurant should be greeted politely and be accompanied to their seats.
- Processes should also enable specific customer preferences to be accommodated (within reason), thereby providing customers with a unique experience.
- McDonald's pledge to serve customers their fast food within 90 seconds (or 3.5 minutes for their drive-thru service) is an example of process in their marketing mix.

Physical evidence: The importance of tangible physical evidence in marketing a service (AO3)

- The location and physical environment where the service is delivered is a significant factor affecting the level of customer satisfaction. So, for example, banks should feel safe, hotels should look clean, family restaurants should appear welcoming, and a floristry should appear inviting.

- Physical evidence refers to any form of tangible representation of a service which helps to create customer perceptions about that service, for example menus, brochures, corporate stationery, certificates and awards on display, business cards, staff dress code, and company reports.

- Customers use physical evidence to gauge the level of comfort and attractiveness of a service. For example, a calm and soothing environment will help to attract customers to a health spa.

- McDonald's restaurants, for example, are all designed to create a family-friendly environment. Their menus are designed and structured in the same way everywhere, so customers feel more familiar with the physical environment within the restaurants.

- Employees are also directly affected by the physical environment, which impacts their level of motivation. Therefore, people in the extended marketing mix can be directly influenced by physical evidence.

■ **Figure 4.11** This image shows physical evidence for a salon – it looks clean, professional, and inviting

KEY CONCEPT

Investigate how the concepts of **change** and **ethics** have affected the marketing mix for an organization of your choice, such as a school, restaurant chain, airline, or theme park.

Appropriate marketing mixes for particular products or businesses (AO3)

- Recall that the marketing mix refers to all aspects of marketing activity that are used to influence a customer's buying decision. It is comprised of the seven Ps.

- To be effective, the different aspects of the marketing mix must complement and reinforce each other, meaning they must be integrated as part of the firm's marketing strategy in order to adequately meet the needs and wants of customers. This helps to strengthen brand value and customer loyalty.

- Hence, an appropriate marketing mix for any given good or service requires the organization to provide the right product, at the right price, communicated through the right promotional channels, and available at the right places.

- In addition, the organization should hire the right people, pay attention to the right physical or visible aspects of the service provided to customers, and use the right procedures and processes to ensure effective delivery of its products to the right customers.

- The right marketing mix for a product will depend on numerous interrelated factors, including the following:
  - The size of the business, that is, whether it is a sole trader or multinational company. Also, a business with a larger market share has greater customer loyalty, and so may be able to charge higher prices.
  - The size of the market, for example the market for horse saddles or the market for bottled water.
  - The type of product, such as whether it is a physical good (the four Ps) or an intangible service (the seven Ps).
  - The product's position in its life cycle. For example, stars will be promoted more heavily than cash cows (at the maturity phase) or dogs (in the decline phase) (see the Boston Consulting Group matrix in the Business management toolkit).
  - The type of good or service. For example, premium products will be more price inelastic in demand, so businesses can charge higher prices.
  - Consumer profiles, such as gender, age, educational attainment, or income levels, can affect a firm's marketing mix and marketing strategies. For example, social media marketing might be more appropriate as part of the promotional mix for sports shoes aimed at the youth market, while direct marketing might be more appropriate for targeting existing Audi car owners.
- Essentially, all parts of a firm's marketing mix must be effective for the business to prosper. An effective marketing mix allows the firm to reach its marketing objectives, such as increased sales revenue and market share.

4.6 International marketing (HL only)

HL content	Depth of teaching
The opportunities and threats posed by entering and operating internationally	AO3

Diploma Programme *Business management guide* (May 2022)

The opportunities and threats posed by entering and operating internationally (AO3)

- **International marketing** has implications for the operational and strategic decisions of firms, because simply extending current marketing practices is unlikely to work well in overseas markets. However, this will also be affected by the **opportunities** and **threats** posed by entering and operating internationally.
- The increasing presence of multinational companies (see Chapter 1.6) has made international marketing more of an operational and strategic priority for many businesses.
- Branding is an integral part of an organization's international marketing strategy. Global brands have a better chance of competing in global markets.
- Methods of entry into international markets include the following:
  - *Exporting.* This involves a firm selling its products to overseas buyers without having to physically expand in an overseas market.
  - *Direct investment.* This involves setting up overseas production or distribution facilities.

Key terms

International marketing is the marketing of an organization's products in foreign countries.

Opportunities are the positive prospects for an organization. In this context, it refers to the openings or potential benefits as the business seeks to expand in overseas markets.

Threats are the potential challenges confronting a business. In this context, they are the obstacles or challenges the business faces as it seeks to expand internationally.

  ○ *Franchising.* This growth strategy involves licensing a third-party provider to supply the goods and services of the business in return for payment of a licensing fee and royalty payments.

  ○ *Strategic alliance.* This growth strategy involves using foreign partners working together on a particular business venture.

  ○ *Joint ventures.* This involves the formation of a new business with two or more other firms using their shared resources.

◼ The opportunities posed by entry into international markets

● *Profitability.* Selling to overseas markets generates higher sales revenue and the potential for higher profits, especially if the domestic market is saturated.

● *Economies of scale.* Firms can benefit from economies of scale (see Chapter 1.5) by selling their products to larger markets around the world.

● *Spread risks.* Selling in overseas markets allows the business to spread its risks (diversification). For example, if the domestic market goes into a recession, then sales from overseas markets can protect the firm's working capital and profitability.

● *Laws and legislation.* Businesses can take advantage of the more relaxed laws and regulations in some countries which would otherwise constrain their operations.

● *Competition.* There may be less competition by operating in certain countries or regions of the world. Conversely, having an overseas presence can improve the international competitiveness of the organization.

● *Production costs.* Costs of production may be lower in overseas markets, for example cheaper labour costs, low-priced raw material costs, and lower rents.

● *Financial incentives.* Foreign governments may offer incentives for firms locating in their country (to encourage investment and employment), for example tax allowances, refunds, and concessions.

● *Extension strategies.* Entering international markets can also help to extend a product's life cycle, thereby leading to higher profits.

◼ The threats posed by entry into international markets

● *Social, cultural, and demographic factors.* Businesses might have to change their marketing mix in order to better suit the needs of customers overseas who may have a different social and demographic profile. Cultural differences may also present some challenges, which would necessitate a change in the firm's marketing strategies.

● *Language barriers.* Marketing messages do not necessarily translate well across international borders, so market research and local knowledge may be required. This undoubtedly adds to the organization's operational costs.

● *Legal and political barriers.* Businesses entering international markets need to ensure they comply with local laws and regulations regarding consumer protection, codes of conduct on advertising and packaging copyrights, trademarks, and patents. The political environment can also cause challenges for business operating in overseas markets.

● *Financial barriers.* Additional working capital may be needed to expand internationally. It will also cost more for human resource planning and to develop new distribution channels in overseas markets.

● *Competitive rivalry.* Businesses entering foreign markets may face strong competition from well-established firms in these markets. Domestic and foreign firms may have already established a strong customer base and enjoy brand loyalty.

- *Exchange rate fluctuations.* Changes in the exchange rate can alter the competitiveness of a firm's products and prices. This directly impacts its sales revenue and profitability.
- *Additional costs.* The above threats may necessitate additional market research and contingency plans in new international markets. Hence, the increase in costs can offset the potential profitability of operating in overseas markets.

BUSINESS MANAGEMENT TOOLKIT

Examine how SWOT analysis can help managers to assess the opportunities and threats posed by entering and operating internationally.

■ **Figure 4.12** SWOT analysis is a commonly used management tool

BUSINESS MANAGEMENT TOOLKIT

Investigate how Hofstede's cultural dimensions (HL only) have impacted the international marketing strategies for an organization of your choice.

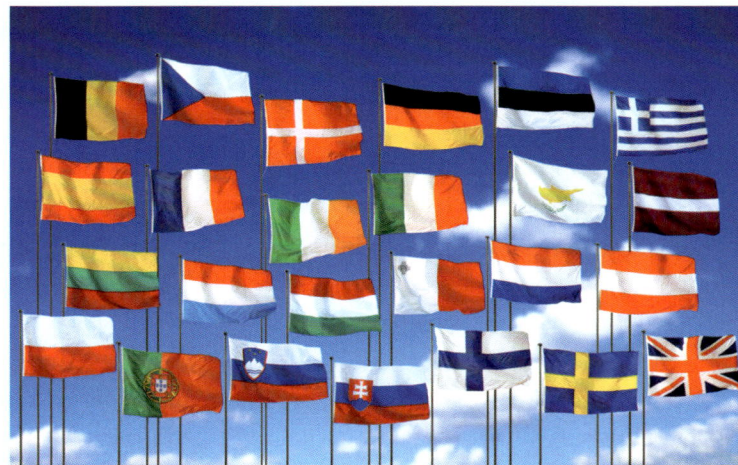

■ **Figure 4.13** Europe is a large international market but the countries of Europe have very varied cultures (© European Community)

BUSINESS MANAGEMENT TOOLKIT

In the context of international marketing, discuss the importance of the Boston Consulting Group matrix for marketers.

5 Operations management

5.1 Introduction to operations management

SL/HL content	Depth of teaching
The role of operations management	AO2

Diploma Programme *Business management guide* (May 2022)

The role of operations management (AO2)

Key term

Operations management refers to the business function of combining inputs (resources) to produce outputs (goods and services) that are valued by consumers.

- **Operations management** (or **production**) involves planning, organizing, co-ordinating, and controlling all activities involved in the transformation process of changing inputs into outputs (see Figure 5.1).

- It focuses on the process of creating goods and providing services using the available resources of the organization; in other words, it is what the business actually does to earn revenues.

- **Goods** are physical products (tangible products) and **services** are non-physical products (intangible products).

- Operations management can be capital-intensive or labour-intensive.
  - ○ **Capital-intensive production** refers to operations processes that have a high proportion of capital cost compared to the costs of labour or land. Examples include car manufacturing, oil and gas extraction, mining, steel production, construction of real estate, as well as telecommunications and internet infrastructure.
  - ○ **Labour-intensive production** refers to operations processes that have a high proportion of labour costs compared to the costs of capital or land. Examples include bespoke tailoring, home cleaning and domestic services, food preparation and cooking, teaching, social care services, and personal care services (such as massage therapy or nail care).

- Operations management must ensure that there is value added (see Chapter 1.1) in the production process. This helps to ensure firms can sell their products and earn profit for their owners.

- It is about acquiring the necessary resources needed for production, in the most efficient and cost-effective way. It impacts the other functional areas of a business, as outlined in the following examples.
  - ○ Marketing function:
    - Physical goods or intangible services are produced based on market research, in order to meet the needs and wants of customers.
    - The good or service needs to be promoted to existing and potential customers.

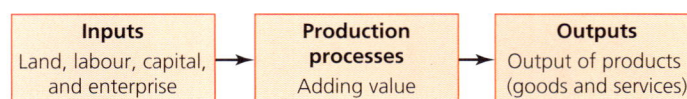

Inputs	Production processes	Outputs
Land, labour, capital, and enterprise	Adding value	Output of products (goods and services)

■ **Figure 5.1** The role of operations management (the transformation process)

- The finished product also needs to be distributed using appropriate channels.
- A suitable pricing method is needed to ensure the products sell well on the market.
  - Finance function:
    - Costs of different operations methods (see Chapter 5.2), for example mass production, are needed in order to gain economies of scale, although this could also require high set-up costs.
    - Funding is needed for all aspects of operations management, including lean production (see Chapter 5.3) and research and development (see Chapter 5.8).
    - Production managers must be held accountable for their expenditure and budgets (see Chapter 3.9).
  - Human resource management function:
    - Production workers need to be hired and trained to work productively.
    - Supervisors and quality controllers may also need to be hired.
    - A crisis management team might need to be formed (see Chapter 5.7).
    - Operations managers are responsible for collaborating and working with managers from other departments to meet organizational objectives.

5.2 Operations methods

SL/HL content	Depth of teaching
The following operations methods: • Job production • Batch production • Mass/flow production • Mass customization	AO3

Diploma Programme *Business management guide* (May 2022)

Operations methods (AO3)

Production (or **operations**) refers to the manufacture or output of a physical good or intangible service. There are four main operations methods: job, batch, mass (flow), and mass customization.

■ **Figure 5.2** This cake, designed especially for a themed party, is an example of a product made using job production

▨ Job production

- Job production is the production of a special or customized good or service suited to the specific requirements of an individual customer.
- Examples of job production include bridges, movies, private tuition, wedding dresses, special occasion cakes, bespoke suits, and portrait painters.
- Each order is a one-off unique good or service.
- It is the most labour-intensive method of production, as it is reliant on highly skilled labour.
- It is also the most expensive operations method, although clients pay relatively high prices for the uniqueness of the product and its quality.

■ **Table 5.1** Advantages and disadvantages of job production

Advantages of job production

- It is the most flexible method of production, as orders are made specifically for a customer.
- Due to its uniqueness, the output is likely to be of outstanding quality.
- A high mark-up price can be charged because of the product's exclusivity and high quality.
- The skilled workers tend to be motivated by the variety and challenges of the job.

Disadvantages of job production

- High labour costs due to the need for highly skilled and experienced workers.
- High production costs due to the absence of economies of scale.
- Production is time consuming because specific requirements need to be catered for.

◼ Batch production

- Batch production is an operations method that involves identical goods being made in sets (batches) rather than in a continuous flow.
- Examples of batch production include the output of casual clothing, cookies (biscuits), bread, shoes, and furniture.
- Goods are produced in consignments (batches), undergoing the production process at the same time, before manufacturing the next batch with different specifications, for example 100 medium-sized red t-shirts, followed by 65 small-sized blue t-shirts.
- It does not involve a system of continuous production.
- Workers are likely to be semi-skilled and output is far more capital intensive compared with job production.

■ **Table 5.2** Advantages and disadvantages of batch production

Advantages of batch production

- Average (unit) costs of production are lower compared with job production, due to there being some economies of scale.
- There is some flexibility to meet a variety of demands, thereby providing some choice to customers.
- It is useful for small businesses that cannot afford to operate continuous production lines and/or where demand for the product is insufficient to justify mass production.

Disadvantages of batch production

- There is less flexibility, as customers have to select from a range of standardized output.
- There is a greater need for stock, especially raw materials.
- There is 'downtime' between batches, as machinery might need cleaning and/or changing prior to the manufacture of the next batch.

◼ Mass (flow) production

- **Mass production** (also known as **flow production**) is used by businesses that focus on large-scale production techniques for mass-market goods.
- It is suitable for the large-scale production of homogeneous (identical or standardized) products such as oil processed at an oil refinery, bottled water, canned drinks, motor vehicles, televisions, light bulbs, ball bearings, and toys.
- Lower prices are charged due to the standardization of mass-produced output.
- There is a high degree of automation as mass production is capital intensive.
- The workforce can be unskilled or semi-skilled, although the workers are highly specialized.
- Marketing support is essential to increase demand, as mass production generates large-scale output.

> **Key term**
>
> **Flow production** is the continuous and automated production process that uses capital intensive production methods to maximize output by minimizing production time. It is associated with large production runs of standardized products.

- It is based on specialization and the division of labour.
- While job production is about quality, mass production is about quantity.

■ **Table 5.3** Advantages and disadvantages of mass production

Advantages of mass production

- Costs per unit of production are lower, due to the existence of production economies of scale.
- It is capital intensive so manufacturing can take place for longer periods.
- Automation means less labour is required in the production process, thus lowering labour costs.
- Relatively easy and cheap to hire labour for mass production.
- Capital-intensive production means there is likely to be efficient use of machinery and equipment.
- As mass production is capital intensive, it is comparatively easy to expand production should the level of demand for the product increase.

Disadvantages of mass production

- Lower profit margins are earned due to the low prices and standardized output.
- Limited, if any, flexibility, as large quantities of identical products are created.
- Requires an efficient system of stock control, as stockpiling of manufactured goods can be very expensive.
- There are likely to be very high start-up costs due to the investment in capital equipment, machinery, and production systems.
- All stages of production are interdependent, so if a problem occurs in one part of the assembly line, production as a whole comes to a halt.
- Workers can become quickly demotivated due to the boring and repetitive nature of the tasks.

> **EXPERT TIP**
>
> In reality, many products are made using more than one operations method. For example, the engines of a Ferrari or Porsche are hand-made using job production. However, the leather is bought in batches of different hides, textures, and colours. The tyres are bought in bulk from mass producers such as Michelin and Pirelli.

▪ Mass customization

- Mass customization is an operations method that combines the benefits of mass production with job production.
- It enables customers to gain from some degree of personalization (custom-made products) at affordable prices, as the base product is mass produced.
- Technological advances and creativity enable many businesses to take advantage of the benefits of mass customization (see Table 5.4).
- Some chocolate manufacturers, like Cadbury, sell customized bars with the name of the customer on the wrapper. Coca-Cola sells customized canned and bottled drinks, also with the customer's name on the packaging.

■ **Table 5.4** Advantages and disadvantages of mass customization

Advantages of mass customization

- Businesses can charge a premium price for a customized product, thereby earning high profit margins on what is mainly a mass-produced item.
- Customization helps to differentiate a product or brand from competitors and can possibly give it a unique selling point (USP), making the business more competitive.
- Flexibility in the production process makes it easier for firms to adapt their products to meet the varying needs and preferences of customers.

Disadvantages of mass customization

- As with mass production, there are high set-up costs, including investment in machinery and technologies.
- There are higher production costs compared to traditional mass production (due to the additional cost of customization).

EXPERT TIP

Exam questions often ask candidates to compare operations methods for a particular product. Be sure to consider the advantages and disadvantages of the various operations methods in your answers.

KEY CONCEPT

Consider how the concept of **change** has influenced the operations methods used by a business organization of your choice.

EXAM PRACTICE QUESTION

Benelao Clothing Co. designs and manufactures fashionable clothing for children in a variety of designs, colours, and sizes.

a Identify the operations method that is most likely to be used by Benelao Clothing Co. [1]

b Explain **two** benefits of this operations method to Benelao Clothing Co. [4]

5.3 Lean production and quality management (HL only)

HL content	Depth of teaching
The following features of lean production: less waste and greater efficiency	AO1
The following methods of lean production: continuous improvement (kaizen) and just in time (JIT)	AO2
Features of cradle-to-cradle design and manufacturing	AO2
Features of quality control and quality assurance	AO2
The following methods of managing quality: quality circle, benchmarking, and total quality management (TQM)	AO2
The impact of lean production and TQM on an organization	AO3
The importance of national and international quality standards	AO2

Diploma Programme *Business management guide* (May 2022)

Features of lean production (AO1)

■ Less waste

- **Lean production**, which originated in Japan, involves streamlining operations in order to reduce all forms of waste and to achieve greater efficiency.
- Lean production is about getting things right first time, and using fewer resources, both of which help to reduce wastage of resources.

> **Key term**
>
> **Lean production** is a philosophy built into the culture of organizations that focus on less wastage and greater efficiency.

- The seven sources of waste (or 'muda' in Japanese) are defective products, overproduction, stockpiling (excessive inventories), unnecessary transportation, over processing (over complex or over complicated), waiting time, and excess movement by workers.
- Methods of waste minimization include total quality management (TQM), cradle-to-cradle manufacturing and just-in-time (JIT) production, all of which are explained in this chapter.

Greater efficiency

- Efficiency is about using resources more effectively to generate output, for example using less capital or labour to produce the same amount of output.
- Efficiency is measured by the productivity rate of resources (see Chapter 5.6). For example, labour productivity can be measured by sales per person or output per worker.
- All members of the organization need to be involved for lean production to work effectively.
- Greater efficiency can be gained in several ways, including:
  - staff training and development
  - higher levels of staff motivation
  - using improved (technologically advanced) machinery and equipment.

Methods of lean production (AO2)

Continuous improvement (kaizen)

- **Kaizen** is a philosophy embedded in the culture of an organization.
- It is a method of lean production and a source of competitive advantage that involves all workers committing to improving quality standards.
- It involves making small, incremental progress (rather than infrequent radical changes) to improve productivity and efficiency.
- As people tend to be resistant to change, workers might be more receptive to small, incremental changes which are less disruptive and risky than large one-off changes.
- It involves empowering workers to make their own decisions for continuous improvement.
- Kaizen can help to reduce costs in the long run by preventing mistakes and outputs of substandard quality.
- It can help to achieve greater efficiency through exploring ways to improve the productivity and efficiency of the organization's processes and operations.
- However, the implementation of kaizen tends to be costly and time consuming. It requires the effort and commitment of all members of the workforce in order to eliminate waste and to make productivity gains.
- The strive for continuous improvement usually causes increased workloads, so can lead to demotivation in the workplace.

Just in time (JIT)

- A **just-in-time (JIT)** stock control system removes the need to have buffer stocks (large quantities of stock on site held as back-up inventory).

> **Key terms**
>
> **Kaizen** is the Japanese philosophy of continuous improvement and changing for the better.
>
> **Just in time (JIT)** is a lean stock control system that relies on stocks (inventories) being delivered only when they are needed in the production process.

- Deliveries of stocks, such as raw materials and components, are made a few hours prior to their use by the purchaser.
- Although JIT can reduce waste, there is always the risk of not having any stock if required urgently. Hence, JIT can be inflexible and expose the firm to greater risks.

Features of cradle-to-cradle design and manufacturing (AO2)

- **Cradle-to-cradle (C2C)** involves production techniques that are waste-free and can be efficiently recycled, for example recyclable plastic water bottles, plastic computer keyboards, and biodegradable bamboo t-shirts.
- The term was coined by Swiss architect Walter R Stahel in the 1970s when examining production techniques that are both efficient and waste free.
- All material inputs in C2C must be either technical (recyclable or reusable with no loss of quality) or biological (consumable or compostable in an ecologically friendly way).
- Although C2C can be time-consuming and expensive to implement effectively, it can provide competitive advantages by differentiating the brand, thereby attracting and retaining customers. C2C also provides sustainable manufacturing over the long term.
- In addition, C2C can generate a positive corporate image to some specific stakeholders, such as employees and environmental protection groups.

Features of quality control and quality assurance (AO2)

■ **Table 5.5** Features of quality control and quality assurance

Features of quality control	Features of quality assurance
• Traditional approach of using quality controllers to check the quality of output.	• **Quality assurance (QA)** uses workers, rather than inspectors, to check the quality of output.
• **Quality control (QC)** is mainly about inspecting and detecting substandard output (defects) rather than preventing it.	• All staff are responsible for quality so QA can therefore be considered as a form of job enrichment (see Chapter 2.4).
• Quality controllers randomly or systematically do the inspecting or checking.	• Firms have various codes of practice that notify customers of quality procedures and specifications.
• It strives to ensure that products meet the quality standards set by the organization.	• QA strives to achieve greater efficiency and less wastage.
• Firms set an acceptable level of wastage or defects (reject rate).	• The aim is zero defects, i.e. the reject rate is zero.
• QC is product orientated rather than process orientated.	• QA is process orientated rather than product orientated.
• QC is reactive rather than proactive, with quality checks done retrospectively.	• QA is proactive rather than reactive.

Methods of managing quality (AO2)

Quality circle

- US government statistician Professor W Edwards Deming (1900–93) noted that American management had typically given managers about 85 per cent of the responsibility for quality control, with only 15 per cent allocated to employees. He argued that this should be reversed.

- The emphasis of **quality circles** is preventing defects from arising in the first place, rather than quality control during post-production checks.

- Deming's ideas were originally developed by Japanese management and manufacturing techniques, with an emphasis on employees working in similar job roles being encouraged to investigate and suggest practices to improve quality.

- For quality circles to work, members must receive appropriate training in problem solving. In addition, senior management must be supportive and fund these teams appropriately, even when requests may seem trivial or budgets are limited.

- Kaizen usually involves the implementation of quality circles.

- A limitation of quality circles for employees is that senior management have a clear target for blame if there are quality issues or problems.

Benchmarking

- **Benchmarking** involves making internal and external comparisons of predetermined criteria (industry standards), with the aim of meeting or exceeding the benchmarks.

- Internal benchmarking involves comparing business practices within the same organization. Best practice is then spread throughout the organization.

- External benchmarking involves comparing business practices outside the organization with other firms considered to be the best in the industry. This approach can take up significant time and resources, to collect, collate and interpret the data and information.

- The ultimate aim of benchmarking is to improve performance. This helps a business to maintain or develop its competitiveness.

- As a strategic management tool, it enables managers to compare the firm's performance, its processes and its products with the best of other companies within the same industry.

- It is usually conducted at regular intervals, for example profits per quarter or market share per year.

- Benchmarks are typically quantifiable, for example star ratings for the hotel industry.

- For benchmarking to be meaningful, comparisons should be made as objectively as possible. However, there is scope for subjective comparisons, for example via customer perceptions and feedback. Importantly, it includes examining the competition from the point of view of customers.

Total quality management (TQM)

- **Total quality management (TQM)** is a philosophy about embedding awareness of quality in all organizational processes – it forms a culture of quality by empowering all workers within the organization to take responsibility for quality issues.

- An essential feature of TQM is zero defects, meaning lean production that is efficient and without any wastage.

Key terms

A **quality circle** is a small group of employees who voluntarily meet regularly to identify, examine, and solve problems related to their work, in order to improve the quality of output.

Benchmarking is the systematic process of comparing a business or its products to its competitors, using a set of standards (called 'benchmarks'), such as sales revenue, profits, labour turnover, or brand loyalty.

Total quality management (TQM) is a quality management approach that aims to involve every employee in the quality assurance process. It involves organization-wide approaches to quality improvements in products, process, people, and philosophy (organizational culture).

- TQM as a form of lean production commits the organization to continuous improvement (kaizen) and benchmarking of all operations relating to the quality of the product. Quality circles can also be a feature of TQM.

■ **Table 5.6** Advantages and disadvantages of TQM

Advantages of TQM	Disadvantages of TQM
• Motivational impact on employees who feel more involved in decision making. • Competitive advantages as it puts customers' needs at the centre of the production process. • Cost-effectiveness as TQM eliminates the need for inspections and the costs of reworking mistakes and defective output. • In the long term, quality is higher while costs should be reduced. • Brand reputation of emphasis on high quality and consistency.	• Requires a change in attitudes and commitment from all staff, which can be difficult to achieve. • Staff training, including management training, and development costs can be high, yet must be properly funded. • Not all workers are motivated by or are suitable for job enrichment and empowerment (see Chapter 2.4). • Accreditation fees paid to awarding bodies such as the International Organization for Standardization (ISO).

EXPERT TIP

Students often write that TQM systems remove complaints about quality. While TQM strives for zero defects, it does not and cannot guarantee that the output will be faultless. For example, toy manufacturer Mattel uses a TQM philosophy but has had to recall faulty products in the market.

The impact of lean production and TQM on an organization (AO3)

- The objective of lean production and TQM is to improve the quality of a firm's goods and services. Quality is a key source of global competitiveness.
- A quality product needs to be fit for purpose, i.e. the product fulfils its intended purpose and function, for example a pen should enable the user to write with it.
- Quality is important for an organization for several reasons:
  - satisfying the needs and wants of customers
  - raising consumer confidence regarding a business and its products
  - improving the motivation of employees
  - gaining a competitive advantage over its rivals
  - lowering production costs, hence higher profitability.
- Poor quality output will result in higher costs for the business due to customers seeking compensation for substandard products. Examples of poor quality include:
  - the product breaking down unexpectedly
  - the product being delivered late
  - a lack of instructions or directions for use.
- Ultimately, lean production and a culture of TQM give an organization competitive advantage over its rivals. Attracting customers and retaining their loyalty becomes easier as consumers trust reputable businesses and their brands.

The importance of national and international quality standards (AO2)

- National and international quality standards are a form of benchmark. A good or service must meet a set of predetermined criteria of quality in order to be awarded certification of quality standards recognized within the country or throughout the world.

- ISO 9000 is the international quality standard awarded to organizations that ensure their goods and services consistently achieve quality standards to meet the needs of customers.

- It is an internationally recognized quality accolade, awarded by the International Organization for Standardization (ISO).

- To be certified for ISO 9000, organizations must ensure there is evidence that quality is consistently improved.

■ **Table 5.7** Advantages and disadvantages of national and international quality standards

Advantages of meeting quality standards	Costs of meeting quality standards
• Quality standards can provide the firm with major marketing advantages. • They can help to differentiate the organization from its rivals, thus minimizing potential competition. • They provide opportunities to build brand loyalty and to charge higher prices. • Motivational impacts on workers who feel proud working for a business recognized for its quality.	• Operational costs of meeting national or international quality standards can be very high, e.g. funding staff training or buying the necessary technology. • Inspection costs must be paid to outside agencies such as the ISO. • There are ongoing costs of obtaining certification, licenses, or awards. • Some customers may be put off by the higher prices.

> **KEY CONCEPT**
>
> For an organization of your choice, investigate the impacts of **change** on its quality management.

5.4 Location

SL/HL content	Depth of teaching
The reasons for a specific location of production	AO2
The following ways of reorganizing production, both nationally and internationally: outsourcing/subcontracting, offshoring, insourcing, and reshoring	AO3

Diploma Programme *Business management guide* (May 2022)

The reasons for a specific location of production (AO2)

- To access cheaper and/or better-quality resources, such as land, labour, or raw materials.
- To be closer to customers domestically or in overseas markets to gain competitive advantages, for example easier access to customers and reduced transportation costs.
- To avoid trade protectionist policies (when foreign governments impose trade restrictions on imported goods) by locating in those overseas countries.
- To benefit from the local infrastructure (the essential physical and organizational structures in an economy that are necessary for it to function), for example transportation and communications networks.
- To benefit from government incentives for locating in a specific place, such as subsidies, grants, tax concessions, or interest-free loans. Such incentives are provided to firms that locate in assisted areas (locations identified by the government as being in need of regeneration, perhaps due to particularly high rates of unemployment).
- Due to **industrial inertia** – when a business continues to stay in the same location even when there are no financial advantages for doing so, for example due to well-established relationships with suppliers and locally based employees.
- To benefit from clustering – when a business locates near to other organizations that function in similar or complementary markets, for example shoe stores and clothes retailers.
- Firms in **bulk-reducing industries** locate near the source of raw materials in order to reduce transportation costs. For example, production plants are located near copper ore mines to reduce the weight (or bulk), so the transportation costs involved in making copper are also reduced.
- Firms in **bulk-gaining industries** locate near their customers because the finished product is bulkier (heavier) than the raw materials used to make it, as in the case of carbonated soft drinks.
- Qualitative factors also affect the location decision, for example the nature of the local infrastructure, and management preferences about a particular location.
- Traditional retailers such as restaurants and clothes stores need to be located near their customers.
- By contrast, a footloose organization is one that does not have any advantage to being located in any particular area, for example e-commerce businesses or computer chip makers.

Ways of reorganizing production, both nationally and internationally (AO3)

▨ Outsourcing (or subcontracting)

- **Outsourced** business activities are those deemed to be non-essential tasks that can be passed on to an external provider in order to cut costs and gain from their expertise.

Key term

Outsourcing is the practice of subcontracting non-core activities of an organization to a third-party provider (an external organization) in order to improve operational efficiency and reduce costs.

- The outsourced firms (known as **subcontractors**) carry out these activities more effectively and cost-effectively, with examples that include security firms, school and hospital caterers, office cleaners, and ICT technical support.

- Subcontractors are the people or organizations that carry out outsourced work more cost-effectively than the business itself, without compromising the quality.

■ **Table 5.8** Advantages and disadvantages of outsourcing

Advantages of outsourcing	Disadvantages of outsourcing
• Using an outsourced provider means the business can concentrate on its core activities and competitive strategy. • The firm benefits from the specialized services of the outsourced partner. • Improved customer service from subcontractors can attract new potential customers and strengthen brand loyalty. • It helps the firm to streamline its business operations, thereby cutting costs and improving its profitability.	• Potential conflict with external parties such as subcontractors can arise. • There could be quality issues with subcontractors. • The firm may have to deal with staff redundancies due to the use of outsourced providers. • There are costs to monitoring and maintaining relationships with the subcontractor.

Offshoring

- Examples of offshored functions include manufacturing, telesales, call centres, research and development (R&D), and accounting services.

- **Offshoring** can, but does not necessarily, involve third-party providers.

- The relocation decision requires the firm to consider both the risks and uncertainties of moving to unfamiliar territories and weighing these up against the potential rewards.

■ **Table 5.9** Advantages and disadvantages of offshoring

Advantages of offshoring	Disadvantages of offshoring
• As with outsourcing, offshoring means the firm can concentrate on and develop its core business activity. • Labour laws may be more relaxed overseas, making it easier to hire and fire staff. • Employee costs may be lower, resulting in lower prices for consumers and a boost in sales. • Relationships with local customers can be improved, as the workforce is accustomed to cultural issues and differences in the offshored country. • Lower operational costs can lead to higher profit margins.	• It is often associated with unethical practices, e.g. the exploitation of child labour in low-income countries. • There could be cultural issues and concerns about transferring functions to an external party. • It would involve making some employees redundant, which has to be handled with care and can be costly. • Overseas operations may lead to greater difficulties in conducting quality control. • The firm could lose some control over workers, as they are based overseas.

Insourcing

- **Insourcing** involves the retention of a task, function, or project within the organization.

- It is often delegated to internal stakeholders who have the expertise (such as ICT, accounting, or consultancy skills) rather than outsourcing the function to an external third-party provider.

Key terms

Offshoring is the practice of relocating part or all of a firm's business functions and processes overseas. These functions can remain within the business (operating in overseas markets) or be outsourced to an overseas organization.

Insourcing is the use of a firm's own resources to fulfil a certain role, function, or task which would otherwise have been outsourced.

- Insourcing happens because it can sometimes be cheaper and more productive to have the work done in-house.
- It has become popular with businesses that have been dissatisfied or unsuccessful with outsourcing, for example if they have experiencd substandard quality or supply chain disruptions.
- It is most suitable when the function, task, or project is only temporary, or when there is no significant capital investment involved.
- It is also suitable for smaller businesses and start-ups with little or no experience of outsourcing.

■ **Table 5.10** Advantages and disadvantages of insourcing

Advantages of insourcing	Disadvantages of insourcing
• Using existing employees and resources can be cheaper than outsourcing. • It enables a business to have better control of what it would have otherwise outsourced. • It helps to develop a team of skilled and experienced workers. • There is job creation in the local/domestic economy.	• Internal staff might not have the necessary skills or experience (external specialists may be more effective and productive). • Multinationals that want to establish or maintain their international presence cannot rely on insourcing. • Implementation costs are likely to be high, affecting profits at least in the short term.

■ Reshoring

Key term

Reshoring occurs when a business brings back production or other business functions into the home country from an overseas location.

- The main reasons for **reshoring** are concerned with cost and competitive advantages. For example, if labour costs in the overseas location have become unaffordable or uncompetitive.
- Another common reason for reshoring is for the domestic business to regain better control. For example, there may have been problems related to quality with previously offshored operations.
- The domestic government may also provide financial incentives for a business to reshore production or other aspects of business activity.
- Managers will usually consider the external environment (see STEEPLE analysis in the Business management toolkit chapter) when making reshoring decisions, such as the political climate in overseas locations.
- Unlike insourcing, reshoring can still make use of outsourcing (except the outsourced suppliers are located in the domestic economy).

■ **Table 5.11** Advantages and disadvantages of reshoring

Advantages of reshoring	Disadvantages of reshoring
• Being located in the home country means there is less risk of supply chain disruptions. • Shorter delivery times. • Greater certainty about the quality of inputs (resources) and outputs (goods and services). • Reduced costs, e.g. transportation, packaging, and communications.	• The initial upfront costs of reshoring can be extremely high. • Technical expertise and skilled labour may not be readily available in the domestic country. • Increased control of production processes puts additional demands and pressures on managers. • Reshoring does not take advantage of an ever more integrated and interrelated world.

> ## KEY CONCEPT
> Examine how the concepts of **ethics** and **change** have impacted the international location decisions of a business you have studied.

5.5 Break-even analysis

SL/HL content	Depth of teaching
Total contribution versus contribution per unit	AO2
A break-even chart and the following aspects of break-even analysis: break-even quantity/point, profit or loss, margin of safety, target profit output, target profit, and target price	AO2, AO4
The effects of changes in price or cost on the break-even quantity, profit, and margin of safety, using graphical and quantitative methods	AO2, AO4
Limitations of break-even analysis as a decision-making tool	AO3

Diploma Programme *Business management guide* (May 2022)

Total contribution versus contribution per unit (AO2)

Break even exists when a business sells enough goods and/or services in order to cover all its costs of production; this is the output level where the business does not make a profit or a loss.

> ## WORKED EXAMPLE
>
> Suppose an entrepreneur sells doughnuts and we are given the following information:
> - The price of each doughnut is $6.
> - The variable cost of each doughnut equals $2.
> - The rent for the doughnut stall is $400 per week.
>
> If the vendor only sells one doughnut, she earns $4 after paying the direct costs: $6 – $2 = $4. This is not profit, but **contribution per unit**. After all, she still has fixed costs to pay (rent for the doughnut stall) before declaring any profit.
>
> As fixed costs are $400, it means she has to sell 100 doughnuts to break even: $4 × 100 doughnuts = $400.
>
> Hence, to work out the **break-even quantity (BEQ)**, the following formula is used:
>
> $$\text{Break even} = \frac{\text{Fixed costs}}{\text{Selling price} - \text{Variable costs per unit}}$$
>
> - This means that a firm breaks even when its **total contribution** equals its total fixed costs.
> - By contrast, contribution per unit only considers the difference between the sales price of one unit and the variable costs needed to produce that unit of output.

Key terms

Contribution per unit refers to the amount of money a business earns from selling each unit of output. It is the difference between the selling price (P) and the average variable cost (AVC).

> Contribution per unit = P – AVC

The surplus is used to contribute towards the payment of fixed costs.

The **break-even quantity (BEQ)** refers to the amount of sales or output required to break even.

Total contribution is calculated by multiplying the unit contribution by the quantity sold. It is used to work out profit or loss.

> Total contribution = (P – AVC) × Q

Profit or loss can then be worked out by taking away fixed costs from total contribution.

Aspects of break-even analysis (AO2, AO4)

- Break-even analysis is a visual tool that enables managers to interpret the relationship between fixed costs, variable costs, price, revenues, and profits.
- It is a strategic decision-making tool. For example, if the analysis shows a very high break-even quantity (BEQ) with a very low margin of safety (MOS), the decision might be to refrain from implementing such a high-risk decision. The MOS is the difference between a firm's sales volume and its break-even quantity.

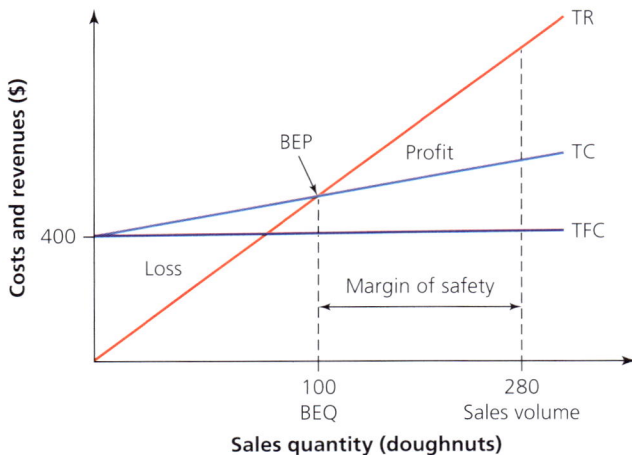

■ **Figure 5.3** Break-even chart for JT Doughnuts

- The model works well for the analysis of single-product firms.
- It is useful for analyzing and predicting the impacts of changes in the price on the profitability of the business.
- Similarly, it is useful for predicting the effects on profitability if the business changes its costs.

The following points refer to Figure 5.3 for a hypothetical business.

- Costs and revenues are measured along the y-axis, expressed in a given currency.
- The level of sales or output is shown along the x-axis, with an appropriate unit of measurement.
- The total fixed costs (TFC) line is drawn as a horizontal line because these costs do not change when the level of output or sales changes.
- The **break-even point (BEP)** occurs where total sales revenue (TR) equals total costs of production (TC).
- The break-even quantity (BEQ) is labelled on the x-axis, indicating the sales volume needed for the business to reach break even.
- Similarly, the break-even revenue is shown on the y-axis, representing the value of the output needed to break even.
- If the firm sells less than the BEQ, it makes a **loss**. If it sells more than the BEQ, the business earns a **profit**.
- If the firm sells 280 doughnuts in a week, but only needs to sell 100 to break even, its MOS is 180 doughnuts.

Key terms

The **break-even point (BEP)** is where the total costs of production equals the total revenue.

A **loss** occurs if total costs exceed total revenues: TC > TR.

Profit is the positive difference between a firm's total sales revenue (TR) and its total costs (TC). It is the reward for successful risk-taking in a business. Profit can be calculated in two ways:

Profit = TR – TC

or

Profit = Total contribution – TFC

EXPERT TIP

The y-axis should be correctly labelled as 'Costs and revenue ($)' and it should include an appropriate currency. The x-axis should be appropriately labelled too, so make sure to include the correct unit of measurement (such as tonnes, kilos, number of customers, or even doughnuts, depending on the context of the question). This is an area where students often have marks deducted, so pay attention to the labels and units of measurement.

EXPERT TIP

The margin of safety (MOS) is measured along the x-axis. This means the correct unit of measurement for the MOS is the units of output. Too often, students incorrectly express the MOS in terms of a currency.

EXAM PRACTICE QUESTION

VHS Cupcakes has variable costs of $0.25 per cupcake and sells them for $1.50 each. Its fixed costs are $10,000 per month. The business sells an average of 9,500 cupcakes per month.

a Calculate the contribution per unit for VHS Cupcakes. [2]

b Calculate how many cupcakes VHS Cupcakes must sell each month in order to break even. [2]

c Calculate the margin of safety for VHS Cupcakes. [2]

d Illustrate the above answers on an accurately plotted break-even chart. [5]

Key terms

Target profit is the desired or expected profit from a business, i.e. how much profit it aims to earn. It can be determined from a break-even chart by comparing the total cost and total revenue curves at each level of output.

Target profit output (or **target profit quantity**) refers to the sales volume (quantity) needed in order to reach a firm's target profit.

$$\text{Target profit quantity} = \frac{\text{Fixed cost} + \text{Target profit}}{\text{Price} - \text{Variable cost (per unit)}}$$

Target price is the amount charged to customers in order to reach break even (or any desired target profit). The target price for break even is found using the formula:

Target price = Average fixed cost + Average variable cost

or

Target price = (Total fixed cost ÷ Output) + Average variable cost

---

EXAM PRACTICE QUESTIONS

1 Calculate the total contribution required for Anson Miu & Co. based on the following data: Fixed costs = $10,000 per month and target profit = $35,000 per month. [2]

2 Li & Tse Jewellers has a target profit of $200,000 per year, earns a unit contribution of $500, and incurs fixed costs of $50,000. Calculate the target profit output for the firm. [2]

3 Bhadwarj Watches has fixed costs of $3,500 per month, direct costs of $120 per watch, a sales target of 60 watches per month, and a target profit of $2,500. Calculate the target price for Bhadwarj Watches. [2]

4 Paine & Co. Consultancy charges $500 per person for its training courses, with unit variable costs of $420. The firm's fixed costs are $12,000 per month.

    a Calculate how many people must pay for training with Paine & Co. Consultancy each month in order for the firm to reach break even. [2]

    b If Paine & Co. Consultancy has a target profit of $20,000, calculate how many people are required to pay for training courses each month. [2]

The effects of changes in price or cost on the break-even quantity, profit, and margin of safety, using graphical and quantitative methods (AO2, AO4)

- A higher price will reduce the break-even quantity. Diagrammatically, the total revenue (TR) line will be steeper due to the higher price, so break even occurs at a lower level of output.

- The opposite is true for a reduction in price, meaning the firm would have to sell more in order to break even.

- This also means that a higher price will reduce the margin of safety (because the firm reaches break even earlier). However, this assumes that the sales volume does not fall due to the increase in price (see Chapter 4.5 – price elasticity of demand).

- Higher costs of production (fixed and/or variable costs) will increase the break-even quantity.
  - Diagrammatically, the total cost line will be steeper if only variable costs increase.
  - It will shift upwards if there is an increase in fixed costs.

EXAM PRACTICE QUESTION

Study the data below for Alyssa Stephen's Fried Chicken Stand and answer the questions that follow.

- The price of each portion of fried chicken is $6.
- The variable costs of each portion of fried chicken are $2.
- Alyssa's rent is $400 per week.
- Sales quantity = 280 portions of fried chicken per week.
  - **a** Suppose Alyssa Stephen's Fried Chicken Stand raises its price to $7. Construct a fully labelled diagram to show the old and new break even following the firm's decision to raise its price. [6]
  - **b** Assuming there is no change in the demand for fried chicken at Alyssa Stephen's Fried Chicken Stand, calculate the new margin of safety. [2]

The limitations of break-even analysis (AO3)

- The model assumes that costs and revenues are static, meaning it assumes unchanging conditions in the market. In reality, variables such as inflation and interest rates will affect the forecasts (see STEEPLE analysis in the Business management toolkit chapter).

- Prices and costs are assumed to be constant, so the TR and TC lines are linear. In reality, a firm is likely to experience economies of scale (or diseconomies of scale) as its output level increases. Businesses are also likely to offer price discounts to customers who buy in bulk.

- It is not always easy to classify certain costs as being only fixed or only variable. For example, charges for electricity have a fixed element (minimum monthly charge) and a variable element (based on the level of energy use per month). Hence, this can create problems for the construction of break-even charts.

- As most businesses sell a range of products, this might require fixed costs to be allocated to different cost and profit centres (see Chapter 3.9). Therefore, break-even analysis might not be so useful for multi-product businesses.

- The effectiveness of the model depends on the accuracy of the data used. Prices and costs are only estimates (forecasts), which the business might not have computed accurately, thus limiting the usefulness of the predictions.

- The model also assumes that only one standard product is produced and sold by the business. For example, hotels have different prices for different types of rooms (which vary at different times of the week, month, and season), as well as other related services such as laundry and catering services.

- As a quantitative tool, break-even analysis ignores qualitative issues in decision making. For example, the impact of working at higher levels of output may cause huge amounts of stress and demotivation for employees.

BUSINESS MANAGEMENT TOOLKIT

Discuss the value of break-even analysis as part of a start-up company's business plan.

5.6 Production planning (HL only)

HL content	Depth of teaching
The local and global supply chain process	AO2
The difference between JIT and just in case (JIC)	AO3
Stock control charts based on the following: lead time, buffer stock, reorder level, and reorder quantity	AO2, AO4
Capacity utilization rate	AO2, AO4
Defect rate	AO2, AO4
Labour productivity, capital productivity, productivity rate, operating leverage	AO2, AO4
Cost to buy (CTB) and Cost to make (CTM)	AO3, AO4

Diploma Programme *Business management guide* (May 2022)

The local and global supply chain process (AO2)

- The **supply chain process** is the management process of overseeing the logistics from the manufacturing stage to the finished product being delivered to the consumer. This can happen at a local or global level.

- It includes managing the storage and movement of raw materials, semi-finished goods and finished goods from the raw material phase to the point of consumption.

- The process involves the sourcing, purchasing, and management of stock (raw materials, components, and finished products ready for sale), as well as the services from suppliers to customers (see Figure 5.4).

- At a local level, the supply chain process involves establishing relationships with suppliers and intermediaries located within a close geographical area, such as local suppliers and service providers in the same region.

- At a global level, the supply chain process involves establishing relationships with suppliers and intermediaries of materials, products, and services from around the world. This process is a lot more complex as it involves understanding the different regulatory and economic environments of different countries and the impact of international trade on global supply chains.

- A long supply chain and/or ineffective supply chain management can be costly, as it increases the chances of things going wrong for the business.

Manufacturer   Wholesaler   Distribution   Retailer   Consumers

■ **Figure 5.4** Example of the supply chain process

The difference between JIT and just in case (JIC) (AO3)

- JIT enables a business to get hold of raw materials and component parts only when the need arises. However, this also means that JIT relies on detailed production planning and scheduling.
- Having access to local and reliable suppliers is essential for JIT, as the system relies on an efficient stock ordering and delivery arrangement so that the inventory is ordered and arrives for the start of the production process.
- As no inventory is required in the operations process, JIT allows businesses to avoid the costs of storage, maintenance, and wastage.
- It is an important aspect of lean production (see Chapter 5.3), as it focuses on eliminating waste, defect rates, and delays in production. Hence, JIT can help to improve quality and levels of customer satisfaction.

■ **Table 5.12** Advantages and disadvantages of just in time

Advantages of just in time	Disadvantages of just in time
• There is no need for buffer stocks, thus cost of stock management is reduced.	• There is complete reliance on third-party suppliers.
• There is no need for stockpiling, thus improving cash flow and working capital.	• Administrative and implementation costs of JIT are high.
• JIT fosters lean production and productive efficiency.	• There is the inability to meet unexpected changes in demand.
• The above benefits combine to lower costs, so help to raise the firm's profits.	• Suppliers can charge premium prices for urgent deliveries of stocks.

Key term

Just in case (JIC) is a stock control system that relies on having spare stocks (inventory) so that output can be raised immediately in the event of a sudden or unexpected increase in demand.

- A **just-in-case (JIC)** stock control system is designed to have a reserve stock level (known as a **buffer stock**). The purpose of this is to ensure that sufficient resources are available to respond to any unforeseen problems or events.
- It ensures the firm has sufficient amounts of inventory to meet the demands of customers whenever required.
- Storage costs associated with JIC include insurance and maintenance and/or security to prevent damage or theft.
- JIC is best suited to stocks that are not perishable, such as cotton, rubber, ball bearings, or wines. It is less suitable for perishables, such as fresh flowers or fresh meat.
- It is not suitable for industries where customer trends and preferences are continually changing, for example in the fashion and high-tech industries.

■ **Table 5.13** Advantages and disadvantages of just in case

Advantages of just in case	Disadvantages of just in case
• There is flexibility to meet any sudden or unexpected rise in consumer demand. • It enables production to continue if there is a delay in deliveries from suppliers. • Customer satisfaction is maintained as they do not have to wait for stocks to arrive. • It prevents the potential loss of customers compared to when a JIT system is used. • Firms can benefit from purchasing economies of scale (bulk buying).	• There are higher costs for a JIC stock control system, due to the storage, maintenance, security, and insurance costs. • There is the risk of large volumes of stocks becoming obsolete. • Not all stocks or products may be sold, so there is wastage with JIC. • Stocks are subject to damage or theft. • There could be liquidity issues because JIC ties up valuable working capital.

EXAM PRACTICE QUESTION

Explain the difference between just-in-case (JIC) and just-in-time (JIT) stock control systems. [4]

Stock control charts (AO2, AO4)

Key term

A **stock control chart** is a graphical representation of the quantity of stock held by a business at different time periods.

- **Stock control charts** are used as a management tool to monitor and control the level of inventory held by a business.
- A typical stock control chart (see Figure 5.5) will show the quantity of stock held along the y-axis and the time period along the x-axis.
- The information in a stock control chart can be used to identify whether the business is overstocking, understocking, or holds the optimal level of stock. Hence, this tool helps businesses to have improved management of their inventory levels.

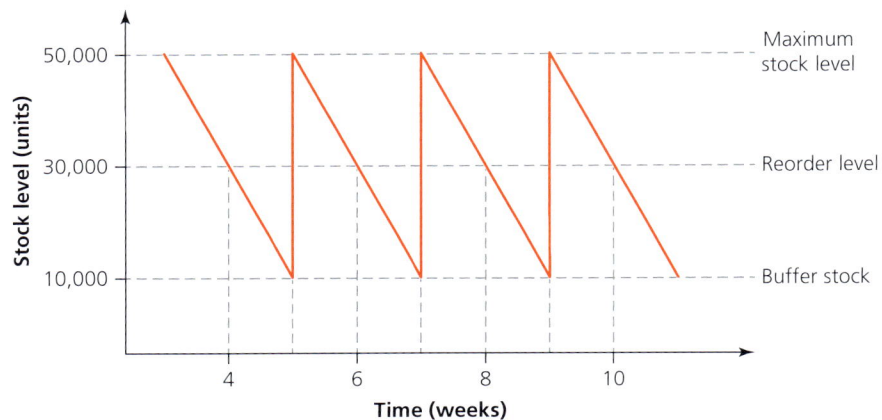

■ **Figure 5.5** Stock control chart

- The **lead time** refers to the length of time it takes between a firm ordering new stock and the firm receiving the stock for production. In Figure 5.5, the lead time is 1 week.
- The longer the lead time, the earlier the reorder needs to be and/or the larger the reorder quantity needs to be.
- **Buffer stock** is the minimum stock level held by a firm in case of unforeseen events, such as late deliveries from suppliers, damaged stock, or a sudden and unexpected increase in demand. In Figure 5.5, the buffer stock is 10,000 units.
- The **reorder quantity** is the volume of the order to replenish stocks. In Figure 5.5, the reorder quantity is 40,000 units (i.e. 50,000 minus 10,000 units).

- The **reorder level** refers to the stock level at the time when the firm places its reorder of stock. In Figure 5.5, this occurs when the firm's stock level reaches 30,000 units.

- The **usage rate** refers to the speed at which stocks (inventories) are depleted in the production process. The usage rate increases during peak periods but drops during recessions and off-peak periods. In Figure 5.5, the usage rate is 40,000 units per 2 weeks (or 20,000 units per week).

- A **stock-out** occurs when a firm has no more stock for production or sale, in other words when it is out of stock. This creates problems for the firm as production also comes to a stop. To prevent a stock-out, some businesses buy extra stock prior to peak trading periods.

- Conversely, **stockpiling** means that a business builds up excessive levels of inventory. However, holding too much stock results in working capital being tied up.

EXAM PRACTICE QUESTION

Study the stock control chart for Beyond Bakeries below, in order to determine the following:

a the lead time   [1]
b the buffer stock   [1]
c the reorder quantity.   [1]

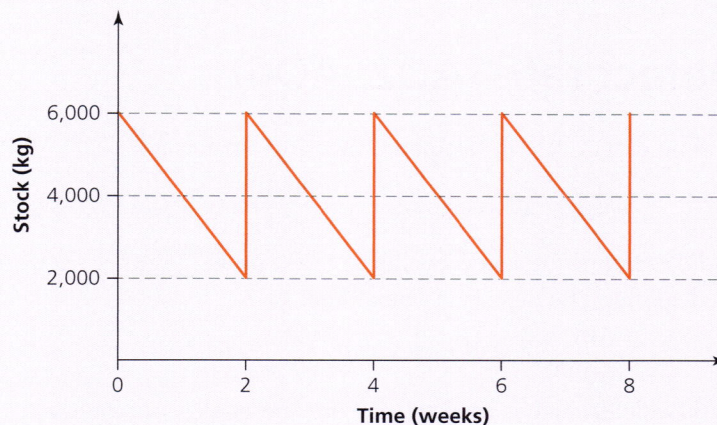

Capacity utilization rate (AO2, AO4)

Key term

The **capacity utilization rate** expresses a firm's actual output as a percentage of its maximum potential output, at a particular point in time.

- Capacity utilization measures the extent to which a firm is operating at its maximum potential level.

- It can be calculated by using the following formula:

$$\text{Capacity utilization rate} = \frac{\text{Actual output}}{\text{Productive capacity}} \times 100$$

- A business that has a 100 per cent **capacity utilization rate** is operating at full capacity, with all its resources being used.

- Capacity utilization for a business operating at full capacity, or experiencing high growth rates, can be improved by subcontracting work (see Chapter 5.4).

■ **Table 5.14** Advantages and disadvantages of full capacity utilization

Advantages of full capacity utilization	Disadvantages of full capacity utilization
• Average (unit) costs of production are likely to be at their lowest, so the business is operating efficiently. • Lower costs per unit (economies of scale) will likely lead to higher profits for the firm.	• Employees can become overworked and stressed due to working at full capacity. • Machinery and equipment are likely to deteriorate at a faster pace, which increases maintenance and replacement costs.

EXAM PRACTICE QUESTIONS

1 a Calculate the capacity utilization rate for Tartinelli Milk Company, which can produce 200,000 pints of milk in its factory each day, but has an output level of 180,000 pints per day. [2]

  b Calculate Odegaard Cheese Company's capacity utilization rate if it produces 2,800 kilos per month, but has a maximum productive capacity of 3,500 kilos per month. [2]

2 Zinchenko Foods Inc. has fixed costs of $10,000 and a productive capacity of 5,000 units per month. Calculate the change in the firm's average fixed costs if it operates at only 80 per cent capacity compared to operating at full capacity. [4]

Defect rate (AO2, AO4)

- The **defect rate** is calculated by using the formula:

$$\text{Defect rate} = \frac{\text{Defective items}}{\text{Total items produced}} \times 100$$

- For example, if a firm produces 1,000 units of output each week and 15 units are defective, the defect rate would be:

$$\frac{15}{1,000} = 0.015, \text{ or } 1.5\%$$

- The defect rate is used to measure the quality of a product. In general, the lower the defect rate, the higher the level of quality of the product.

- Calculating the defect rate is important, as it helps businesses to identify any problems in quality control and quality assurance (see Chapter 5.3), because high defect rates are costly.

- Lowering the defect rate is crucial for an organization's reputation and profitability.

> **Key term**
>
> The **defect rate** measures the number of faulty or substandard items as a percentage of the total number of items produced. The lower the defect rate, the better this is for producers and consumers.

EXAM PRACTICE QUESTION

Kinetic Bearings Inc. produces 2.5 million ball bearings per month in its factory. An average of 500 ball bearings are of substandard quality. Calculate the firm's defect rate. [2]

Labour productivity, capital productivity, productivity rate, operating leverage (AO2, AO4)

- **Productivity** is a measure of the efficiency of production. Examples of such measures include labour productivity, capital productivity, the productivity rate, and operating leverage.

- **Labour productivity**, for example, is a measure of the efficiency of workers in an organization. The most common measure of labour productivity uses the following formula to calculate output per worker:

$$\frac{\text{Output per period (units)}}{\text{Number of employees at work}}$$

- Labour productivity can also be measured by sales revenue per worker, or the volume produced per labour hour. Labour-intensive firms prefer to use this measure of productivity.

- Labour productivity matters because labour costs are usually a significant part of a firm's total costs.

- Similarly, **capital productivity** measures how efficiently a firm's non-current assets generate output for the business. Capital-intensive firms prefer to use this measure of productivity.

- The capital productivity rate is calculated by using the formula:

$$\text{Capital productivity} = \frac{\text{Total output}}{\text{Capital input}}$$

- The **productivity rate** measures the amount of output generated per unit of input. It is calculated by using the formula:

$$\text{Productivity rate} = \frac{\text{Total output}}{\text{Total input}} \times 100$$

- The higher the productivity rate, the more efficient the business is. This is important, as there is a positive correlation between a firm's efficiency level and its profitability and competitiveness.

- **Operating leverage** is a measure of how an increase in a firm's sales volume will affect its operating profit (profit before interest and tax).

- It is calculated by using the following formula:

$$\text{Operating leverage} = \frac{\text{Quantity} \times (\text{Price} - \text{Variable cost per unit})}{\text{Quantity} \times (\text{Price} - \text{Variable cost per unit}) - \text{Fixed costs}}$$

Or simplified as:

$$\text{Operating leverage} = \frac{\text{Sales} - \text{Variable costs}}{\text{Profits}}$$

- The formula for operating leverage shows that if a firm generates enough sales to cover its fixed costs, it will earn a profit.

- Operating leverage is lower if any variable helps to improve a firm's profits, for example higher sales volume (quantity sold), higher price (as the firm reaches break even quicker), or lower average variable costs.

- Similarly, a high operating leverage means that a small increase in sales will have a large impact on the firm's profits, while a low operating leverage indicates that a large increase in sales is needed to have an impact on the profits.

- Operating leverage also helps investors to analyze the risk and rewards associated with an organization as it measures the ability of the firm to generate profits from its sales. In particular, high operating leverage indicates relatively high risk, and vice versa.

EXAM PRACTICE QUESTION

Arteta Trading Co. sells an average of 1,000 units of output each month at a selling price of $20. Its variable cost per unit is $8 and the monthly fixed costs are $8,000.

a   Calculate the company's operating leverage.   [2]

b   Comment on what this figure shows.   [2]

EXPERT TIP

While productivity is important, it can be difficult to measure the output in some professions, for example in the cases of public sector workers such as teachers, firefighters, nurses, and doctors. For these occupations, the quality of service is regarded as more important than output or profits.

EXAM PRACTICE QUESTIONS

1   SWCH Co. produces $500,000 worth of output in one week in a total of 1,000 labour hours. Calculate the firm's labour productivity rate.   [2]

2   The 25 sales employees at TIL Co. manage to sell $120,000 worth of goods in one week. Calculate the company's labour productivity rate.   [2]

Cost to buy (CTB) and Cost to make (CTM) (AO3, AO4)

> **Key term**
>
> A **make or buy decision** is a management decision that involves choosing whether to manufacture a product (make) or to purchase it (buy) from an external supplier. Essentially, it is a decision about whether to insource or outsource production.

- A **make or buy decision** requires managers to compare the cost to make (CTM) with the cost to buy (CTB).
- If the CTM is greater than the CTB, then it makes financial sense for the business to buy the product instead of producing it, and vice versa.
- The CTB a product from a supplier is calculated by the formula:

  CTB = Price × Quantity

- The CTM a product is calculated by the formula:

  CTM = Fixed costs + Variable costs

- Quantitative methods that can be used to help with decisions about the CTM and CTB include break-even analysis (see Chapter 5.5) and investment appraisal (see Chapter 3.8).
- However, this quantitative decision-making tool does not typically consider non-quantitative factors as these are difficult to measure, for example quality issues, reliability and reputation of suppliers, the impact on the workforce, and the level of experience and expertise of employees.

EXAM PRACTICE QUESTION

Organic Fruit Bars Ltd can purchase equipment for $25,000 intended for in-house production. It can manufacture the goods for $1 each. Alternatively, a local supplier can produce these for $1.50 each. Demand for the fruit bars is forecast to be 45,000 units. Suggest whether it is better for Organic Fruit Bars Ltd to make or buy.   [3]

5.7 Crisis management and contingency planning (HL only)

HL content	Depth of teaching
The difference between crisis management and contingency planning	AO2
The factors that affect effective crisis management: transparency, communication, speed, and control	AO2
The impacts of contingency planning for a given organization or situation in terms of: cost, time, risks, and safety	AO3

Diploma Programme *Business management guide* (May 2022)

■ **Figure 5.6** A fire is one example of a crisis in the workplace

The difference between crisis management and contingency planning (AO2)

- Crisis management is the response taken by a business in the event of an actual crisis occurring.

- Contingency planning is the development of predetermined strategies to deal with a crisis, should it ever occur.

- Examples of crises include financial crises, economic recession, severe weather conditions, power failure, major product recalls, the outbreak of infectious diseases, fire, employees on strike, and natural disasters.

■ **Table 5.15** Features of crisis management and contingency planning

Crisis management	Contingency planning
• Focuses on how an organization responds to an actual crisis, especially one that threatens its survival.	• Involves formulating risk assessments in order to be better prepared for crises, should they ever occur.
• Emphasis is placed on dealing with actual catastrophes (threats and disasters) that businesses face.	• Uses scenario planning, i.e. examining 'what if' scenarios and developing continuity plans to minimize the impacts of a crisis if it occurs.
• Focuses on the way in which an organization responds with its various stakeholder groups during a crisis situation.	• Involves devising actionable plans and making the effort to minimize the negative impacts of potential crises.

EXPERT TIP

Make sure you can distinguish between contingency planning and crisis management. The former helps to prepare a business to deal with crises should they ever occur. This differs from crisis management, which is about responding to a real crisis.

Factors that affect effective crisis management (AO2)

The fundamental factors affecting the effectiveness of crisis management include transparency, communication, speed, and control.

◼ Transparency

Key terms

Quantifiable risks are financially measurable threats that can jeopardize the survival of an organization. For example, there is a statistically low chance of a fire breaking out in a hospital, but a much higher likelihood of taxi drivers being involved in a motor accident.

Unquantifiable risks are factors that can threaten the survival of an organization, but are extremely difficult to measure or calculate, for example the threat of a terrorist attack or the outbreak of a new infectious disease.

- Transparency is about the ethical obligation of businesses to be honest and to inform their stakeholders of the truth during a crisis.

- Most risks in business are **quantifiable risks** – for example, the costs of theft or fire damage to a factory. However, not all risks are easily quantifiable – for example, the costs following the outbreak of an infectious disease. This is because **unquantifiable risks** are prohibitively expensive to calculate and highly unlikely to happen.

- Transparency about the truth can help a business to maintain its integrity, reputation and public perceptions, especially if the crisis was beyond the firm's control.

- Employees, the general public, and the media are far more forgiving if a business owns up to its mistakes and responds with transparency and honesty.

◼ Communication

- During and after a crisis, public relations (PR) plays an important role in communicating with and reassuring all stakeholders.

- Prompt and effective communication with stakeholders is vital in a crisis – contacting the emergency services, informing employees, notifying insurers, and communicating appropriately with the media.

- Speedy and honest communication is important to prevent a possible loss of goodwill and a public relations crisis.

- Within the organization, a specialist media or PR team is often used to communicate with the general public, politicians, and the mass media.

- Communicating corporate social responsibility (see Chapter 1.3) is an important part of crisis management. It might not always be necessary to communicate with the general public, although all responses and actions must be implemented in a socially responsible way.

◼ Speed

- A speedy response is essential in order to contain the crisis and to ensure it is not prolonged or worsened by causing collateral damage.

- A swift strategy applied with common sense can prevent huge expenses resulting from a crisis. As an example, BP was slow in responding to an oil spillage in the Gulf of Mexico in 2010, and the company lost 3.19 million barrels of oil and was fined a record $14 bn.

- Speed is far less of an issue if the organization has adequate preparation and simulation through its contingency planning.

- Speed also means the business acts quickly before a biased or untruthful version of the issue gets reported by others in the media, which could potentially lead to greater problems that the organization has even less control over.

- Speed also helps to pre-empt or prevent a crisis from actually occurring.

- A speedy response, backed by honest actions, helps to return the matter to normality.

Control

- Crises can be preventable. For example, contingency planning not only helps a business to be better prepared in the event of a real fire, but helps to prevent fires from actually occurring.
- Quantifiable risks are measurable risks, for example the damage or theft of commercial property. These risks mean that control is a vital factor that affects the effectiveness of crisis management.
- To ensure effective control, it is important for the business to select a suitable team to handle a crisis.
- Control of the situation is vital, especially as bad news will spread extremely quickly via social networks and social media (see Chapter 4.5).

The impacts of contingency planning for a given organization or situation in terms of cost, time, risks, and safety (AO3)

■ **Table 5.16** Advantages and disadvantages of contingency planning

Factor	Advantages	Disadvantages
Cost	Business continuity becomes top priority during a crisis. Contingency funds and emergency financial aid can help to deal with the costs of a crisis. Effective planning can help to minimize losses incurred.	The costs of dealing with a crisis can be huge. It uses up valuable management time and resources. Having insurance does not necessarily cover unquantifiable risks associated with crises.
Time	A properly prepared contingency plan is essential for being prepared to manage a crisis.	The incident planned for might never happen, so crisis planning can be a waste of time and money.
Risks	Enables businesses to be better prepared to deal with setbacks should a crisis ever occur. Planning helps to reduce the risks arising from a crisis.	The plans cannot fully prepare firms for the actual impacts of natural disasters or other crises. It is not realistic for businesses to account for all possible risks.
Safety	Contingency planning can ensure the safety of employees in the event of a crisis. It also helps to protect and reassure customers.	There are opportunity costs involved to ensure contingency plans cover all aspects of safety. There are implementation costs of ensuring safety in the workplace.

EXPERT TIP

Be sure to know the link between crises and contingency plans. Although contingency plans can help with business continuity plans (created to deal with crises), the crises themselves are unpredictable so are disruptive and costly to the organization (otherwise they would not be classified as crises).

KEY CONCEPT

Investigate the role of **ethics** in contingency planning and crisis management for a business of your choice.

EXAM PRACTICE QUESTION

In December 2022, Ford Motor Company announced it would recall over 634,000 sports utility vehicles (SUVs) worldwide due to fuel leaks and fire risks. The recall was announced to prevent increasing the risk of injury to drivers and passengers. Ford acted quickly to reassure customers that the faulty fuel injectors would be replaced by dealers free of charge, and that fires were rare. Owners were also given the option of a courtesy loan car while their SUV was in for repairs at a Ford dealership. The company also admitted to receiving 43 legal claims attributed to the problem.

a   Identify **two** stakeholder groups from the case study.   [2]

b   Explain why a product recall is an example of a crisis.   [4]

c   Explain why crisis management and contingency planning are important to global multinational companies such as Ford Motor Company.   [4]

5.8 Research and development (HL only)

HL content	Depth of teaching
The importance of research and development for a business	AO3
The importance of developing goods and services that address customers' unmet needs (of which the customers may or may not be aware)	AO2
Intellectual property protection: copyrights, patents, and trademarks	AO2
Innovation: incremental and disruptive	AO2

Diploma Programme *Business management guide* (May 2022)

The importance of research and development for a business (AO3)

Key term

Research and development (R&D) is the systematic process of discovering new knowledge about products, processes, and markets, and then applying the knowledge to make new and improved goods and services to fulfil market needs.

- **Research** focuses on creating new knowledge and new products. It is a prerequisite to development.

- **Development** is about adapting existing ideas and products to create commercially viable products. Its primary function is to improve new commercially viable products, helping to increase the firm's future earning potential.

- **Research and development (R&D)** is important for the longevity and competitiveness of a business, irrespective of the sector in which it operates (primary, secondary, tertiary, or quaternary).

- R&D is an essential part of innovation (the commercialization of a business idea that appeals to consumers).

- Competitive rivalry in an industry can drive firms to spend more on R&D in order to survive in the long term.

- Market leaders often use R&D expenditure as a barrier to entry so that they can continue to dominate the industry, as with airline manufacturers such as Airbus and Boeing, for example.

■ **Table 5.17** Advantages and disadvantages of R&D

Advantages of R&D	Disadvantages of R&D
• It can improve a firm's productivity rate (see Chapter 5.6). • It can enhance a firm's corporate image, e.g. brand perception as an innovator. • It can help to gain a first-mover advantage or achieve a competitive advantage. • Premium prices can be charged. • R&D expenditure can prolong a product's life cycle (see Chapter 4.5). • R&D does not necessarily lead to higher prices, as the discovery of more efficient operations methods can help to cut prices.	• There is an opportunity cost of spending large sums of money on R&D. • There is no guarantee that the R&D expenditure will be recouped due to the high failure rate of product launches. • R&D can be very time consuming in some industries, such as pharmaceuticals. • Rivals might spend more money on R&D, thus wiping out any advantages for the firm. • R&D is not always applicable to all firms, such as those that make budget laptops, as R&D can result in higher costs and prices.

EXPERT TIP

Although the terms 'research' and 'development' are usually used together, make sure you are able to distinguish the meanings of the two terms. Also, note that answers in the exam can be enhanced by using real-world examples of innovations.

The importance of developing goods and services that address customers' unmet needs (of which the customers may or may not be aware) (AO2)

- Many product ideas fail to get commercialized because:
  - there are legal and administrative barriers which discourage R&D expenditure
  - the amount of money needed to fund successful R&D is often unaffordable
  - the market size for the product might be too small to justify the required amount of R&D expenditure
  - the product does not meet the needs or desires of the market, perhaps due to a lack of market research (see Chapter 4.4).
- Market research enabled Samsung, for example, to become the market leader in the smartphone industry, as the company developed phones with larger screen sizes (something that Apple seemingly didn't recognize as an unmet need of the market).
- R&D addresses the fact that not all unmet needs are known by customers. Steve Jobs famously said that Apple would create a product that everyone would want, despite no one knowing they would want it (the iPod, which went on to revolutionize the whole music industry).
- To test whether a new product addresses the unmet needs of customers, businesses often develop a **prototype**. This refers to trial products that are made prior to the final development of a product that is ready for commercial launch in the market.

Intellectual property protection: copyrights, patents, and trademarks (AO2)

- Intellectual property (IP) refers to anything created by someone using their mental intellect (mind), such as pieces made by an artist, musician, or inventor.
- A person or business can register and pay for the intellectual property rights (IPR) of their works or creation. This gives the owner legal protection to stop others from copying or stealing it. This publication is protected by international copyright legislation, for example.
- The main reasons or benefits of IP protection are to:
  - establish a unique selling point or distinctive competitive advantage
  - minimize the threat of competition
  - maximize return on investment spent on R&D.
- The main intellectual property protection are copyrights, patents, and trademarks.

Copyrights

- Copyrights refer to the legal protection of original works of authorship. This covers creative works such as advertising, computer software, films, manuals, music, novels, paintings, photographs, promotional literature, radio broadcasts, reports, sculptures, songs, television broadcasts, and textbooks.
- Users of copyrighted materials need prior permission depending on licensing laws. In some cases, the use of copyrighted works involves the user paying royalties or a fee to the copyright owner.
- Infringement of copyright laws is a criminal offence in some countries.

Patents

- Patents are a type of intellectual property protection that relates to inventions and innovations.
- They provide the owner of the IP exclusive use of the intangible asset for a finite period of time.
- The owner of a patent owns the IPR so can take legal action against anyone who uses the invention or innovation without their prior permission.
- However, patents can be difficult and expensive to obtain.

Trademarks

- A **trademark** is any mark (such as a symbol, image, word, or phrase) that is legally registered to an organization or its products. Examples include Nike's 'swoosh' logo and McDonald's golden arches.
- A business protects its brands (the names of its products) by registering trademarks for these with the authorities.
- As with all forms of IP, the registered owner of a trademark can take legal action against anyone who uses the brand, logo, or slogan of the business without its permission. Counterfeit products infringe the IP protection of registered trademarks.

Innovation: incremental and disruptive (AO2)

- **Innovation** is the successful commercial creation of a new business idea or product, which adds value to the organization. The purpose is to create or fulfil existing needs and desires that are not currently being satisfied.

- **Incremental innovation** is about adjusting and improving something that already exists.
  - This takes place incrementally (in stages). For example, Apple's iPad Mini was developed from the original, larger-sized iPad.
  - Many workplaces had to introduce incremental changes due to the COVID-19 pandemic, such as measures to allow employees to work from home.

- **Disruptive innovation** is about creating a new product or process. For example, Apple's iTunes Store changed the way consumers around the world buy their music, movies, and games.
  - It occurs in a radical manner, creating a whole new market. This can disrupt the market dominance of leaders in the existing markets.
  - Examples include Uber disrupting the taxi market, Airbnb disrupting the holiday accommodation market, and budget airline carriers disrupting the commercial air-travel industry.

- The underlying difference between incremental innovation and disruptive innovation is the pace and degree of change involved in the innovation process.

EXPERT TIP

While disruptive innovation can create huge competitive advantages for a business, radical changes do not always work better than incremental innovation, especially if such changes cause huge disruptions, anxieties, and uncertainty for employees.

BUSINESS MANAGEMENT TOOLKIT

Investigate how the **culture** of a multinational company, such as Google or Apple, has shaped its corporate strategy. You may find it useful to refer to Hofstede's cultural dimensions in your response.

5.9 Management information systems (HL only)

HL content	Depth of teaching
Data analytics	AO1
Database	AO1
Cybersecurity and cybercrime	AO1
Critical infrastructures, including artificial neural networks, data centres, and cloud computing	AO2
Virtual reality	AO2
The Internet of Things	AO2
Artificial intelligence	AO2
Big data	AO2
Customer loyalty programmes	AO3

HL content	Depth of teaching
The use of data to manage and monitor employees; Digital Taylorism	AO3
The use of data mining to inform decision making	AO3
The benefits, risks, and ethical implications of advanced computer technologies (collectively referred to here as 'management information systems') and technological innovation on business decision making and stakeholders	AO3

Diploma Programme *Business management guide* (May 2022)

Data analytics (AO1)

- **Data analytics** is the process of analyzing, developing, and transforming data to extract useful information and draw meaningful conclusions in order to support decision making.

- It involves the use of various statistical methods and tools such as machine learning to analyze data from various sources to make predictions or decisions.

- To carry out data analytics, specialists need to have a good understanding of the data, including its composition, quality, and limitations. As with all forecasting tools, the predictions are only as good as the data used to make such projections.

- The use of descriptive statistics (such as infographics, bar charts, and pie charts) is an important aspect of data analytics, as these help to present data in an easy-to-understand format.

- The exponential rise in the amount of data available means that more sophisticated tools are needed to make data analytics more accessible and effective for business decision making.

- Managers use data analytics to make more informed decisions and to improve operational efficiency. This helps the business to gain competitive advantages.

Database (AO1)

- A database is a computerized and structured collection of data that are stored and organized in a way that allows for the efficient retrieval, use, and management of the data.

- Databases can be physically hosted on the premises of the business, or online in the cloud (see later in this section). There are many cloud-based databases available, such as Amazon's Relational Database Service (RDS) and Google's Cloud SQL (Structured Query Language) databases.

- However, the storage of such huge volumes of private data means there is an increasing need for data integrity and security. Techniques such as data encryption and backups are used to protect sensitive information and to protect the interest of businesses and their clients.

- Databases can be integrated with other aspects of management information systems (MIS), such as data analytics and data visualization software tools, to provide insights and support business decision making.

- With the rise of big data (see later in this section) and advanced techniques of data analytics, databases have become increasingly important for managing and extracting (or mining) value from large and complex data sets.

Cybersecurity and cybercrime (AO1)

- Cybercrime refers to any criminal activities that are committed using the internet or other forms of online or digital platforms. Examples of cyber threats include hacking, identity theft, phishing scams, viruses, malware (malicious software), ransomware, and cyberstalking.

- Cybercriminals target individuals, businesses, or government organizations and can steal or destroy sensitive and private information, disrupt their operations, or extort money (bribery).

- To prevent potential crises, businesses need be aware of the risks associated with cybercrime and have policies and procedures in place to protect their assets and data (by using appropriate cybersecurity measures). Effective contingency plans will help businesses to respond to a cyberattack, should it occur, and minimize the impact of such an incident.

- Businesses face an increasing need to educate their managers and employees about the threats of cybercrime and the importance of maintaining cybersecurity.

- Cybersecurity refers to the management process of protecting an organization's internet-connected systems, including its hardware, software, and data, from cyberattacks. This includes theft, damage, or unauthorized access to private data.

- In an increasingly integrated and digital world, businesses need to regularly review and update their security procedures and protocols to ensure they are keeping pace with evolving cyber threats. Examples include:

  - having appropriate security measures in place (such as firewalls, regular software updates, anti-virus software, and other methods of security management systems) to protect against cyber threat

  - training employees regarding the need to have strong passwords as a basic step that can be taken to improve cybersecurity

  - using the professional services of a cybersecurity provider or consultant to help the business to identify and mitigate risks of cybercrimes.

- Cybercrime is a global issue and businesses should be aware that they may be subject to laws and regulations in numerous jurisdictions, requiring them to protect the private information of their employees, customers, suppliers, and other stakeholders.

- Very importantly, businesses need to have contingency plans (see Chapter 5.7) in place to respond to any form of cybercrime, including measures to contain the attack, assess the damage, and recover from the attack.

Critical infrastructures, including artificial neural networks, data centres, and cloud computing (AO2)

- Critical infrastructures refer to the systems and structures that are necessary for the efficient functioning of an organization. Examples include artificial neural networks (ANN), data centres, and cloud computing.

- The extent to which an organization's management information system is effective depends on the infrastructure that lies behind it. This will also determine how well the organization is able to protect itself against potential cybercrimes.

- Given the growing importance of data, this means the organization's critical infrastructure becomes even more significant.
- Artificial neural networks (ANNs) are an aspect of computing systems that are designed to simulate how the human brain processes and analyzes data and information.
  - Examples include image and speech recognition.
  - ANNs make predictions based on large sets of data, such as market trends and financial performance.
  - Hence, ANNs help managers with decision making and improve the overall performance of a business.
- Data centres are physical facilities that store large amounts of data, such as telecommunications and storage systems.
  - They are crucial to the operation of many businesses as they store and process vast amounts of data to support problem solving and decision making.
  - A key limitation of data centres is that they require significant investments in hardware, software, and infrastructure, such as power and cooling systems, security measures, and stable telecommunications connectivity.
- Cloud computing refers to the delivery of computing resources and services via the internet. Examples include the storage and retrieval of data, processing power, and software.
  - It allows businesses to access and use these cloud resources and services on demand, without the need to invest in and maintain their own critical infrastructures.
  - Data and applications are stored and processed by a third-party provider.
  - However, cybersecurity is a major threat for critical infrastructures such as cloud computing, which is often targeted by cybercriminals looking to steal sensitive and private data or to disrupt the operations of a business.
- The growing use of and reliance on critical infrastructures mean that there can be major consequences if these are attacked, damaged, or destroyed. Such consequences include disruptions to the organization's operations, as well as financial losses. Hence, it is vital that a firm's critical infrastructures, be they physical or virtual, are maintained, updated, and protected with the latest security measures and technologies.

Virtual reality (AO2)

- **Virtual reality** (VR) is the use of computer-generated environments that enable users to immerse themselves and interact in simulated settings in real-time.
- VR can be used for a variety of business applications, such as staff training and development (see Table 5.18).
- The market for VR is expected to grow rapidly, driven by continual advances in technology and increasing demand from businesses across many industries. For example, VR is becoming more popular in marketing as it allows advertisers and marketers to create brand-immersive experiences and product demonstrations that engage potential customers.
- A key benefit for businesses that use VR is that it provides a safe and controlled environment for employees to learn, practice, and develop a range of essential skills, such as pilots in simulated flights or surgeons performing virtual operations.
- A limitation of VR is that it requires significant capital expenditure on specialized computer hardware and software, as well as data storage.

■ **Table 5.18** Examples of VR in the business world

Examples of VR in the business world
• Architecture and construction, such as virtual walkthroughs of buildings.
• Immersive experiences such as movies and music concerts in the entertainment industry.
• Medical and health care services, such as simulated surgeries.
• Product visualization, design, and prototyping.
• Sports and fitness training for individuals and professional athletes.
• Virtual educational visits to historical/famous landmarks.
• Virtual tours of properties (real estate).

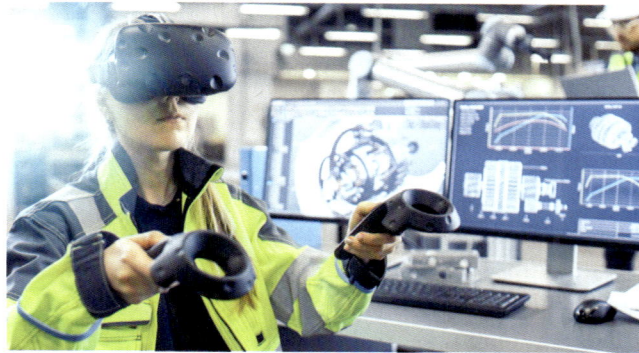

■ **Figure 5.7** An industrial engineer using a VR headset for industrial design and prototyping

The Internet of Things (AO2)

- The **Internet of Things** (IoT) refers to the network of interconnected devices and appliances over the internet.

- These devices and appliances (such as smartphones and smart home devices) are also able to collect, analyze, and share data.

- IoT devices use sensors, embedded processors, and communication technologies (such as Wi-Fi, Bluetooth, and cellular networks) to connect with each other.

- The connectivity enables users to control IoT devices remotely, allowing for improved efficiency, cost savings, and new business opportunities.

- The use of IoT devices, such as customers interacting with their Alexa smart speakers, can lead to a vast amount of data (see the section on big data below). This can be used by businesses to gain a better understanding of the needs and preferences of their customers.

- However, IoT devices can be vulnerable to cyberattacks. Therefore, cybersecurity and data privacy are major concerns for businesses that use and rely on the IoT.

- Also, as IoT technologies are continually evolving, businesses need to be aware of the latest devices and applications so as to be able to take advantage of the opportunities offered. However, this can be rather time consuming and expensive for an organization to execute.

- In addition, the IoT requires well-designed critical infrastructures, which include the hardware, software, networking, and other aspects of management information systems.

Artificial intelligence (AO2)

- **Artificial intelligence** (AI) refers to management information systems that enable the simulation of human intelligence in machines that are programmed to think and learn in similar ways to human beings.

- AI is intended to develop the ability of machines to replicate and perform any intellectual task that a human can, such as navigating maps, processing natural language, and scientific decision making.

- AI is used in a wide range of industries (for example education, finance, health care, retail, and transportation) to improve efficiency and decision making by analyzing and interpreting large amounts of data.

- Machine learning (ML) is an aspect of AI that allows management information systems to learn from big data and improve their performance and decision making without the need to be explicitly programmed.

- However, AI requires large volumes of data and powerful computing systems to operate and facilitate ML. AI systems can also be vulnerable to biases if the data used are not representative.

- As AI is only one aspect of MIS, it is often integrated with other systems such as big data, data mining, data analytics, and IoT in order to provide comprehensive solutions for an organization to manage and analyze business information to support business decision making.

Big data (AO2)

- **Big data** refers to the large and complex sets of data that are generated by business activity and which are difficult to process or manage using traditional methods. The data can be generated from a variety of sources, including social media platforms, IoT devices, and business transactional systems.

- Big data therefore requires efficient MIS in order to turn the raw data into insightful and useful information for businesses to use and to nurture better decision making.

- It is widely used in the business world to help with problem solving and decision making, as well as to improve customer engagement.

- Big data, as an element of MIS, is characterized by five dimensions that make it different from traditional data. These attributes are known as the 5 Vs:

  - *Volume.* Big data entails large amounts of data that are generated and collected to support problem solving and decision making.

  - *Velocity.* The speed at which data is generated and processed has intensified with developments in technology and the widespread use of IoT devices, for example.

  - *Variety.* The different types of data, be they structured, semi-structured, or unstructured data, generate a huge breadth of data.

  - *Veracity.* This refers to the quality of data, given the volume and variety available and the velocity at which data is generated. The quality of data is dependent on factors such as the source of the data and the data collection methods used. The veracity of data determines how reliable and significant the data really are.

  - *Value.* This is the potential benefit derived from big data, based on the insights and advantages gained from the data.

- Other aspects of MIS, such as AI and machine learning, are used to analyze big data and make predictions.

- As with other aspects of MIS, there is a need for effective data management and cybersecurity to ensure the quality and protection of big data.

> **KEY CONCEPT**
>
> Discuss the **ethical** considerations (such as privacy and bias) when using big data.

Customer loyalty programmes (AO3)

- A **customer loyalty programme** is a rewards scheme offered by a business to encourage repeat purchases from its customers.

- The main purpose of offering customer loyalty programmes is to increase customer retention and sales revenue by incentivizing customers to continue buying from the business.

- These loyalty schemes can take many forms, such as reward points for discounts on future purchases, exclusive access to sales promotions and events, or personalized offers and concessions.

- MIS play a key role in the design, execution, and management of customer loyalty programmes:
  - MIS can be used to store customer information, which can be used to provide a personalized service that rewards customers for their loyalty.
  - Big data, databases, and data analytics can be used to determine the purchase history of customers in order to suggest other or related products they may be interested in.
  - It enables the business to tailor the rewards programme to the specific needs and preferences of different customers.
  - MIS can be used by businesses to identify any gaps or opportunities in their customer loyalty programme. This information can then be used to improve the rewards scheme, thereby allowing the business to make it more effective and appealing for customers.
  - Having a better understanding of changing customer needs and preferences can inform businesses of their future marketing strategies.
  - It can also be used to measure the degree of success of these rewards programmes.

The use of data to manage and monitor employees; Digital Taylorism (AO3)

- **Digital Taylorism** refers to the use of management information systems, such as data analytics, to manage and monitor employees in order to increase the operational efficiency and productivity of a business.

- The term comes from FW Taylor's principles of scientific management (see Chapter 2.4). This approach to management is based on three pillars:
  - Measurement of what can be done better and how.
  - Monitoring operations to ensure that performance targets are met.
  - Control by using rigorous analysis of the organization's inputs, outputs, and costs.

- Digital Taylorism is used to track and monitor employee performance and to optimize workflow using the same approach as advocated by Taylor, but in the modern digital era, using management information systems.
- As with all methods of electronic data management, using employee data can help the business to make better-informed decisions. This includes surveillance systems that provide managers with real-time visibility of employee activities, thereby allowing managers to take corrective measures where appropriate.
- At the same time, digital Taylorism can be used to collect and examine data to evaluate the decisions made by managers, thereby holding them accountable for their actions. This also helps to ensure that decisions and actions are based on reliable evidence and data (scientific decision making), rather than on hunch, instinct, or personal biases.
- Using MIS to manage and monitor employees and to automate aspects of an organization's operations not only increases production levels, but also improves accuracy. This helps to reduce wastage (see Chapter 5.3) and lower production costs in the long term.
- As digital Taylorism involves the collection, storage, and analysis of large amounts of data about employees, it can raise ethical concerns about data privacy and surveillance. Hence, it is important for businesses to consider the moral implications of the use of digital Taylorism in the workplace.

The use of data mining to inform decision making (AO3)

- Data mining is the management process of extracting useful information and insights from large sets of raw data in order to support strategic decision making.
- It is used to determine broad trends, patterns, and correlations (relationships) that would be difficult to uncover manually.
- Data mining can be used to identify new market opportunities and to make predictions about future trends and consumer behaviours. This helps businesses to improve their operations, marketing, and level of customer engagement.
- Data mining relies on the use of machine learning algorithms to process and analyze large amounts of raw data and to transform these into practical information for managers.
- As with big data, the process of data mining can raise concerns about data privacy and protection. Hence, there is a need for procedures and processes to handle and safeguard data in a responsible and safe manner.
- In many countries, data mining is subject to legal and regulatory compliance. For example, businesses in the UK are subject to the Data Protection Act (1998) and the General Data Protection Regulation (GDPR) regarding the use of personal data for data mining purposes. These laws stipulate that businesses must ensure that personal data are collected and used lawfully, fairly, and transparently. These laws also enable individuals to have certain rights related to the use of their information.
- Data mining is used with other elements of management information systems, such as data analytics, artificial intelligence, and cloud computing, to create even more valuable insights to support problem solving and decision making.

The benefits, risks, and ethical implications of advanced computer technologies (collectively referred to here as 'management information systems') and technological innovation on business decision making and stakeholders (AO3)

- Advanced computer technologies, collectively known as management information systems (MIS), can bring benefits as well as costs to businesses and their stakeholders.

- There are also ethical considerations associated with MIS and **technological innovations** in business organizations.

- To remain competitive, businesses need to actively engage with their stakeholders (see Chapter 1.4) by using aspects of MIS to gain a better understanding of their needs, preferences, and concerns. This will enhance the use of advanced computer technologies to align with the interests of customers, employees, and other stakeholder groups.

- Managers and decision makers also need to be aware of the long-term implications of technological innovations (such as the widespread use of the IoT devices and the growing presence of artificial intelligence) and have strategic plans in place to remain competitive in sustainable ways.

The benefits of MIS for business decision making and stakeholders

MIS provide numerous benefits to businesses and various stakeholders. These include, but are not limited to, the following points.

- MIS can help businesses gain competitive advantages by providing them with a better understanding of their customers, employees, suppliers, and other stakeholders. Such insights, provided in real time, can help businesses to anticipate their customers' needs and to develop corporate strategies to embrace changing trends.

- Advanced computer technologies, such as the use of AI and ML, can be used to help a business to improve its operational efficiency and to make cost savings.

- MIS can be used to create new goods and services for customers, such as automated customer checkout services in retail outlets. This can lead to a reduction in costs (by streamlining processes) and an increase in sales (due to the added convenience for customers).

- Aspects of MIS, such as customer loyalty programmes, can be used to improve the level of customer service and engagement, as well as to strengthen customer loyalty.

- Ultimately, MIS can help businesses to gain strategic advantages by allowing them to make more informed choices and to respond quickly to changes in the market.

The risks of MIS for business decision making and stakeholders

There are also risks associated with the use of and reliance on MIS. These risks include the following:

- Advanced computer technologies are vulnerable to the risks of cyberattacks, such as security breaches and theft of personal and sensitive data.

- Businesses need to be aware of the legal and regulatory requirements related to the use of MIS and ensure compliance with such laws and regulations. There is also a moral obligation to protect the interests of their customers and employees.

- The widespread use and reliance on MIS can reduce the need for employees. For example, MIS can be used to automate production processes, such as invoicing, tracking customer orders, and inventory (stock) management. Although this can benefit businesses (by saving time and money by reducing or eliminating the need for manual labour), employees are likely to lose out due to the mass job losses.

- There is always the risk of system failures, such as software or hardware malfunctions, as well as possible power outages which would bring critical infrastructures to a standstill.

- The risks associated with using and relying on advanced computer technologies mean that it is important for organizations to have robust and state-of-the-art security protocols and cybersecurity systems in place. This helps to protect the interests of customers, employees, and other key stakeholder groups of the organization.

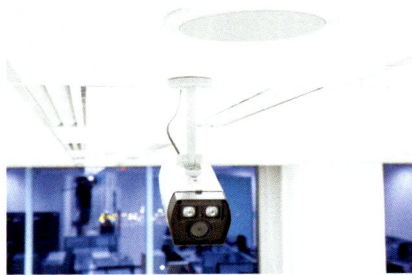

■ **Figure 5.8** Digital Taylorism can raise ethical concerns in the workplace

▓ The ethical considerations of MIS for business decision making and stakeholders

Finally, there are ethical considerations of MIS for business decision making and stakeholders. These include the following:

- The ethical considerations of advanced computer technologies require businesses to ensure that the data being collected, processed, stored, and shared are handled in a fair and principled manner. For example, data collection from the IoT devices and how these are then used need to comply with local, national, and/or international laws and regulations.

- The use of MIS, such as digital Taylorism, can raise ethical concerns such as data privacy, surveillance (of customers and employees, for example), and partiality in the decision-making process. For example, data must be used for legitimate business purposes only.

- Similarly, managers need to ensure that their advanced computer technologies (MIS) are not used to discriminate, exploit, or harass vulnerable individuals or other stakeholders.

- Businesses should also strive to ensure that when data is shared or used by third parties this is done in a socially responsible and transparent manner.

- A further ethical consideration is that MIS must not be used to gain unfair advantages over competitors or to manipulate the market in any way. Such behaviours are likely to be not only unethical, but illegal.

- Hence, there is a moral obligation for businesses to consider the ethical implications of their use of advanced computer technologies to ensure they protect the interests of their customers, suppliers, and employees, as well as ensuring these practices align with the organization's core values.

Business management toolkit (BMT)

1 SWOT ANALYSIS

SL/HL content	Depth of teaching
SWOT analysis	AO2, AO4

Diploma Programme *Business management guide* (May 2022)

■ SWOT analysis of a given organization (AO2, AO4)

A **SWOT analysis** is a situational business management tool used to assess where a business is at the present time and how it is affected by the external business environment. It is sometimes referred to as **situational analysis** as it examines the position of an organization at one point in time. SWOT stands for:

- **S**trengths – internal factors that reveal what the organization does well compared to its rivals, such as having a high market share.

- **W**eaknesses – internal factors that reveal what the organization does not do so well compared to its rivals, for example poor customer service or low employee motivation.

- **O**pportunities – external factors that may enable an organization to grow and prosper, for example an economic boom (see Chapter 1.5).

- **T**hreats – external factors that may hinder an organization's ability to achieve its goals, for example higher interest rates (see Chapter 1.5) or increasing competition in the industry.

■ **Table BMT.1** Example of SWOT analysis

Strengths	Weaknesses
• Brand loyalty/brand reputation	• A lack of new products being developed
• Customer loyalty/brand loyalty	• High gearing (high level of borrowing)
• Dedicated and productive workforce	• High labour turnover (demotivated staff)
• Efficient distribution channels	• High wastage rate/high defect rate
• High liquidity	• Low profitability
• High market share	• Poor customer service
Opportunities	**Threats**
• Economic growth	• Demographic changes
• Entering new overseas markets	• Economic recession
• Internet technologies	• Higher raw material costs
• Lower interest rates	• Minimum wage legislation
• Strategic alliances	• Pressure group action

■ **Table BMT.2** Advantages and disadvantages of SWOT analysis

Advantages of SWOT analysis	Disadvantages of SWOT analysis
• A simple and useful tool to assist managers in the planning process.	• It is only a snapshot of the current situation for an organization.
• A tool that gives decision makers an overview of an organization's actual position in the market.	• It may need to be revised regularly, accounting for changes in the internal and external business environments.
• It encourages an examination of the strategic opportunities for an organization, e.g. growth (expansion) or relocation.	• It is subject to some bias as the analysis is based on opinions, not only facts and figures.

KEY CONCEPT

Investigate how **change** presents both opportunities and threats for a multinational company of your choice.

2 ANSOFF MATRIX

SL/HL content	Depth of teaching
Ansoff matrix	AO2, AO4

Diploma Programme *Business management guide* (May 2022)

■ Ansoff matrix (AO2, AO4)

● The Ansoff matrix is a management growth tool, first published in an article titled 'Strategies for Diversification', featured in the *Harvard Business Review* (1957).

● It is used by businesses to identify and decide their product and market growth strategies. It is shown in Figure BMT.1.

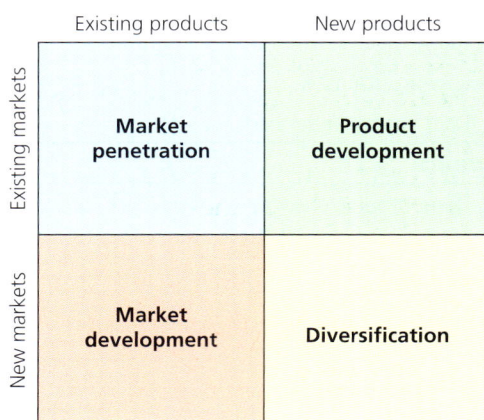

■ **Figure BMT.1** The Ansoff matrix

■ Market penetration

● Market penetration focuses on existing markets and existing products, meaning it focuses on what it knows and does well.

● It is a low-risk strategy so requires little, if any, investment in new market research as the organization aims to increase revenues by focusing on sales of its existing products to existing customers.

● The strategy concentrates on increasing the organization's sales revenue or market share of its existing products, for example by using competitive pricing methods, introducing customer loyalty schemes, widening distribution channels, or using a more effective promotional campaign.

Market development

- Market development is a growth strategy that involves a business selling its existing products into new markets, meaning the product remains the same, but it is sold to a new group of customers.

- An example is a car manufacturer that exports its cars to overseas markets or has production plants in various countries.

- There is an element of risk with market development because customer tastes may vary in different regions and countries. There are also the added costs of market research. In the case of foreign direct investment, market development presents even higher financial risks.

- Nevertheless, the business knows its products well, so should be familiar with customer needs. This helps to minimize some of the risks involved with market development.

Product development

- Product development is a growth strategy where a business introduces new products into existing markets – it targets new products at existing customers.

- It is common for businesses, such as carmakers, to develop and innovate new products to replace their existing ones. These new products are then marketed to existing customers.

- An example is Apple's introduction of the iPhone, iPad, and Apple Watch.

- Product development often involves a business developing modified products as part of its product extension strategy.

- It is a medium-risk strategy as product development often involves significant investment in research and development (R&D).

Diversification

- Diversification involves businesses marketing completely new products to new customers. It is a high-risk growth strategy, as the business enters markets in which it has little or no experience.

- Related diversification means that organizations remain in a market (industry) that they are familiar with. Unrelated diversification involves businesses entering new industries in which they have no previous market experience.

- For example, Honda launched its HondaJet (aircraft) division in 2015. Lenovo introduced smartphones, watches, and sports shoes in 2015! Although Hitachi is a household name for consumer electronics, the Japanese company also produces elevators (lifts), escalators, auto parts, defence technology, semiconductors, supercomputers, and railway systems!

- Diversification can be an important strategy for business growth and survival (see Table BMT.3).

■ **Table BMT.3** Examples of diversification

Company	Original business	Company	Original business
American Express	Postal services	Peugeot	Toolmaker
Shell	Collectable shells	Nintendo	Playing cards
Nokia	Rubber and paper	Lamborghini	Tractors
Wrigley's	Soap and baking powder	Mitsubishi	Shipping

209

■ **Table BMT.4** Summary of the Ansoff matrix

Market penetration	Product development	Market development	Diversification
Same products for existing customers	New products for existing customers	New customers for existing products	New products for new customers
Familiar markets	Product-extension strategies and product development	Familiar products	Spreading of risks
Minimal risk	Moderate risk	Moderate risk	High risk
Seeking to maintain or raise market share	Innovation to replace existing products	Entering overseas markets	Spreading of risks
Intense competition	Product improvements	New distribution channels	Use of subsidiaries and strategic business units
Adapting the firm's marketing mix	Using brand-extension strategies	Adapting the firm's marketing mix	Shifting away from core markets and competencies

KEY CONCEPT

The needs and wants of customers change over time. Investigate how the Ansoff matrix is connected to the concepts of **change** and **creativity** for an organization of your choice.

EXAM PRACTICE QUESTION

The COVID-19 pandemic caused Connie's Candles to respond to the decline in sales by announcing that it would launch a new range of sustainably made premium soy wax candles, made from natural ingredients. Connie Walker, the founder and CEO, believes this move can help the company to gain higher market share in an industry worth over $3 billion per year. This new range of premium candles will allow Connie's Candles to make up for some of the losses incurred during the pandemic, while maintaining its extensive range of candles.

a   Suggest which growth strategy in Ansoff's matrix best describes Connie's Candles' launch of its premium soy wax candles.   [2]

b   Explain one possible reason why the launch of premium soy wax candles may improve the company's market share.   [2]

c   Explain **two** reasons why Connie Walker may underestimate the risks involved with this growth strategy.   [4]

3 STEEPLE ANALYSIS

SL/HL content	Depth of teaching
STEEPLE analysis	AO2, AO4

Diploma Programme *Business management guide* (May 2022)

STEEPLE analysis (AO2, AO4)

- As a brainstorming framework, **STEEPLE analysis** is straightforward to construct and interpret.

- It can help managers and decision makers be more objective, proactive, and comprehensive in their analysis of external opportunities and threats for the business.

- Hence, this tool enables managers to be more informed and better prepared to deal with changes in the external business environment.

- The STEEPLE factors in the text below can provide both opportunities and threats for businesses.

Social factors

Demographic changes are classified as a social factor. Changes in fashions and trends are also social factors affecting businesses. Other examples are shown below, which may not necessarily apply to all countries or regions of the world.

- An increasing number of people now live in single-person households.

- In many parts of the world, such as France, the UK and Japan, there has been an increase in the retirement age.

- An ageing population is common in many economically developed countries, which has affected recruitment practices in these nations. Similarly, there is an increasing number of older and retired people living in these countries.

- Some women in modern societies are choosing to have children at a later age due to the higher costs of raising children and the desire to advance their careers before having children.

- A common trend is the increasing movement of young workers to cities and away from rural areas.

Technological factors

- The increasing use of mobile devices and internet technologies provides huge opportunities for businesses engaged in e-commerce (electronic commerce).

- The increasing number of businesses that are striving to have a greater online presence means an investment in management information systems (MIS) (see Chapter 5.9) as well as development of their e-commerce strategies.

- Advances in automation and industrial technologies improve efficiency and productivity in the manufacturing process.

- Unemployment can arise in certain industries due to the use of automation and more capital-intensive methods of production.

- The increasing ability to communicate with customers all around the world, using social networks and social media.

- Artificial intelligence and other developments in MIS can also present opportunities and threats to businesses across all industries.

■ Economic factors

- The level of consumer confidence influences the level of demand in an economy.
- Higher costs of production will tend to force prices up. Higher prices (inflation) will also tend to damage a country's international competitiveness.
- A currency appreciation reduces the competitiveness of an exporter's prices – for example, an appreciation of the US dollar against the Japanese yen will tend to lead to a fall in US exports to Japan.

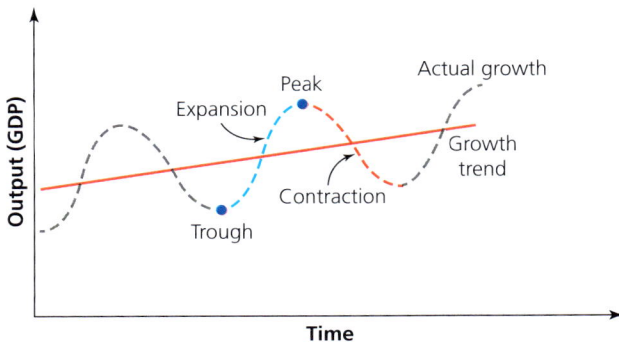

■ **Figure BMT.2** The business cycle

- An increase in interest rates makes borrowing more expensive, thus discouraging investment expenditure. In addition, firms with existing loans have larger repayments.
- An economic boom is associated with an expanding economy (see Figure BMT.2) – higher levels of consumption and investment create many opportunities for businesses.
- By contrast, an economic recession occurs when the level of economic activity contracts for at least two consecutive quarters (six months), caused by lower levels of consumption and investment expenditure in the economy.

■ **Table BMT.5** Phases in the business cycle

Indicator	Trough (slump)	Expansion (recovery)	Peak (boom)	Contraction (recession)
Consumer and business confidence	Very low confidence (pessimistic)	Increasing levels of confidence	Very high confidence (optimistic)	Low and falling confidence levels
Consumer spending	Very low	Increasing	High	Falling
Economic growth	Negative GDP growth	Rising levels of GDP	Positive growth, high GDP	GDP begins to fall
Unemployment	Very high	Falling	Low	Rising
Inflation	Low or negative (deflation)	Rising prices	High price levels	Price levels begin to fall
Number of firms failing	High	Falling	Low	Rising
Business investment	Very low, if any	Rising	High	Falling

EXAM PRACTICE QUESTION

Bristol Cars, a specialist British car maker, sold its sports cars at an average price of £120,000 to customers in the USA. Calculate the change in the price that would have been paid by US customers if the US dollar depreciated from £1 = $1.2 to £1 = $1.4. [2]

■ Environmental factors

- The depletion of scarce and non-renewable resources raises concerns about the sustainability of business activity.
- Inclement weather and climate change are environmental factors that can cause major threats to businesses, for example severe flooding, droughts, typhoons, tsunamis, and snowstorms.

■ **Figure BMT.3** Business can be affected by inclement weather

- An increasing number of businesses use green technologies as part of their operations in order to protect the planet, for example renewable energy sources or cradle-to-cradle design and manufacturing (see Chapter 5.3).

- Businesses also have to consider their ecological footprint as part of their corporate social responsibility (CSR), and must be aware of the impact of their activities, such as waste production or air pollution, on the natural environment. Firms that take such an approach can benefit from having a positive corporate image, while those that do not may face financial penalties.

▩ Political factors

- The political climate in a country has direct implications for businesses. For example, political instability due to regional conflicts can be a major threat to business activity.

- The government's use of taxes can also create opportunities or threats for businesses. For example, some countries such as Bahrain, Brunei, Kuwait, and the Bahamas have a zero rate of income tax to attract the migration of workers. Low rates of corporate tax can also incentivize multinational companies to invest in such countries.

- Some governments use trade protectionist measures to safeguard domestic businesses and jobs, for example imposing a tariff on imported cars protects domestic car producers.

- Similarly, governments may impose quotas (quantitative limits) on the number of foreign products sold in the country. For example, quotas are imposed on the number of Hollywood movies that are released in China, in order to protect the domestic film industry.

- Governments can also provide subsidies as a form of protection for certain domestic industries. For example, the French government subsidizes domestic farmers.

- The government itself is a large consumer with its various forms of expenditure, such as on education and health care services, thereby providing huge opportunities for many businesses.

▩ Legal factors

- Organizations must meet certain legal standards that help to reduce any adverse effects of business activity.

- Many countries impose data protection laws as a form of consumer protection. This has major implications for how businesses collect, store, and use data about their employees and customers (see Chapter 5.9).

- Laws such as censorship or bans on the production or sale of certain goods and services can be a threat to many businesses.

- Employers must operate within the constraints of employment laws, for example national minimum wage legislation, laws on maximum working hours, health and safety regulations, and anti-discrimination employment laws.

- Smoking bans in restaurants, shopping malls, and public parks enforced in many countries across the world can have a significant impact on businesses.
- Environmental protection legislation can impact on the production and investment decisions of many businesses.

■ Ethical factors

- Ethical factors are about doing what is right or morally correct from society's point of view.
- Businesses need to consider the impact of their activities on society and the environment.
- Businesses are often presented with ethical dilemmas, for example determining how much of the firm's profits to keep for investment purposes and how much to distribute to shareholders in the form of dividends.
- Bribery, fraud, embezzlement, and theft are examples of unethical and illegal practices – all of which create threats to any organization.
- An increasing number of businesses choose to adopt environmental practices and to prioritize their corporate social responsibilities (CSR).

EXPERT TIPS

- It is not always easy to classify external factors into the STEEPLE categories. For example, an increase in vehicle duty can be regarded as a political, legal, or economic factor. However, what matters is how well you justify your answer.
- The contextualized nature of the Business Management course means that you will need to be able to examine how changes in any combination of the STEEPLE factors impacts the objectives and strategies of a particular business.

KEY CONCEPT

Investigate how **change** in any combination of the STEEPLE factors has affected the business objectives for an organization of your choice.

4 BOSTON CONSULTING GROUP (BCG) MATRIX

SL/HL content	Depth of teaching
Boston Consulting Group (BCG) matrix	AO2, AO4

Diploma Programme *Business management guide* (May 2022)

■ Boston Consulting Group (BCG) matrix (AO2, AO4)

- The Boston Consulting Group (BCG) matrix is a marketing tool used to examine an organization's product portfolio.
- For example, the Volkswagen Group's product portfolio includes vehicles produced by Audi, SEAT, Skoda, Bentley, Bugatti, Lamborghini, Porsche, Ducati, and Scania.
- There are two dimensions to the BCG matrix: a product's market share and the market growth:
  - Market share examines whether the product in question has a low or high market share.
  - Market growth examines the numbers of potential customers in the market and whether this is growing, stagnant, or shrinking.

- There are four quadrants in the BCG matrix:
  - ○ Question marks are products that have low market share in a high growth market. Managers try to convert these products into stars, although this requires investment expenditure.
  - ○ Stars are products with high or increasing market share in a high growth market. They have yet to become market leaders, but have the potential to become cash cows for the business.

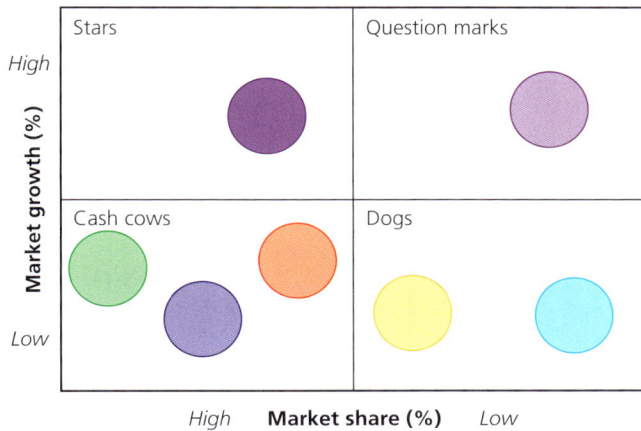

■ **Figure BMT.4** The Boston Consulting Group matrix

- ○ Cash cows are products with high market share in a low growth (mature) market, so these are the products that earn the most cash for a business.
- ○ Dogs are products at the end of their product life cycle, so they operate in low growth markets and have low market share. Hence, dogs are products that drain cash from the organization.
- The BCG matrix is a useful tool for managing a diverse range of products in an organization's portfolio, helping to provide balance to the firm's product portfolio.
- In addition, it is used to help an organization to allocate resources among its various products and to prioritize its investments in the product portfolio.

■ **Table BMT.6** Categories of the BCG matrix

Stars	Question marks
• High market growth	• High market growth
• High market share	• Low market share
• Growth stage in the product life cycle (PLC)	• Introduction stage in the PLC
• Investment needed to turn these into cash cows	• Drains the firm's cash flow
Cash cows	**Dogs**
• Low market growth	• Low market growth
• High market share	• Low market share
• Maturity stage in the PLC	• Decline stage in the PLC
• Main generators of cash	• Divest to prevent further losses

■ **Table BMT.7** Benefits and drawbacks of a broad product portfolio

Benefits of a broad product portfolio	Drawbacks of a broad product portfolio
• Developing a group of products in the portfolio can help a business to increase brand awareness.	• Managers may need to spread their resources and expertise too thinly, i.e. it can cause a lack of focus.
• It reduces the risks of relying on a single product or limited range of products.	• Bad publicity for one product in the portfolio may harm the organization's overall image.
• It increases the firm's revenue streams (see Chapter 3.3).	• There are high costs of developing and selling a broad range of products.
• Having a variety of products helps to limit the impact of seasonal fluctuations in demand.	• There are additional administrative and accounting costs.

■ **Table BMT.8** Benefits and drawbacks of the BCG matrix as a business management tool

Benefits of the BCG matrix	Drawbacks of the BCG matrix
• It is a useful tool for analyzing a firm's product decisions. • It provides a snapshot of a firm's current product portfolio position.	• Market share and market growth are not the only indicators of a competitive advantage. • The product life cycle varies for different products.

5 BUSINESS PLAN

SL/HL content	Depth of teaching
Business plan	AO2, AO4

Diploma Programme *Business management guide* (May 2022)

▨ Business plan (AO2, AO4)

> **Key term**
>
> A **business plan** is a formal document that details how an organization intends to meet its business objectives.

- **Business plans** are often used to attract funds from banks, venture capitalists, or other investors.
- A business plan adds substance to a business idea and helps with strategic thinking and decision making.

A typical business plan will include the following elements:

- *Executive summary.* An overview of the business organization, its objectives, and corporate strategies. It is essentially a summary of the business plan.

- *Business description.* A brief introduction to or description of the organization, its legal status and ownership, and its goals and objectives. It may also include the firm's mission or vision statement (see Chapter 1.3). For larger firms, the business plan might also include details of the management team or board of directors.

- *Business environment.* Details of the market or industry in which the organization operates. For example, it might list market leaders or market share data. This section of the business plan is likely to include a SWOT analysis or a STEEPLE analysis (see earlier sections of the Business management toolkit).

- *Risk analysis.* Identification and assessment of the potential impact of possible risks and the likelihood of them occurring, as well as the options available to mitigate the identified risks.

- *Product description.* Details of the product offering (goods and/or services) to prospective customers. The plan should identify what makes the product unique or distinguishable from rival products that might be available on the market.

- *Marketing plan.* This section details the state of the market, including projected sales figures and marketing opportunities. It may include information about the use of market research, branding, prices, distribution channels, promotions and advertising, as well as social media platforms.

- *Finance plan.* This part of the business plan outlines the finances of the organization, including its forecast balance sheet and income statement (see Chapter 3.4) for business start-ups. This helps investors to determine the financial status of the organization.

- *Operations plan.* Production processes and operational costs appear in this section of the business plan. It may cover matters such as quality assurance, break-even analysis, stock control (inventory management), and supply-chain management (see Chapter 5.6).

- *Human resources plan.* This section of the business plan contains information about staffing and may include an organizational chart.
- *Appendix.* This section of the business plan includes any additional supporting documents, such as market research data, pricing information, technical product specification, or copies of required permits, leases, and contracts.

> **KEY CONCEPT**
>
> Explore how **change** has impacted a business start-up of your choice.

6 DECISION TREES

SL/HL content	Depth of teaching
Decision trees	AO2, AO4

Diploma Programme *Business management guide* (May 2022)

Decision trees

- A **decision tree** is a quantitative decision-making tool that allows managers to visualize possible options and their probable outcomes.
- In a decision tree diagram, a circle represents a chance node. A square represents a choice or decision.
- Probabilities of the various outcomes are shown. For example, 0.35 means there is a 35 per cent chance (likelihood) of the outcome actually materializing. Probabilities for each chance node must add up to 1.0 – 100 per cent likelihood.
- Figure BMT.4 illustrates the decision of a firm to pursue either Project Chicago (which costs $55m) or Project Delhi (which costs $51m). The following can be seen from the decision tree:
  - There is a 65 per cent chance of success if the firm chooses Project Chicago, which would gain the firm $70m in sales revenue. Thus, the likely outcome is $70m × 0.65 = $45.5m.
  - There is a 35 per cent chance of failure for Project Chicago, with expected revenues of only $45m. Hence, the probable outcome is $45m × 0.35 = $15.75m.
  - Therefore, the combined outcome for Project Chicago is $45.5m + $15.75m = $61.25m. After the costs of the project are accounted for, the likely yield (return) of Project Chicago is $61.25m – $55m = $6.25m.
  - For Project Delhi, there is a 55 per cent chance of success in earning $80m. Hence, the likely outcome is $80m × 0.55 = $44m.
  - If the project fails, the likely outcome of earning $35m in sales revenue is $35m × 0.45 = $15.75m.
  - Hence, the combined likely outcome is $44m + $15.75m = $59.75m. The likely profit is therefore $59.75m – $51m = $8.75m.
- Two parallel lines that cross through a branch represent the options that are rejected based on quantitative grounds.
- Examining the decision tree in Figure BMT.4 shows that Project Delhi should be pursued on financial grounds. Despite the relatively higher risk of failure, the investment cost is lower and the likely yield is an extra $2.5m ($8.75 return for Project Delhi compared to $6.25m for Project Chicago).

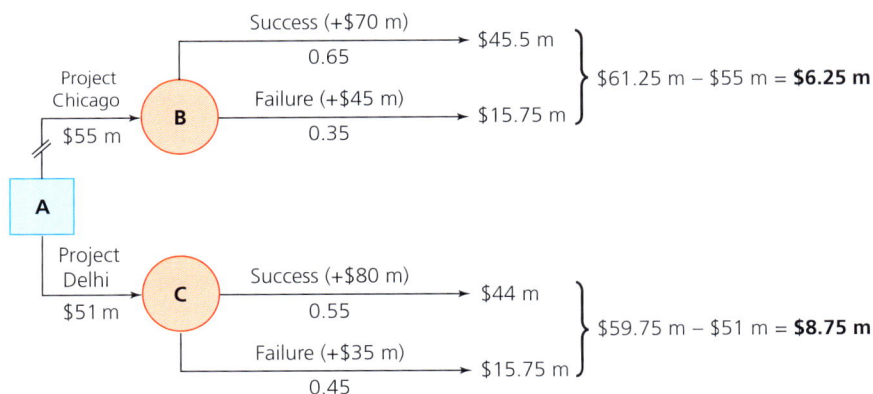

■ **Figure BMT.4** Example of a decision tree

EXPERT TIP

Remember when constructing a decision tree that squares are used for decisions while circles are chance nodes for which probabilities are assigned.

■ **Table BMT.9** Advantages and disadvantages of decision trees

Advantages of decision trees	Disadvantages of decision trees
• It formalizes the decision-making process and makes it possible for outcomes to be compared objectively. • It offers a visual and logical representation of various decisions with quantifiable outcomes, thus making things easier to follow. • The management team is forced to consider the risks of different options.	• Qualitative factors affecting decision making are ignored, e.g. business objectives and stakeholder views. • Data on likely outcomes are only forecasts so actual outcomes can be quite different. • Data can become out of date by the time a decision is actually taken. • External factors and non-financial information are ignored in the diagram.

EXAM PRACTICE QUESTION

Kingman Educational Resources (KER) is considering expanding into one of three locations. The expected costs and revenues are shown in the table below. KER only has the resources to pursue one of these growth options.

Project	Probability (%)	Cost ($m)	Revenue ($m)
Ashtown		100	
Success	50		215
Failure	50		80
Brigcity		80	
Success	65		180
Failure	35		75
Centrapolis		90	
Success	60		175
Failure	40		90

Using the data above, construct a decision tree showing which project is best on financial grounds. Show all your working and include an appropriate key in your diagram.

[6]

7 DESCRIPTIVE STATISTICS

SL/HL content	Depth of teaching
Descriptive statistics. These include the following: mean, mode, median, bar charts, pie charts, infographics, quartiles, and standard deviation.	AO2, AO4

Diploma Programme *Business management guide* (May 2022)

◾ Descriptive statistics (AO2, AO4)

- **Descriptive statistics** is a division of statistics that summarizes and expresses data in usable ways to support analysis and decision making.

- It involves the use of measures such as averages (mean, mode, and median), graphical tools to visually represent the data (such as bar charts, pie charts, and infographics), and measures of dispersion or spread in a data set (such as quartiles and standard deviation).

- The purposes of descriptive statistics are to provide a general understanding of the data and to identify any patterns or trends within the data.

- These statistical tools help managers to identify any patterns and trends in the data set that might not be immediately obvious or easy to determine from the raw data.

◾ Mean

- The **mean** (or arithmetic mean average) is the most common measure of the average value in a set of data.

- It is calculated by adding up all the values in a data set and then dividing this total by the number of items in the set of data.

- For example, the following data show the number of years that each worker in the sales department of a firm has been with the company: 3, 5, 7, 9, and 11. To calculate the mean:
  - Add up all the values: $3 + 5 + 7 + 9 + 11 = 35$
  - Divide the total (35) by the number of items in the data set (5)
  - Hence, the mean = $35 \div 5 = 7$

- The mean can be used to express the average figure in variables such as financial data, production data, and survey responses.

- It can also be used to make comparisons between different groups or sets of data, such as the monthly average sales revenue of different branches of a coffee company.

EXAM PRACTICE QUESTION

The average daily sales of a convenience store in a typical week are shown below.

Mon	Tues	Wed	Thurs	Fri	Sat	Sun
$3,500	$3,000	$4,500	$5,000	$8,000	$8,600	$2,300

Calculate the mean value of sales for the convenience store. [2]

Mode

- The **mode** is the second method of measuring the average figure in a data set. It is the value that appears most frequently in the data set.

- For example, the mode can be used to identify the most popular item in an organization's product portfolio, the most frequent age group of the firm's customers, or even the most common category of customer complaints.

- A business is able to use the mode to prioritize production and marketing efforts for its most popular product. Conversely, it might also use the mode to consider discontinuing products that are least popular.

- It is possible to have more than one mode in a data set (multimodal data set) or even no mode at all (non-modal data set). This is a limitation of using the mode to express an average value.

EXAM PRACTICE QUESTION

The data below show the number of toys sold by a retailer during the past month:

A	B	C	D	E
50	60	80	70	40

Describe the mode from the data above. [2]

Median

- The **median** is the third and final measure of the average figure in a set of numbers. It is the middle value when the items in a data set are placed in numerical order from the lowest to the largest value.

- It is used to identify the typical or middle value in a data set, which can then be useful for making comparisons or identifying patterns. For example, the median can be used to determine the average income of a firm's employees or the median sales revenue of the different products sold by the business.

WORKED EXAMPLE

A firm has the following sales revenue over the first five trading months of the year and wants to determine its median sales value.

Month	1	2	3	4	5
Sales ($)	12,000	15,000	13,000	16,000	14,000

First, place the values in numerical order: $12,000, $13,000, $14,000, $15,000, $16,000.

Identify the value in the middle as the median value, i.e. $14,000.

- Using the median is particularly useful when there are outliers in the data set or if it is skewed (which would affect or distort the value of the mean).
- If there is an even number of data items in the data set, the median is the average of the two middle values.

WORKED EXAMPLE

Month	1	2	3	4	5	6
Sales ($)	12,000	15,000	13,000	16,000	14,000	14,500

In this example, the median would be calculated as follows:

Placing the values in numerical order gives two middle values: $12,000, $13,000, **$14,000**, **$14,500**, $15,000, $16,000.

The median is the average of these two middle values, i.e. ($14,000 + $14,500) ÷ 2 = $14,250.

◼ Bar charts

- A **bar chart** is a graphical representation of processed data. The length of each bar in the chart shows the frequency or quantity of different categories of the data, for example sales revenue or sales volume.
- Bar charts are particularly useful in business management for visualizing data that can be divided into categories or groups. They can also be used to show the distribution of data across different categories (see Figure BMT.5).
- The bars in a bar chart are typically positioned horizontally or vertically, with the values shown along the axes.
- The chart in Figure BMT.5 shows that Product C is the best-seller in a firm's product portfolio, as sales revenue is $80,000. This is higher than any other product it sells. By contrast, Product D is the least popular item, with sales of only $10,000. By looking at the bar chart, management can easily compare the revenue of each product and make decisions accordingly.

Sales, $'000

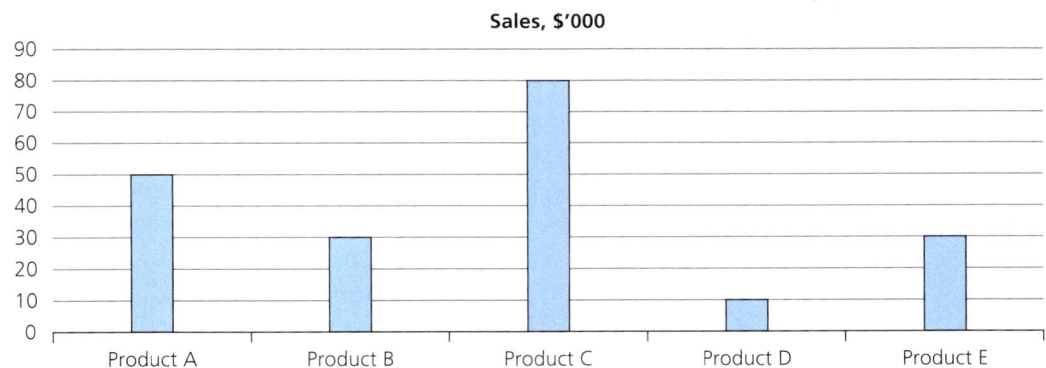

◼ **Figure BMT.5** A bar chart

◼ Pie charts

- A **pie chart** is a type of visual diagram that displays processed data in the form of a circular graph.
- It is particularly useful for displaying data in proportions or percentages that add up to 100 per cent of the items in the data set being represented.
- A pie chart is divided into segments, with the size of each segment being proportional to the quantity it represents from the data set.

- In business management, pie charts are often used to display data such as market share, sales revenue by product or location, cost and revenue data, customer demographics, or any other metrics used to gauge customer preferences. The pie charts can then be used by managers to make decisions accordingly.

- When dealing with a large number of categories, it can be challenging to represent the segments using a pie chart. In such cases, a bar chart might be more appropriate.

EXAM PRACTICE QUESTION

Use the following data from a school to create a pie chart to represent the percentage of candidates who opt to write an extended essay based on each IB subject group.   [4]

IB Subject Group (EE)	Percentage
Group 1	20
Group 2	10
Group 3	45
Group 4	15
Group 5	5
Group 6	5

Infographics

- An **infographic** is a visual tool used to represent data by combining information (text) and graphics (images).

- Infographics are designed to make complex information and data easier to interpret and understand.

- As a form of descriptive statistics, infographics use visual tools to summarize and convey key insights and findings about a specific topic or data set.

- They can be used to present data in a variety of formats, including charts, graphs, diagrams, timelines, flowcharts, maps, and coloured illustrations.

- Infographics are more engaging and accessible as a form of communication to a wide audience.

Quartiles

- A **quartile** divides the data collected in a data set (such as sales revenue for a given period of time) into four parts, in order to facilitate statistical analysis and business decision making.

- Quartiles split the data into four, in the same way that the median splits the data into two.

- Note that three quartiles are used to divide the data set into equal parts, or quarters (see Figure BMT.7). The three quartiles are known as the:

  o first quartile (Q1) or the 25th percentile – the bottom 25 per cent of the values in the data set appear to the left of Q1

  o second quartile (Q2) or the 50th percentile – the middle range in the data set appears to the left and right of Q2 (which is also the median value of the data)

Which Countries Have Been Female-Led?

Number of elected/appointed female heads of government/state* by country since 1946

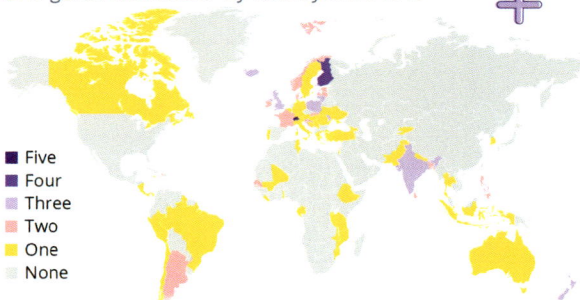

- Five
- Four
- Three
- Two
- One
- None

As of Jan 2023
* excludes monarch or those appointed by them, acting/interim/honorary positions
Source: Council on Foreign Relations

statista

■ **Figure BMT.6** An example of an infographic, showing the number of elected/appointed female heads of government/state by country since 1946

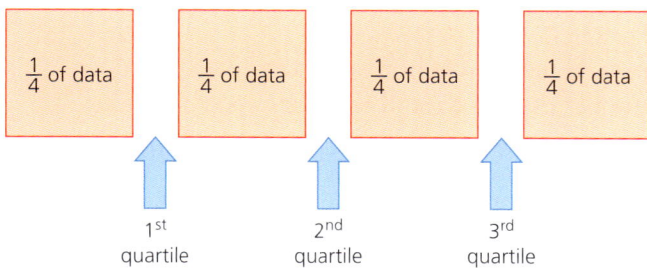

■ **Figure BMT.7** Quartiles

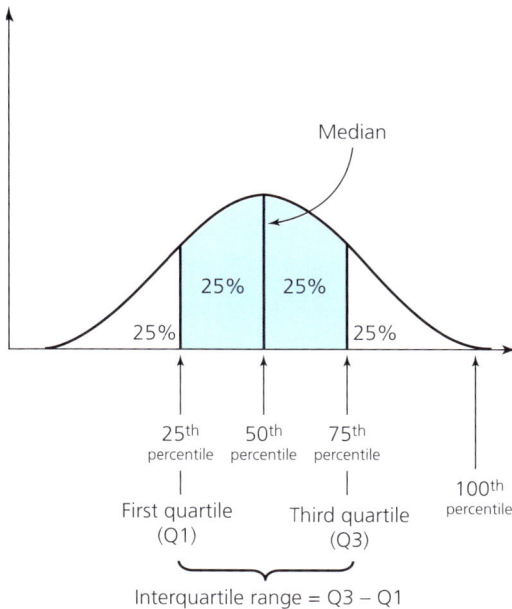

■ **Figure BMT.8** The interquartile range

○ third quartile (Q3) or the 75th percentile – the top 25 per cent of the values in the data set appear to the right of Q3.

● Using quartiles enables managers to see the distribution of items in a data set, such as the ranking of different branches of a restaurant or retail outlet, based on the value of the sales revenue they account for.

● Figure BMT.8 shows a typical or normal distribution of the data dispersed in a data set, using quartiles.

● The **range** in a data set is a measure of variation, meaning how spread out the data are. The range is equal to the highest value minus the lowest value in a data set. However, the range is affected by extreme values (called **outliers**). To deal with this problem, statisticians use the interquartile range.

● The **interquartile range** is used to show the spread of data in a data set. It measures the difference between the first and third quartiles, thereby showing the middle spread of the data.

Interquartile range = Third quartile − First quartile

or

Interquartile range = Q3 − Q1

WORKED EXAMPLE

As an example, the following are the results of an aptitude test, marked out of 100, taken by 11 employees: 33, 97, 37, 71, 13, 77, 84, 55, 57, 27, and 94. To find the interquartile range, the following steps are taken:

● First, place the test scores in numerical order: 13, 27, 33, 37, 55, 57, 71, 77, 84, 94, and 97.

● The median value or score is 57.

● The data set has 11 items, so we can find the position of Q1 and Q3.

● The first quartile (Q1) value is 33 (there are two employees who scored less than this and two people who scored more than this in the test, but less than the median score of 57).

● The third quartile (Q3) value is 84 (there are two employees who scored higher than this and two employees who scored less than this, but higher than the median score).

● Therefore, the interquartile range is 84 − 33 = 51.

● This indicates that the values between the first and third quartiles are spread out over a large range (51 out of 100), so managers may need to consider retraining opportunities for the employees. In particular, the two employees who scored less than the 25th percentile may need additional training.

■ Standard deviation

- **Standard deviation** (σ) is a statistical measure of how spread out data points are within a set of data. It shows whether there is a small or large spread of results.
- A low standard deviation implies that the data items in a data set are clustered closely around the mean (average).
- Conversely, a high standard deviation indicates that the data points are spread out over a wide range, which can be caused by outliers within the data set.
- It is important to note that the standard deviation for a data set is prone to outliers. A single outlier in the data set can significantly change the standard deviation, even if the rest of the data points are clustered around the mean value.
- In general, managers prefer a low standard deviation, as this indicates more consistency within the raw data. Note that this is a reason why it can be useful to also measure the interquartile range, which is not generally sensitive to outliers.

WORKED EXAMPLE

To calculate the standard deviation, consider the data items representing the monthly sales revenue from a business that has five retail outlets.

Store	A	B	C	D	E
Sales ($'000)	120	110	130	125	115

- First, calculate the mean (average) of the data set: $(120 + 110 + 130 + 125 + 115) \div 5 = 120$.
- Next, work out the variance for each data point by subtracting the mean from the data point, then squaring the result:
  - $(120 - 120)^2 = (0)^2 = 0$
  - $(110 - 120)^2 = (-10)^2 = 100$
  - $(130 - 120)^2 = (10)^2 = 100$
  - $(125 - 120)^2 = (5)^2 = 25$
  - $(115 - 120)^2 = (-5)^2 = 25$
- Next, add all the squared differences and then divide by the number of data points: $(0 + 100 + 100 + 25 + 25) = 250 \div 5 = 50$
- Finally, calculate the square root of the result to get the standard deviation: $\sigma = \sqrt{50} = 7.07$

EXAM PRACTICE QUESTION

The data below show the sales of five employees at a retail store.

Employee	Sales ($'000)
A	25
B	30
C	15
D	30
E	50

a Describe what is meant by standard deviation in a data set. [2]

b Use the data above to calculate the standard deviation. [4]

8 CIRCULAR BUSINESS MODELS

SL/HL content	Depth of teaching
Circular business models: circular supply models, resource recovery models, product life extension models, sharing models, and product service system models	AO2, AO4

Diploma Programme *Business management guide* (May 2022)

Circular business models (AO2, AO4)

> **Key term**
>
> **Circular business models (CBMs)** are a modern approach to conducting business by focusing on sustainability and reducing waste.

- **Circular business models (CBMs)** enable organizations to conduct their business in such a way that it is sustainable and future proofed.

- In a linear business model, items are produced, consumed, and then disposed of. However, in a circular business model, the goal is to keep products, components, and materials in use for as long as possible. Hence, a CBM makes more efficient use of the planet's scarce resources and minimizes waste for a more sustainable future.

- CBMs involve the reuse and remanufacture of products, components, and materials, as well as using and reusing recyclable resources.

- For example, upcycling is the process of reusing materials or components from one product to create a different product, for example turning used ties into wallets. This helps to reduce waste and conserve the planet's resources.

- By using CBMs, businesses reduce their environmental footprint (the impacts of business activities on the natural environment), such as waste, pollution, land erosion, and climate change. CBMs also help to create greater economic and social benefits for a clean and green future in sustainable ways.

- The five CBMs that feature in the Business Management course are the ones advocated for by the Organization for Economic Co-operation and Development (OECD): circular supply models, resource recovery models, product life extension models, sharing models, and product service system models.

Circular supply models

- **Circular supply models** reduce the need for and reliance on the extraction of resources in the long run, by replacing traditional raw material inputs with renewable or recovered materials.

- These models help to reduce the demand for virgin resources such as fossil fuels and other non-renewable resources. This is achieved by making use of materials that have already been used, for example renewable, recyclable, or bio-degradable resources.

- Reducing the amount of raw material and the number of components used in the production process can significantly reduce the environmental impacts resulting from business activity.

- A circular supply model consists of four main stages: production, use, reuse, and recycling (see Figure BMT.9).

- The manufacturer process, from product design to final output, uses the fewest materials and resources possible, while still ensuring the output meets the required quality standards.

Production → Use → Reuse → Recycling

■ **Figure BMT.9** Circular supply model

Resource recovery models

- **Resource recovery models** involve recycling waste into secondary raw materials, which postpones or reduces final disposal and waste. Such an approach also means there is less of a need for extraction and processing of scarce natural resources for production.

- Resource recovery models focus on maximizing the value of resources used in the production process, by reducing or minimizing waste, as well as reusing or recycling waste materials. Therefore, resource recovery models are beneficial for the conservation of scarce and non-renewable resources.

- Examples of business activities that use resource recovery models include:
  - optimizing packaging so that it can be reused for production and to reduce waste
  - composting by breaking down organic waste and converting this into nutrient-rich soils for agricultural use
  - working with suppliers to ensure materials are sourced from renewable and recycled sources.

- As a category of circular business models, resource recovery models enable businesses to have positive environmental impacts, as well as financial benefits due to reduced waste and lower costs.

Product life extension models

- **Product life extension models** involve methods that prolong the useful life of existing products. This helps to reduce the rate at which scarce resources are extracted from the Earth, as well as reducing the generation of waste.

- Extending the life of a product can be achieved through several means, including repairing, refurbishing, remanufacturing, or renovating; all of which help to reduce the need for new production and waste. For example:
  - Creating products that are more durable (built to last) so that they can be repaired and upgraded promptly, which means being able to easily fix broken or damaged products and restore them to a usable condition.
  - Some electric vehicle manufacturers offer owners of older e-vehicles the option to upgrade their battery pack for improved performance, without the need to replace the entire car.
  - Some smartphone manufacturers, such as Apple and Samsung, offer customers the option to have their old devices repaired or refurbished to near-new working condition.

- This also means that product life extension models create new revenue streams for the business (from customers who pay for repairs and upgrades, for example).

- By focusing on extending the useful life of more products, society can transition to a more sustainable and circular economy. This brings about social benefits, such as less pollution and a lower carbon footprint for a more sustainable future.

Sharing models

- **Sharing models** involve customers sharing products that tend to be underutilized, thereby reducing the demand for more new products. This also helps to reduce the demand for the scarce resources that would otherwise be used to produce these products.

- Examples include car sharing, bike sharing, music equipment sharing services, clothes sharing, office sharing, and tool sharing (such as power tools, ladders, etc.).

- Sharing models enable businesses to gain from lower production costs, additional revenue streams, and an improved corporate image due to the lower environmental impact of their business activities.

- Sharing models can also provide customers with access to goods and services that they might not otherwise be able to afford.

- Sharing goods and services, rather than buying them outright, helps to reduce the need to purchase new goods and services. This puts less pressure on the demand for productive resources and also helps to reduce waste.

▨ Product service system models

- **Product service system models** focus on providing customers with the functional and intrinsic benefits of a product, rather than just selling the product itself.

- The emphasis is on efficient product use by focusing on the service provided rather than the physical product being sold as a one-off purchase.

- In a product service system model, a business may choose to lease or rent a product to a customer (rather than selling it), while providing maintenance and repair services to keep the product in good working condition.

- This category of circular business models reduces the environmental impacts of business activity due to lower levels of consumption and production, as well as providing customers with access to products they might not otherwise be able to afford to purchase outright.

- Examples include on-demand car rental services, such as Car2Go or Zip, that enable customers to rent cars by the minute. This can be beneficial to customers as they do not need to worry about the costs of owning and maintaining a car full time.

- Furthermore, as a circular business model, product services also help to reduce the need for customers to purchase and dispose of physical products.

9 GANTT CHARTS (HL ONLY)

HL content	Depth of teaching
Gantt charts	AO2, AO4

Diploma Programme *Business management guide* (May 2022)

▨ Gantt charts (AO2, AO4)

- A **Gantt chart**, devised by American engineer Henry L. Gantt, is a visual planning tool that illustrates the sequencing and schedule of a particular project.

- Links established between dependent tasks allow managers to sequence the various activities (tasks) of a particular project, and show what must be completed before the next task(s) can begin.

- The required time and resources can then be linked to each of the tasks in the project.

- Ultimately, a Gantt chart helps project managers to determine how long a project should take to complete.

- An example of the data used to create a Gantt chart is shown in Table BMT.10. The Gantt chart representing this project (Project X) is shown in Figure BMT.10.

■ **Table BMT.10** Activities for Project X

Activity	Preceded by	Duration (days)
A	-	3
B	-	3
C	-	3
D	A	2
E	B	4
F	C	3
G	D, E, and F	7

Gantt chart for Project X (days)

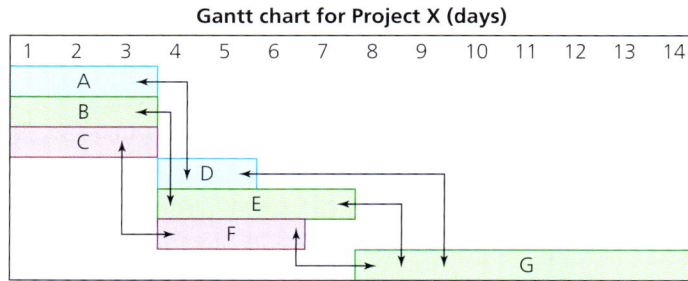

■ **Figure BMT.10** Example of a Gantt chart for Project X

■ **Table BMT.11** Advantages and disadvantages of Gantt charts

Advantages of Gantt charts	Disadvantages of Gantt charts
• A Gantt chart shows the dependencies between different activities in order to minimize the time needed to complete a project.	• The length of time (each bar) does not necessarily correlate with the amount of work or resources involved for each activity.
• There are wide applications, e.g. scheduling production processes, employee work rosters, and holiday schedules.	• A Gantt chart needs to be monitored and may need regular updating.
• It helps managers to set realistic deadlines for the various activities of a project.	• Complex projects may be difficult to display on a one-page Gantt chart.
• Gantt charts are simple to interpret and understand.	• Its simplicity means that a Gantt chart may not provide enough detail or information for complex projects.
• A Gantt chart allows managers to monitor progress and take corrective measures.	• It is based on and is reliant on the estimates of the timings of each task.

EXAM PRACTICE QUESTION

Construct a Gantt chart for Project A from the data given in the table below. [4]

Activity	Preceded by	Duration (weeks)
A	-	3
B	A	2
C	A	1
D	B	3
E	C	2
F	D and E	5

10 PORTER'S GENERIC STRATEGIES (HL ONLY)

HL content	Depth of teaching
Porter's generic strategies	AO2, AO4

Diploma Programme *Business management guide* (May 2022)

Competitive advantage

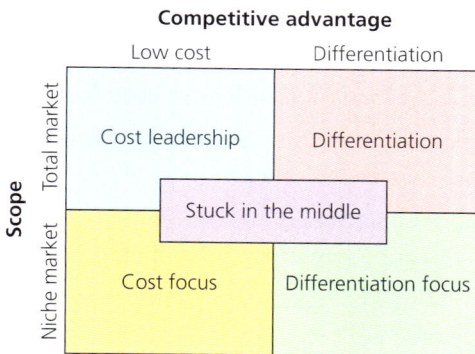

■ **Figure BMT.11** Porter's generic strategies

Porter's generic strategies (AO2, AO4)

- Devised by management guru and Harvard University professor Michael Porter, this management tool provides a relatively simple analytical framework for decision makers to assess an organization's competitive potential.

- The three generic strategies are cost leadership, differentiation, and focus. The latter strategy is further split into cost focus or differentiation focus. Not pursuing any of these generic strategies causes a business to be 'stuck in the middle'.

- Each of **Porter's generic strategies** (sometimes referred to as **competitive strategies**) has its own benefits and limitations, so needs to be considered carefully.

Cost leadership

- **Cost leadership** is the generic strategy used by a business to gain a competitive advantage by producing products at a lower cost and selling these at a lower price than competitors. It concentrates on reducing costs and improving efficiency in order to gain a competitive advantage.

- Strategies used by businesses that pursue cost leadership include opportunities to exploit economies of scale, opting for outsourcing, or improvements to production processes.

- Therefore, cost leadership can help businesses to gain a competitive edge and increase their profitability in the long term.

- Examples of businesses that use cost leadership as a competitive strategy include budget airlines and discount supermarkets.

- However, it is important for businesses to maintain a balance between cost cutting and product quality. Cutting costs to the extent that it compromises product quality can actually cause competitive disadvantages.

> **Key term**
>
> **Porter's generic strategies** is a management decision-making tool that refers to different strategic approaches that any business can use to compete and gain a competitive advantage.

Differentiation

- **Differentiation** is the generic strategy used by a business to gain a competitive advantage by focusing on creating unique products that customers cannot easily find elsewhere. These approaches give the business a unique selling point or distinctive appeal.

- To gain competitive advantages, it is important for a business to differentiate its goods and services in ways that add value for its customers and increase profitability for the organization.

- Differentiation can be achieved by methods such as creating innovative product features, superior levels of customer service, or brand appeal.

- This generic strategy is commonly used by high-tech and innovative companies such as Apple and Tesla.

■ Focus

- **Focus** is the generic strategy used by a business to gain a competitive advantage by targeting a specific market segment with customized goods and services.
- This competitive strategy relies on identifying a specific market segment to target, and creating a strong and loyal customer base.
- Focus enables businesses to customize their goods and services to meet the specific needs and preferences of the target market segment. This helps to build brand loyalty.
- There are two subcategories of a focus strategy: cost focus and differentiation focus.
- **Cost focus** is a generic strategy that seeks to gain a competitive edge by producing and selling products in a mass market at a lower cost than competitors.
  - This strategy involves the business reducing production and operational costs and improving efficiency, both of which help to create competitive advantages.
  - Businesses that use this strategy rely on economies of scale, outsourcing, and other methods of cost cutting to achieve cost focus.
  - Examples of businesses that use a cost-focus strategy include Walmart, Lidl, Amazon, Ryanair, Primark, IKEA, and McDonald's.
- **Differentiation focus** is a generic strategy that seeks to gain a competitive edge by producing and selling products in a specialized or niche market at higher prices.
  - It relies on a business to create unique goods or services that offer exceptional and exclusive value to customers, such as highly innovative product features, high-end quality, and superior customer service.
  - For example, both Apple and Tesla have successfully differentiated their products over many years, allowing these companies to charge premium prices, while enjoying a high degree of customer loyalty.

■ Stuck in the middle

- **Stuck in the middle** refers to a business or an organization that takes none of the actions in Porter's model, and fails to excel in any of these generic strategies.
- It usually happens when a business tries to offer low prices (by focusing on lowering costs) and high quality at the same time, or low prices for differentiated products. These are not sustainable competitive strategies.
- Businesses that are stuck in the middle struggle to gain any competitive advantage, so will tend to suffer from low profitability in the short term and liquidity problems in the long term.
- According to Porter's model, it is important for all businesses to concentrate on one of Porter's generic strategies and excel at this, rather than to try to do a combination, or even all of them, at the same time.

11 HOFSTEDE'S CULTURAL DIMENSIONS (HL ONLY)

HL content	Depth of teaching
Hofstede's cultural dimensions	AO2, AO4

Diploma Programme *Business management guide* (May 2022)

■ Hofstede's cultural dimensions (AO2, AO4)

- The model was created by Dutch psychologist and former IBM manager Geert Hofstede (1928–2020).

Key term

Hofstede's cultural dimensions is a model consisting of six elements of difference in cultural values between countries and regions.

- The purpose or value of **Hofstede's cultural dimensions** as a situational tool is to help businesses to gain a better understanding of the differences between cultures, thereby enhancing communications with a diversified workforce and negotiations with international clients. This is particularly important for multinational companies (see Chapter 1.6).

- The six cultural dimensions provide a framework for understanding how people in and from different cultures interact and connect with each other, such as their varying approaches and attitudes towards communications, management and leadership, and decision making.

- By understanding different cultural dimensions, businesses can also gain insight into the potentially different behaviours of individuals from different cultures and what might motivate or demotivate them (see Chapter 2.4).

- The six cultural dimensions are power distance, individualism versus collectivism, masculinity versus femininity, uncertainty avoidance, long- versus short-term orientation, and indulgence versus restraint.

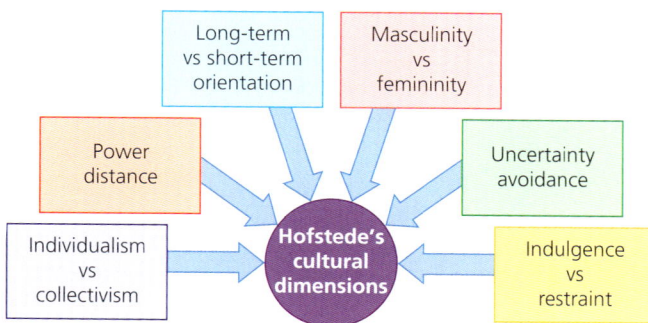

■ **Figure BMT.12** Hofstede's cultural dimensions

■ Power distance

- **Power distance** is a cultural dimension that measures the level of inequality between members of a society, in terms of the power they hold, and how willing people are to accept it.

- Power is the ability to influence the thoughts and actions of others. This is typically done through persuasion or coercion.

- Power distance is higher in countries where there is a greater difference between those with official power and those without. For example, power distance is very high in Malaysia, Qatar, Romania, Saudi Arabia, and Singapore, where people are generally expected to show considerable respect to those in positions of authority. It also exists in organizations with tall, hierarchical structures (see Chapter 2.2).

- By contrast, the lower the power distance, the more likely people are to challenge authority and question the decisions made by those in positions of power or authority. For example, power distance is relatively low in Austria, Denmark, Ireland, and New Zealand, where people are generally more likely to challenge and question the decisions made by those in positions of authority.

■ Individualism versus collectivism

- **Individualism versus collectivism** is a cultural dimension that measures the extent to which there is interdependence and unity among members of a society.

- Individualistic societies are focused on the interests, needs, and preferences of the individual, with people willing to take higher levels of risk.

- For example, people in France, Latvia, and the USA are generally more focused on the rights and needs of the individual, and there is greater emphasis on autonomy and independence.

- Conversely, collectivist societies are focused on the needs and wants of the community, group, or team. Collectivist cultures place more emphasis on conformity, harmony, and co-operation.

- As a cultural dimension, individualism versus collectivism can be used to understand differences in communication styles, decision-making processes, and approaches to management and leadership in different cultures.

- For example, collectivism is more highly valued by people in Bangladesh, China, Singapore, Thailand, and Vietnam, where people are generally more focused on the rights and needs of the community and put greater emphasis on conformity, cohesion, and co-operation.

Masculinity versus femininity

- **Masculinity versus femininity** is the cultural dimension that measures the extent to which people in a country or community value traditional gender roles.

- Masculine cultures put greater emphasis on traits such as success, status, power, competition, assertiveness, and money. For example, in Austria, Japan, Germany and the USA, masculinity is more dominant, meaning people place more emphasis on competition, success, power, and wealth.

- On the other hand, feminine cultures put more emphasis on qualities such as caring, communication, co-operation, community, nurturing, and sharing. For example, femininity is more highly valued in Denmark, Finland, Norway, Sweden, and the Netherlands, where there is greater emphasis on co-operation and nurturing, with less importance placed on hierarchical structures.

- Masculine cultures tend to have a tall, hierarchical structure, whereas feminine cultures are more likely to have a more open and democratic arrangement.

Uncertainty avoidance

- **Uncertainty avoidance** is a cultural dimension that measures the degree to which people in a country or community feel vulnerable to, or threatened by, uncertainty and ambiguity.

- Countries and communities with high uncertainty avoidance cultures have more rigid rules and regulations (with hierarchical structures) so people are more risk averse. They tend to have a strong sense of national identity. Examples include Colombia, France, Italy, Japan, Kuwait, South Korea, Singapore, and Turkey.

- By contrast, countries and communities with low uncertainty avoidance cultures are more open minded and tolerant of differences, so are more open to risk taking. They are likely to have more democratic structures, and are more receptive to outside influences. Examples include Australia, Canada, Denmark, Iceland, Jamaica, the Netherlands, Norway, Singapore, Switzerland, and the UK.

Long-term versus short-term orientation

- **Long-term orientation** is a cultural dimension that emphasizes adherence to traditional values, having respect for cultural heritage, and the importance of long-term goals to people in a country or community. Hence, there are likely to be tall, hierarchical structures.

- Countries and communities with a culture in favour of long-term orientation have strong respect for tradition and heritage. There is also emphasis on thrift and perseverance – there is a cautionary approach to decision making.

- Examples of countries with a culture of long-term orientation include Angola, China, Germany, Japan, South Korea, and Taiwan.

- By contrast, societies with a culture in favour of **short-term orientation** place strong emphasis on gratification and fulfilment in the immediate time period. In such cultures, people are more receptive and open to change.

- Examples of countries with a culture of short-term orientation include India, Mexico, Morocco, the Philippines, and Venezuela.

Indulgence versus restraint

- **Indulgence versus restraint** is the final cultural dimension in Hofstede's model, and considers a country's level of adherence to different rules and regulations, and the extent to which people value indulgence or restraint.

- Examples of countries that have a culture of high indulgence include Angola, Mexico, Mozambique, New Zealand, and Zambia. This means that people, in general, put more emphasis on pleasure and pampering in their desires.

- By contrast, restraint cultures put more emphasis on self-control and discipline (moderation rather than overindulgence). Societies with restrained cultures are more likely to adhere strictly to rules and regulations.

- Examples of countries that have a culture of low indulgence include Bulgaria, China, Czech Republic, India, and Kazakhstan. This means that people, in general, put more emphasis on doing what is considered appropriate in terms of societal 'norms'.

EXPERT TIP

As with any tool, be aware of the limitations of the model. In this case, the calculations used to measure the six cultural dimensions in Hofstede's model are based on limited data (that might even be out of date), and therefore may not be representative of all cultures or subcultures that exist in different communities and countries.

12 FORCE FIELD ANALYSIS (HL ONLY)

HL content	Depth of teaching
Force field analysis	AO2, AO4

Diploma Programme *Business management guide* (May 2022)

Force field analysis (AO2, AO4)

- Force field analysis (FFA) was devised by German–American psychologist Kurt Lewin as a planning and decision-making framework for examining the factors for and against change.

- The factors (or forces) that support change towards a goal are called **driving forces**, whereas those that block or hinder change are called **restraining forces**.

- FFA allows managers to identify and evaluate the driving and restraining forces that affect a particular change situation or decision.

- These forces are numerically weighted in order to calculate the relative strengths of driving and restraining forces, thereby aiding decision making in an objective and quantifiable way.

- The tool provides a more comprehensive understanding of the change situation or decision, enabling managers to consider each of the forces impacting the situation.

- Once the driving and restraining forces have been identified, managers can consider strategies for strengthening the driving forces and weakening the restraining forces in order to achieve the desired outcome.

- In Figure BMT.13, the weights range from 1 to 5, with 5 being of most significance to the business. In this particular example (whether the business should relocate overseas), as the driving forces outweigh the restraining forces, the objective or logical decision is to relocate the business.

Driving forces
(Forces for change)

Restraining forces
(Forces against change)

Cheaper rent = 4

Improved competitiveness = 4

Access to overseas markets = 4

Decision:
Overseas relocation

Resistance from staff = 3

Staff training costs
(new location) = 3

Staff redundancies
(current location) = 3

Cultural adjustments = 2

Total: 12

Total: 11

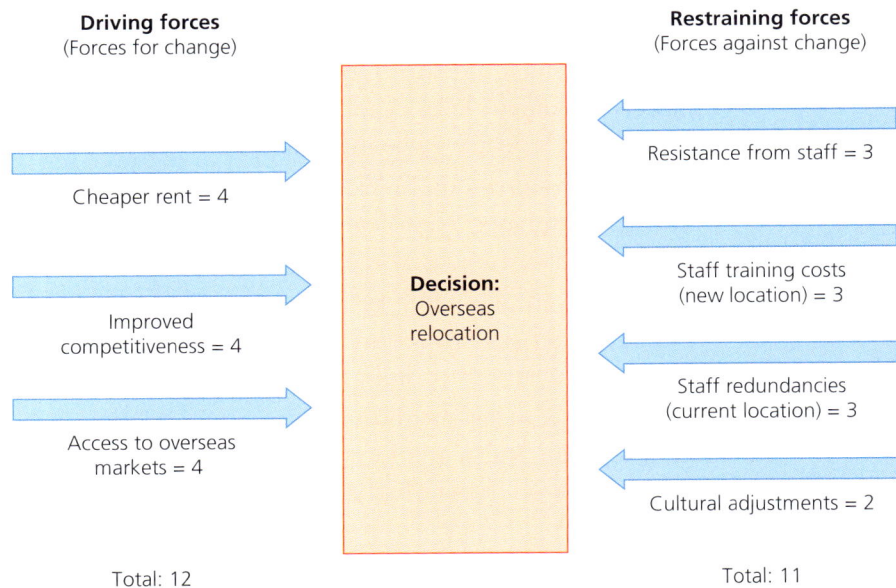

■ **Figure BMT.13** Force field analysis for a decision about overseas relocation

■ **Table BMT.12** Advantages and disadvantages of force field analysis

Advantages of FFA	Disadvantages of FFA
• As a quantitative planning tool, FFA makes the decision-making process more objective and logical. • It offers a simple visual representation of the forces for and against change. • Weighting (allocating numerical values to) the forces helps managers consider the relative importance of factors affecting the decision.	• Qualitative factors affecting decision making are ignored and/or are difficult to quantify. • The omission of certain driving or restraining forces can alter the outcome quite drastically. • The weighting of the forces is subjective, leaving room for potential bias.

BUSINESS MANAGEMENT TOOLKIT

Discuss the potential benefits of including a force field analysis as part of an organization's business plan.

13 CRITICAL PATH ANALYSIS (HL ONLY)

HL content	Depth of teaching
Critical path analysis, including the following: • Completion and analyses of a critical path diagram (drawing of the diagram is not expected) • Identification of the critical path • Calculation of free and total float	AO2, AO4

Diploma Programme *Business management guide* (May 2022)

Critical path analysis (AO2, AO4)

● **Critical path analysis (CPA)** is a widely used project management tool that supports managers to schedule and resource complex and time-sensitive business projects or ventures.

Key term

Critical path analysis (CPA) is a strategic planning tool used to identify the sequence of tasks in a project that need be completed on time so as to prevent any delays to finishing the project.

- It involves project managers identifying the following items before a network diagram can be constructed:
  - ○ All tasks that are required in order to complete the project.
  - ○ The order in which each task must be completed.
  - ○ Dependencies – tasks that cannot start until preceding ones have been completed.
  - ○ The duration of each task – how long it takes to complete each job within the project.
  - ○ Tasks that can be carried out concurrently so as to complete the project in the quickest time possible.
- Therefore, CPA helps project managers to schedule resources and minimize delays in order for the project to be finished in a time-efficient manner. Ultimately, CPA helps managers to determine the minimum time required to complete a project.

Completion and analyses of a critical path diagram

- A critical path diagram (also known as a network diagram) is a visual representation of a project schedule that displays the sequence of tasks, their durations, and dependencies between tasks.
- It is used to help project managers determine the timeline of a project and to identify the critical path – the minimum amount of time needed to complete a project (or quickest time that a project can be completed in).
- By focusing on the critical path, project managers can ensure that each task stays on track so that the overall project is completed on time.
- When constructing a network diagram (see Figure BMT.14), the following features are used:
  - ○ A circle (called a 'node') represents the start and end times of an activity. Each node is split into three sections:
    - The node number is shown on the left-hand side of the semi-circle.
    - The **earliest start time** (EST) is shown in the top half of the semi-circle on the right side of the node.
    - The **latest finish time** (LFT) is shown in the bottom half of the semi-circle on the right side of the node.
  - ○ An arrow represents the activity itself, with the duration (a numerical value) also shown.
  - ○ Nodes and activities are constructed in the diagram from left to right.
    - The EST shows when an activity can commence, which is dependent on the completion of the previous task.
    - The LFT shows when the previous activity in the project must be completed.

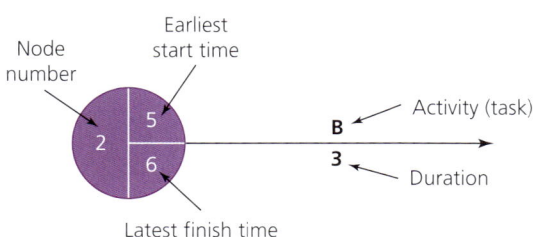

■ **Figure BMT.14** Conventions in a network diagram

● To construct a network diagram, a production schedule is required (such as the example shown in Table BMT.13). This shows the various tasks or activities in the project, the duration of each task, and the sequencing (order).

■ **Table BMT.13** Sample production schedule

Task	Duration (days)	Preceded by
A	1	-
B	3	A
C	2	A
D	3	B
E	3	C
F	4	D, E

● The network diagram for the project in Table BMT.13 is shown below.

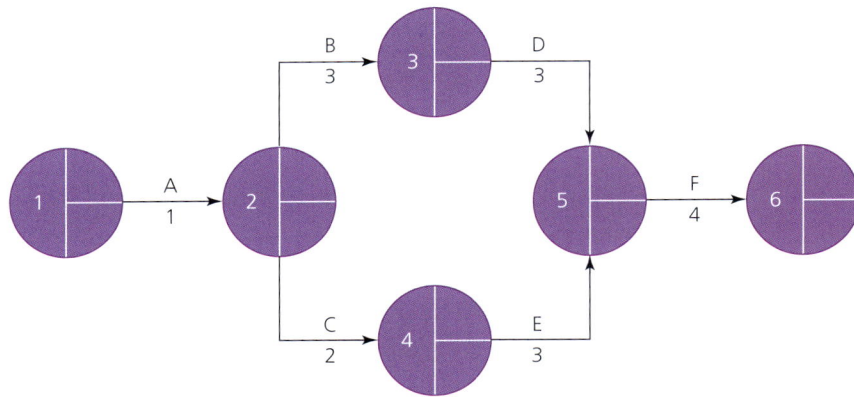

■ **Figure BMT.15** Network diagram

● The next step is to enter the ESTs for all nodes, from left to right and beginning with Node 1. This is shown in Figure BMT.16.

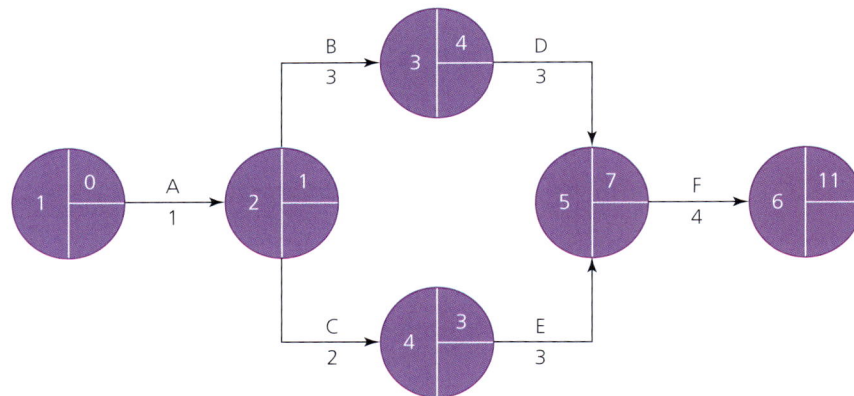

■ **Figure BMT.16** Network diagram, with EST shown

● For example, Node 2 shows that Activity A can be completed on Day 1. Hence, the earliest start time for Activity B is after this time. Similarly, Node 5 shows that Activity F cannot start until the 7th day of the project.

- The next step in the process is to enter the LFTs for all nodes from right to left, beginning with Node 6.

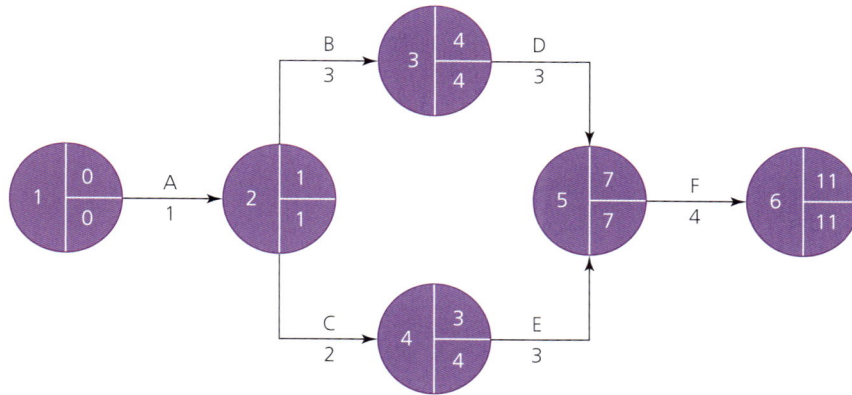

■ Figure BMT.17 Network diagram, with LFT shown

- As shown in Figure BMT.17, the project can be finished on the 11th day, as activity F takes four days, the latest finish time of the previous activities must be day 7 (11 − 4 = 7 days).

- The shortest length of time that a project can be completed in is shown in the final node (farthest right). In this case, Node 6 shows that the project can be completed in 11 days.

- The critical path is identified by the path or sequence of activities where the EST and LFT are the same. The network diagram in Figure BMT.17 shows that all nodes have equal EST and LFTs except for Node 4. Therefore, the critical path in this example is A, B, D, F.

- Node 4 shows that there is spare capacity of one day (the difference between the EST and LFT) for Activity E, so this means it cannot be on the critical path. Even if Activity E was started on the fourth day, as Activity E takes three days to complete it would not delay the start of Activity F on Day 7.

- Note that the critical path in a network diagram is the sequence of tasks that takes the longest time to complete. Hence, any delay to the activities that are on the critical path will prolong the completion of the project.

- Project managers can use the information from network diagrams to prioritize tasks, allocate resources, identify potential bottlenecks, and adjust schedules if need be, in order to ensure that the project is completed on time and therefore within budget.

Dummy activity

- As the name suggests, a **dummy activity** is not an actual task, but is used to represent a logical dependency between two tasks in the schedule of a project.

- A dummy activity does not consume any resources or time (as it is not an actual activity).

- It is shown in a network diagram using a broken dotted arrow and is used to link tasks that are connected with a specific sequence.

- As an example, study the tasks, duration, and sequencing shown in Table BMT.14.

■ **Table BMT.14** Sample schedule

Activity	Duration (weeks)	Preceded by
A	2	-
B	4	-
C	3	A
D	3	A
E	2	B, D
F	4	C, E
G	2	C
H	3	F, G

- This schedule is represented by the network diagram shown in Figure BMT.18.

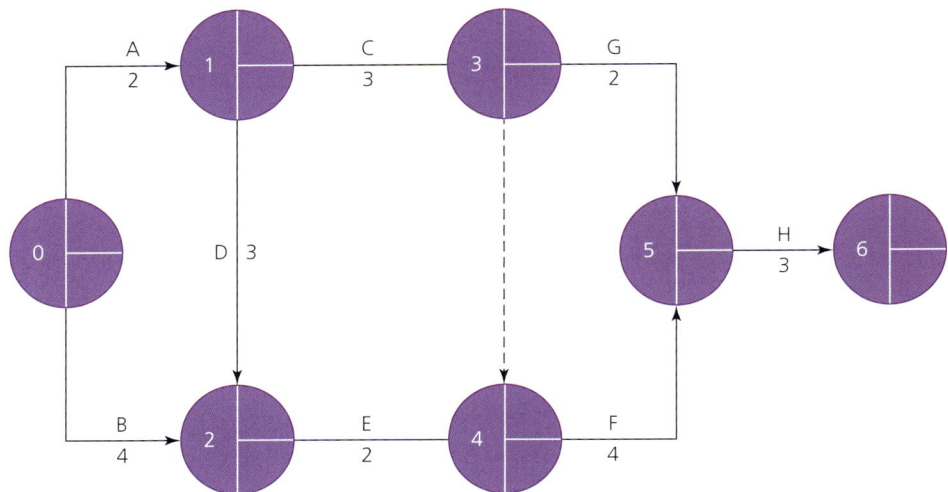

■ **Figure BMT.18** Network diagram

- Notice that Task F is dependent on both Task C and E being completed first. The use of a dummy activity shows this relationship by connecting Nodes 3 and 4 in the network diagram.

EXAM PRACTICE QUESTION

a Complete the network diagram shown in Figure BMT.18 by calculating the earliest start times and latest finish times. [4]

b Identify the critical path from your network diagram. [1]

■ Calculation of free and total float

- An activity or task without spare time is considered to be critical.
- Any activity not on the critical path will have some spare time, referred to as **float**. There are two types of float times – the free float and the total float.
- The **free float** is the amount of spare time available for an activity without it delaying the *next activity* in the project.
- The **total float** is the amount of spare time available for an activity without it delaying the *whole project*.
- The free float and total float for activities on the critical path is always zero.

  Free float = EST of the next activity – (EST at start of activity + Duration of activity)

  Total float for an activity = LFT – Duration – EST

EXAM PRACTICE QUESTION

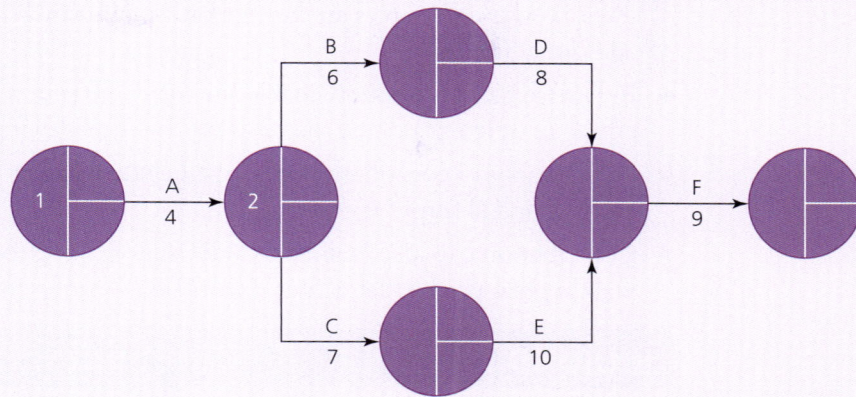

a Complete the network diagram above. Durations are in weeks. [4]
b Calculate the total float for Activity B. [2]
c Calculate the free float for Activity D. [2]

EXPERT TIP

Remember the actual meaning of the term *critical* path – this will then clarify why there cannot be any float time for any of the tasks along the critical path.

14 CONTRIBUTION (HL ONLY)

HL content	Depth of teaching
Contribution, including the following:	AO2, AO4
• Make or buy analysis	
• Contribution costing	
• Absorption costing	

Diploma Programme *Business management guide* (May 2022)

■ Contribution (AO2, AO4)

Key term

Contribution is the numerical difference between a firm's revenue and its variable costs of production.

- **Contribution** (or **contribution analysis**) is a strategic tool used to analyze the profitability of a firm's goods and services, or specific projects. It is measured in one of two ways:
  ○ **Total contribution** is measured by the numerical difference between a firm's total revenue (TR) and its total variable costs (TVC):

    Total contribution = TR – TVC

  ○ **Contribution per unit** refers to the amount of money a business earns from selling each unit of output. It is the difference between the selling price (P) and the average variable cost (AVC):

    Contribution per unit = P – AVC

- In both cases, the surplus is used to contribute towards the payment of the firm's fixed costs. Once sufficient amounts of contribution are generated to pay all fixed costs, the firm reaches its break even (see Chapter 5.5). Any sales beyond the break-even point mean that the contribution generated becomes profit for the business.

- Contribution analysis is used to identify profitable business activities and products, or areas of the business that require improvement. It also helps managers to identify where resources are best invested, and which products or departments need additional funding.
- In particular, contribution enables managers to gain a better understanding of the effects of different pricing methods on the firm's level profits.
- Applications of contribution analysis include make or buy analysis, contribution costing, and absorption costing.
- Contribution can also be used as a decision-making tool to forecast the financial viability of a product launch or a particular business project.

WORKED EXAMPLE

- A business plans to launch a new product, which will cost a total of $150,000. The expected sales revenue from the sale of the new product is $220,000.
- In this case, total contribution is $220,000 − $150,000 = $70,000
- This informs managers that so long as total fixed costs are less than $70,000 the project is profitable (or financially viable).

Make or buy analysis

- **Make or buy analysis** is a management decision-making tool used to determine whether it is more cost effective for a business to produce a product or project itself (in-house), or to pay an external supplier to produce this.
- The make or buy decision is based on the cost to make (CTM) the product in-house versus the cost to buy (CTB) the product from a supplier or producer.
- Make or buy analysis can also consider qualitative factors such as quality, lead times (including delivery time), and the reputation of the external supplier. For example, if an external supplier can provide the product at a lower cost, with higher quality, and in a quicker timeframe, it would make financial sense for the business to buy the product from the external supplier rather than to make it in-house.

Contribution costing

- **Contribution costing** is a method of analyzing and allocating costs to different products, cost centres, or profit centres (see Chapter 3.9). The purpose is to support management decision making, such as with pricing decisions.
- In particular, contribution costing is used to determine the allocation of the indirect costs of the business as a whole, and how much each product or division contributes to these costs.
- In the following example, the business produces three products. As can be seen, contribution for each product is calculated by the difference between sales revenue and direct costs. Assume that the firm's total fixed costs are $150,000.

■ Table BMT.15

Product	A	B	C
Sales revenue ($)	500,000	200,000	300,000
Direct costs ($)	275,000	130,000	150,000
Contribution ($)	225,000	70,000	150,000

- The three products earn a total sales revenue equal to $1,000,000 for the business. The total direct costs are $555,000, which means the business earns a total contribution of $445,000. Product A earns the highest amount of this contribution for the business, whereas Product B earns the least.

▨ Absorption costing

- **Absorption costing** is an aspect of contribution analysis that takes contribution costing one step further, by deducting indirect costs to calculate the profits earned from each product or division of the business.

- It calculates the total cost of producing each product, including the costs for direct materials, labour, electricity, and rent. These costs can then be spread out over the total number of units produced, allowing managers to calculate the cost per unit. This helps them to make informed judgements, such as pricing decisions.

- Absorption costing involves the allocation of indirect costs (such as rent) to determine the amount of profit that each product earns for the business. Continuing with the previous example in Table BMT.15, the simplest way to do this is to divide the indirect costs (of $150,000) equally between the three products.

■ **Table BMT.16**

Product	A	B	C
Sales revenue ($)	500,000	200,000	300,000
Direct costs ($)	275,000	130,000	150,000
Contribution ($)	225,000	70,000	150,000
Indirect costs ($)	50,000	50,000	50,000
Profit ($)	175,000	20,000	100,000

- It then becomes clear that Product A is the most profitable for the business ($175,000), whereas Product B is the least profitable ($20,000). This analysis can help managers to determine the financial returns from the firm's product offerings.

- Alternatively, the allocation of indirect costs can be based on the percentage of sales revenue attributed to each product. For example, Product A earns $500,000 in sales revenue, which represents 50 per cent of the firm's total sales revenue. Therefore, it is allocated 50 per cent of the firm's indirect costs (50 per cent of $150,000 is $75,000), as shown in Table BMT.17.

■ **Table BMT.17**

Product	A	B	C
Sales revenue ($)	500,000	200,000	300,000
Direct costs ($)	275,000	130,000	150,000
Proportion of revenue	50%	20%	30%
Contribution ($)	225,000	70,000	150,000
Indirect costs ($)	75,000	30,000	45,000
Profit ($)	150,000	40,000	105,000

- By allocating indirect costs in this way, it can be seen that the profit earned by Product B is significantly higher.

- Therefore, absorption costing can be a valuable tool for managers, as it provides greater insight into the full cost of producing a product.

- However, note that this example shows that the choice of methods used to allocate indirect costs is somewhat subjective, and has a clear impact on the amount of profit earned from each product.

■ **Table BMT.18** Differences between contribution costing and absorption costing

Contribution costing	Absorption costing
Only direct costs are allocated to the product.	Both direct and indirect costs are allocated to the product.
Focuses on earning profit for each product.	Focuses on earning profit for the business as a whole.
Typically used in short-term decision making.	Typically used in long-term decision making.

- Contribution analysis can also be used for forecasting purposes, to see whether a particular business proposal is financially viable – whether it can generate enough sales revenue to cover its direct and indirect costs. Hence, contribution analysis helps managers to make more informed decisions about the best use of their resources.

15 SIMPLE LINEAR REGRESSION (HL ONLY)

HL content	Depth of teaching
Simple linear regression: scatter diagrams, line of best fit, and correlation/extrapolation	AO2, AO4

Diploma Programme *Business management guide* (May 2022)

◼ Simple linear regression (AO2, AO4)

- Simple linear regression is a statistical tool used to investigate the relationship between an independent variable (such as advertising expenditure) and a dependent variable (such as sales revenue). So, a business could use simple linear regression to see if there is any relationship between the impact of its advertising and the firm's sales revenue. This will also enable the business to make forecasts about future sales revenue based on changes in the firm's advertising expenditure.

- As the name suggests, a straight line is used in simple linear regression to show the extent to which there is a relationship between the independent and dependent variables (such as the amount of money spent on staff training and the impact on labour productivity in the organization). The slope of the straight line represents the strength and direction of the relationship between the variables, for example whether there is a strong or weak correlation, and whether the relationship is direct (positive) or indirect (negative).

- There are three key aspects of simple linear regression: scatter diagrams, line of best fit, and correlation/extrapolation.

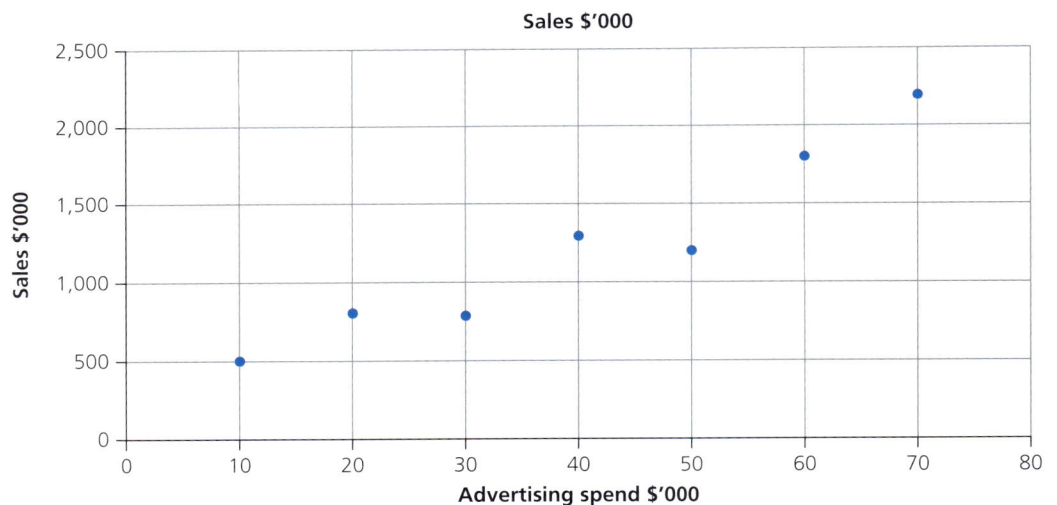

■ **Figure BMT.19** Scatter diagram showing advertising spending and sales

Scatter diagrams

- A **scatter diagram** (sometimes referred to as a **scatter chart**) is a graphical representation of the relationship between two quantifiable variables (see Figure BMT.19).

- The tool is used to visualize the extent to which there is relationship between the two variables being measured – to see if there is a correlation or pattern between them.

- The relationship shown in a scatter diagram can be positive (strong or weak) or negative (strong or weak). A positive correlation exists when the variables tend to increase or decrease together, while a negative correlation exists when one variable increases as the other decreases.

- It is also possible for there to be no clear correlation (relationship) between the two variables in a scatter diagram.

- A scatter diagram may reveal outliers in the data set. Outliers are data points that lie outside the overall pattern of the data. They indicate extreme cases or possible errors in the data. Outliers make it more challenging to establish strong correlations between the variables under investigation.

- Essentially, scatter diagrams are used to illustrate the strength of relationship between two quantitative variables in order to make more informed decisions.

Line of best fit

- The line of best fit is a straight line that is used to identify an underlying pattern showing the relationship between two variables in a scatter diagram.

- It is determined by the sum of the squared distances (or deviations) between the data points and the line that goes through the data points in a scatter diagram (see Figure BMT.20). This means that approximately half of the data points appear above the line of best fit, and the other half appear below it.

- The line of best fit can be used to determine the extent to which there is a correlation between the two variables, as well as to make predictions about future values of the variables.

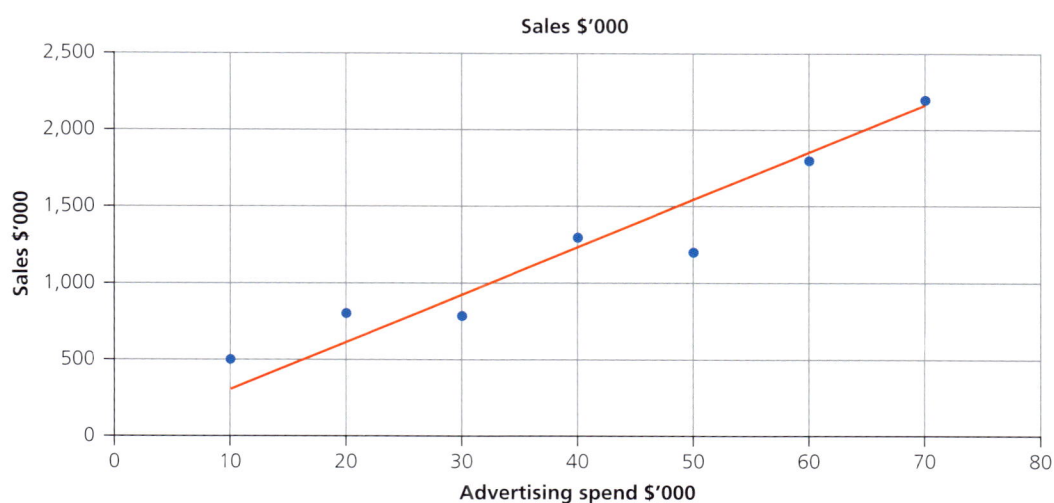

Figure BMT.20 A line of best fit

▨ Correlation/extrapolation

- **Correlation** refers to the strength (strong or weak) and direction (positive or negative) of a relationship between two variables.

- A positive correlation means that as the independent variable increases, the dependent variable also increases. A negative correlation means that as the independent variable increases, the dependent variable decreases. It is also possible for there to be no relationship between the variables under investigation.

- However, correlation does not imply causation – an apparent correlation in a scatter diagram does not mean that one variable (such as the number of days employees spend on training and development) causes the other (such as labour productivity). This is because there may be other factors that are responsible for the relationship between the two variables (such as the level of staff motivation).

- Correlation is used to make predictions by using **extrapolation**.

- Extrapolation is a statistical technique that makes predictions based on trends identified from using past data – it is the use of a line of best fit in a scatter diagram to predict future sales.

- Extrapolation assumes that patterns are stable and past data (such as sales revenues or profits) are indicative of the future.

- Extrapolation identifies the trend by determining the line of best fit and then simply extends this line to make the predictions (see Figure BMT.21).

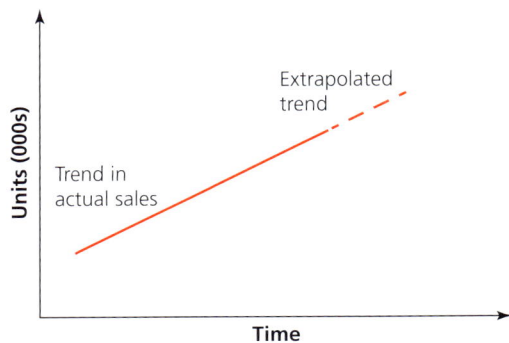

■ **Figure BMT.21** Extrapolation of sales data

- A key assumption of extrapolation is linear regression, that is, that the relationship between the two quantifiable variables is linear.

- Hence, extrapolation can be unreliable if there are significant outliers in the data set, or if there are numerous underlying factors that determine the variable of interest.

- Furthermore, extrapolation assumes that the future looks like the past and ignores the dynamic nature of the external environment (see STEEPLE analysis).

- To reduce the risk of inaccurate predictions, it is important to use caution when making extrapolations and to consider the potential impact of changes in the external environment (see STEEPLE analysis).

EXAM PRACTICE QUESTIONS

1 Define the term *scatter diagram*. [2]

2 The data below depict the number of employees at a firm, and the corresponding output. Use the data to plot a scatter diagram. [4]

Number of employees	Output ('000 units)
5	80
10	110
15	130
20	145
25	160
30	170
35	175

3 Plot the line of best fit. [1]

4 Comment on the findings from your diagram. [2]

Glossary

Acid test ratio – a liquidity ratio that measures a firm's ability to meet its short-term debts. It ignores stock because some inventories are difficult to turn into cash in a short timeframe.

Adverse variance – when the difference between the actual and budgeted figure is disadvantageous to the business, for example when actual sales revenues are lower than planned, or wages are higher than budgeted.

Appraisal – the formal assessment of an employee's performance, with reference to the roles and responsibilities set out in their job description.

Average rate of return (ARR) – an investment appraisal technique that calculates the average annual profit of an investment project, expressed as a percentage of the initial amount invested in the project.

Bad debts – the funds that cannot be recovered from a firm's debtors. As the money is no longer recoverable, it is written off as a loss or expense.

Benchmarking – the systematic process of comparing a business or its products to its competitors, using a set of standards (called 'benchmarks'), such as sales revenue, profits, labour turnover, or brand loyalty.

Break-even point (BEP) – where the total costs of production equals the total revenue.

Break-even quantity (BEQ) – the amount of sales or output required to break even.

Bureaucracy – the administrative systems of a business, such as the set of rules and procedures and formal hierarchical structures in an organization.

Business plan – a formal document that details how an organization intends to meet its business objectives.

Capacity utilization rate – a firm's actual output as a percentage of its maximum potential output, at a particular point in time.

Capital expenditure – spending on non-current assets. Examples include expenditure on buildings, capital equipment, tools, and vehicles.

Centralization – organizational structures where the majority of the decision making is in the hands of a very small number of people at the top of the hierarchical structure.

Chain of command – the formal line of authority through which orders and decisions are passed down, from senior management at the top, to operational workers at the bottom of the hierarchy.

Circular business models (CBM) – a modern approach to conducting business by focusing on sustainability and reducing waste.

Contribution – the numerical difference between a firm's revenue and its variable costs of production.

Contribution per unit – the amount of money a business earns from selling each unit of output. It is the difference between the selling price (P) and the average variable cost (AVC).

Corporate social responsibility (CSR) – an organization's moral or ethical duties to its internal and external stakeholders. Organizations meet their CSR by behaving in a way that positively impacts society as a whole.

Cradle-to-cradle (C2C) – a production philosophy with the view that sustainable production involves designing and manufacturing goods so that they can be recycled to produce the product again.

Creditor days ratio – the average number of days a business takes to repay its creditors.

Critical path analysis (CPA) – a strategic planning tool used to identify the sequence of tasks in a project that need be completed on time so as to prevent any delays to finishing the project.

Culture clash – when there is a difference between the values and beliefs of individuals within an organization.

Current ratio – a liquidity ratio which calculates the ability of a business to meet its short-term debts, meaning debts that have to be paid within 12 months of the balance sheet date.

Cyclical variations – the recurrent fluctuations in sales revenues linked to the business cycle.

Debtor days ratio – the average number of days a business takes to collect debts from its customers who have bought goods and services on trade credit.

Decentralization – organizational structures which include the delegation of decision-making authority throughout an organization, away from a central authority.

Defect rate – the number of faulty or substandard items as a percentage of the total number of items produced. The lower the defect rate, the better this is for producers and consumers.

Delayering – the process of removing one or more layers in the organizational hierarchy to make the structure flatter.

Delegation – the process of entrusting and empowering a subordinate to successfully complete a task, project, or job role.

Depreciation – the decline in the value of a non-current asset over time, mainly due to its continued usage (wear and tear) and newer models or better technologies being available.

Differentiation – the process of making a business or its products distinct from others in the same market.

Discount rate – a number used to reduce the value of a sum of money received in the future in order to determine its present value. This is the opposite of a compound interest rate.

External economies of scale – the fall in unit costs of production for all organizations in an industry as it experiences growth and evolution.

External stakeholders – external stakeholders are not members of a business, but they have a direct stake (interest) in its operations and performance. Examples include customers, suppliers, competitors, the local community, pressure groups, financiers, and the government.

Favourable variance – when the difference between the actual and budgeted figure is beneficial to the business, for example if sales revenues are higher than planned and/or costs are lower than planned.

Flow production – the continuous and automated production process that uses capital intensive production methods to maximize output by minimizing production time. It is associated with large production runs of standardized products.

Gearing ratio – the degree to which a business is financed by loan capital, by comparing debt finance and the total capital employed.

Gross profit margin (GPM) – a profitability ratio that shows a firm's gross profit expressed as a percentage of its sales revenue.

Hofstede's cultural dimensions – a model consisting of six elements of difference in cultural values between countries and regions.

Human resource planning – the management process of anticipating and meeting an organization's current and future staffing needs.

Hygiene factors – aspects of a job that can lead to workers being dissatisfied. These factors need to be addressed in order to prevent dissatisfaction, but they do not motivate.

Insourcing – the use of a firm's own resources to fulfil a certain role, function, or task which would otherwise have been outsourced.

Internal economies of scale – the fall in unit costs of production for a single organization as it grows and evolves, for example managerial and financial economies of scale.

Internal stakeholders – members of the organization, such as employees, managers, directors, and shareholders (the owners of the business).

International marketing – the marketing of an organization's products in foreign countries.

Job description – a document that provides details of a particular job, including, for example, the job title, roles, duties, and responsibilities.

Just in case (JIC) – a stock control system that relies on having spare stocks (inventory) so that output can be raised immediately in the event of a sudden or unexpected increase in demand.

Just in time (JIT) – a lean stock control system that relies on stocks (inventories) being delivered only when they are needed in the production process.

Kaizen – the Japanese philosophy of continuous improvement and changing for the better.

Labour turnover – the rate of change of human resources within an organization, per period of time.

Lean production – a philosophy built into the culture of organizations that focus on less wastage and greater efficiency.

Levels of hierarchy – the management structure of an organization, based on the number of layers of formal authority, usually presented in an organizational chart.

Liquidity ratios – the financial ratios that look at a firm's ability to pay its short-term financial obligations (bills and debts).

Loss – occurs if total costs exceed total revenues.

Make or buy decision – a management decision that involves choosing whether to manufacture a product (make) or to purchase it (buy) from an external supplier. Essentially, it is a decision about whether to insource or outsource production.

Market leaders – the firms with the largest market share in a particular industry.

Market research – the systematic process of collecting, collating, analyzing, and interpreting data and information about existing and potential consumers, competitors, and markets. It is used by businesses to aid their marketing planning and marketing strategies.

Market segmentation – the process of splitting a market into distinct consumer groups to better understand their needs.

Market share – an organization's portion of the total value of sales revenue in a particular industry.

Mass marketing – a marketing strategy aimed at all consumers in a market without trying to differentiate them into separate market segments.

Matrix structure – a flexible organizational structure that uses teams of employees from across traditional departments for a specific business project.

Merchandising – the use of branded products (such as toys, cups, souvenirs, and clothing) linked to a business organization or its products (such as a theme park, blockbuster movie, theatre show, or music band).

Mission statement – a clear and concise declaration of an organization's fundamental purpose – a succinct description of what the organization does, in order to become what it wants to be.

Motivators – factors that help workers to gain job satisfaction, for example recognition and opportunities for personal advancement. These factors satisfy the psychological needs of employees. Herzberg's motivators correspond with Maslow's higher level of needs and the nature of the job or work itself.

Multinational company (MNC) – an organization that operates, owns, or controls production and/or service facilities in two or more countries. Typically, the headquarters (or head office) of the MNC is in its home country.

Net present value (NPV) – an investment appraisal technique that calculates the real value of an investment project by discounting the value of future cash flows. Once the initial cost of the investment project is deducted from the total discounted cash flow, the NPV is found.

Niche marketing – a marketing strategy based on identifying and serving a relatively small and specific target market.

Non-sampling errors – market research mistakes that are not attributed to human errors, for example untruthful answers by respondents which distort the findings.

Offshoring – the practice of relocating part or all of a firm's business functions and processes overseas. These functions can remain within the business (operating in overseas markets) or be outsourced to an overseas organization.

Operations management – the business function of combining inputs (resources) to produce outputs (goods and services) that are valued by consumers.

Opportunities – the positive prospects for an organization. In this context, it refers to the openings or potential benefits as the business seeks to expand in overseas markets.

Organization by function – establishing the organizational structure according to business functions such as marketing, production, and finance.

Organization by product – when an organization groups its human resources based on the distinct goods or services it sells.

Organization by region – establishing the organizational structure according to different geographical areas.

Outsourcing – the practice of subcontracting non-core activities of an organization to a third-party provider (an external organization) in order to improve operational efficiency and reduce costs.

Overtrading – when a business expands too quickly without sufficient sources of finance in place to sustain its operations.

Payback period (PBP) – the estimated length of time it takes for a business to recover the initial cost of an investment project.

Person specification – a document that gives the profile of the ideal candidate for a job, and includes a description of the desired qualifications, skills, experience, knowledge, and other attributes.

Piece rate – a payment system, advocated by Frederick Winslow Taylor, which rewards workers based on their level of output (productivity), for example earning $1 per batch produced or 5 per cent per product sold. Piece rate is used to motivate and reward workers who are more productive.

Point of sale (POS) – the marketing of goods in stores where customers can purchase the goods. It is based on convenience (positioned in a way so they are easily accessible to customers, such as by supermarket checkouts) and prompts impulse buying.

Porter's generic strategies – a management decision-making tool that refers to different strategic approaches that any business can use to compete and gain a competitive advantage.

Position map – a visual representation of customers' perception of a product relative to its competitors, using variables such as price and quality.

Primary market research (or **field research**) – the systematic process of collecting, recording, analyzing, and interpreting new data and information about a specific issue of direct interest to the business, for example through the use of questionnaires, interviews, focus groups, and observations.

Profit – the positive difference between a firm's total sales revenue (TR) and its total costs (TC). It is the reward for successful risk-taking in a business.

Profit margin – a firm's overall profit (after all costs have been deducted), expressed as a percentage of its sales revenue.

Project-based organization – the organization of human resources around specific projects that need to be completed, rather than traditional functional departments.

Public relations (PR) – an organization's planned and sustained process of maintaining mutual understanding with the general public. The PR team tries to gain favourable publicity via the media and other channels, for example via educational programmes, news conferences, community activities, and sponsorship of local events.

Quality assurance (QA) – an approach to quality management that involves the prevention of mistakes in the production process, such as defective output, poor customer service, or delays in distributing goods to customers. It involves agreeing to and meeting quality standards at all stages of production to ensure customer satisfaction.

Quality circle – a small group of employees who voluntarily meet regularly to identify, examine, and solve problems related to their work, in order to improve the quality of output.

Quality control (QC) – the traditional approach to quality management by inspecting a sample of products. It involves quality controllers checking or examining a sample of products in a systematic way, for example once every 15 minutes on the production line, every 500th unit of output or 10 per cent of the amount produced.

Quantifiable risks – financially measurable threats that can jeopardize the survival of an organization. For example, there is a statistically low chance of a fire breaking out in a hospital, but a much higher likelihood of taxi drivers being involved in a motor accident.

Random variations – unpredictable and erratic fluctuations in sales revenues, caused by irregular and unexpected factors.

Remuneration – the entire package of financial rewards received by an employee, including, for example, their basic salary, commission, bonuses, share options, housing allowance, and other fringe benefits.

Research and development (R&D) – the systematic process of discovering new knowledge about products, processes, and markets, and then applying the knowledge to make new and improved goods and services to fulfil market needs.

Reshoring – when a business brings back production or other business functions into the home country from an overseas location.

Return on capital employed (ROCE) – a ratio that measures a firm's profitability and efficiency in relation to its size (as measured by the firm's capital employed).

Revenue expenditure – spending on a firm's daily or routine operations. Examples include expenditure on rent, raw materials, utility bills, and remuneration for employees.

Sales forecasting – a quantitative technique used to predict the level of sales revenue that a firm expects to earn over a certain period of time.

Sampling errors – the mistakes that arise from the sampling design, for example the sample size being too small, the selection of an unrepresentative sample, the use of inappropriate sampling methods, or having bias built into the research.

Seasonal variations – the expected periodic fluctuations in sales revenues over a given time period, such as peak trading periods during certain times of the year.

Secondary market research (or **desk research**) – the collection, collation, and interpretation of existing data and information from previously available sources, such as market analyses, academic journals, government publications, media articles, and online content.

Span of control – the number of subordinates who are directly accountable to a manager.

Stakeholders – individuals, organizations, or groups with a direct interest in the operations and performance of a particular business. They have varying degrees of influence on the organization.

STEEPLE analysis – a situational and planning tool that examines the influences in the external environment in which a business operates, for example the social, technological, economic, ethical, political, legal, and environmental factors.

Stock control chart – a graphical representation of the quantity of stock held by a business at different time periods.

Stock market (or **stock exchange**) – a place for buying and selling shares in publicly held companies. It oversees the IPO of new companies and subsequent share issues of existing companies. It is also the marketplace for buying and selling secondhand shares.

Stock turnover ratio – the number of days it takes a business to sell its stock or the number of times the business replenishes its stock during a given period of time.

Target price – the amount charged to customers in order to reach break even (or any desired target profit).

Target profit – the desired or expected profit from a business, i.e. how much profit it aims to earn. It can be determined from a break-even chart by comparing the total cost and total revenue curves at each level of output.

Target profit output (or **target profit quantity**) – the sales volume (quantity) needed in order to reach a firm's target profit.

Targeting – the practice of devising an appropriate marketing mix and marketing strategies for different market segments.

Technological innovation – the management process of developing and implementing new and improved products or processes for commercialization.

Threats – the potential challenges confronting a business. In the context of entering and operating internationally, they are the obstacles or challenges the business faces as it seeks to expand internationally.

Total contribution – calculated by multiplying the unit contribution by the quantity sold. It is used to work out profit or loss.

Total quality management (TQM) – a quality management approach that aims to involve every employee in the quality assurance process. It involves organization-wide approaches to quality improvements in products, process, people, and philosophy (organizational culture).

Unique selling point (USP) – any positive feature or aspect of a business, brand, or product that makes it distinctive (stand out) from those offered by the competitors.

Unlimited liability – the owner(s) of a business are personally liable for any and all of the business's debts. This means the owner(s) may need to pay for the debts by selling off their personal belongings and assets.

Unquantifiable risks – factors that can threaten the survival of an organization, but are extremely difficult to measure or calculate, for example the threat of a terrorist attack or the outbreak of a new infectious disease.

Vision statement – an optimistic and inspiring declaration that defines the purpose and values of an organization and where it wants to be in the future.